# Flying with the Fifteenth Air Force

# Flying with the Fifteenth Air Force

## A B-24 Pilot's Missions from Italy during World War II

Tom Faulkner
Edited by David L. Snead

Number 13 in the North Texas Military Biography and Memoir Series

University of North Texas Press
Denton, Texas

10 9 8 7 6 5 4 3 2 1

Permissions:
University of North Texas Press
1155 Union Circle #311336
Denton, TX 76203-5017

The paper used in this book meets the minimum requirements of the American National Standard for Permanence of Paper for Printed Library Materials, z39.48.1984. Binding materials have been chosen for durability.

Library of Congress Cataloging-in-Publication Data
Faulkner, Tom, 1925– author.
Flying with the Fifteenth Air Force : a B-24 pilot's missions from Italy during World War II / Tom Faulkner ; edited by David L. Snead.
pages cm.
Includes bibliographical references and index.
ISBN-13 978-1-57441-731-9 (cloth : alk. paper)
ISBN-13 978-1-57441-742-5 (ebook)
1. LCSH: Faulkner, Tom, 1925– 2. Airmen—United States—Biography. 3. Bomber pilots—United States—Biography. 4. United States. Army Air Forces—Airmen—Biography. 5. United States. Army Air Forces. Air Force, 15th—History. 6. World War, 1939–1945—Aerial operations, American. 7. World War, 1939–1945—Campaigns—Europe. 8. World War, 1939–1945—Personal narratives, American. 9. LCGFT: Autobiographies.

D790.22 15th .F38 2018
DDC 940.54/4973092 [B]—dc23
2018025844

*Flying with the Fifteenth Air Force: A B-24 Pilot's Missions from Italy during World War II* is Number 13 in the North Texas Military Biography and Memoir Series

The electronic edition of this book was made possible by the support of the Vick Family Foundation. Typeset by vPrompt eServices.

# Dedication

It may have been my father who once told me, if you live to have only five close friends in this life, you will have been blessed. I feel blessed, with more. This book is dedicated to four of them, all World War II pilots, and to all others who risked their lives in the defense of our great nation during World War II. Even the brief references to them in the Afterword of this book cannot begin to bring them justice.

These are the four. Not only were they my valued friends, each was unique, and a very special person.

| | | |
|---|---|---|
| Charles P. Storey | Pilot | United States Air Force |
| James S. Cleaver | Pilot | United States Marines |
| Stephen W. Schneider | Pilot | United States Navy |
| * Warner H. Marsh | Pilot | United States Air Force |

* Killed in action over German/French border - November 5, 1944

# Special Dedication

This book would never have been written had it not been for Dan Matthews of Minnesota. He had heard through a mutual friend of my concerns about my twenty-eighth and last mission, concerns which had left me with hidden emotional and eventually physical scars from World War II. Dan had researched the details of the death of his uncle, also a member of a B-24 crew of the Fifteenth Air Force in Italy. Without knowing me, he delved into the events of that twenty-eighth mission, probing sources and archives he was familiar with, and after introducing himself to me over the telephone in March of 2013, continued his research. His findings lifted a veil that had hounded me for six decades. He has been invaluable in the discovery of unknown details of that last mission, and also the current location of other pilots in my squadron, or their families, all of whom I have since personally seen or been in communication with. Since first talking to Dan in March of 2013, he has become not only my very good friend, but has actually been responsible for the complete, overnight reversal of my physical and emotional problems; the extent of which I had never completely realized or understood. Until Dan came along, my prognosis was becoming increasingly worse. No other person, outside of my family, has had such an enormous effect. He saved my life, in more ways than one. I am forever grateful.

Thank you once again, Dan Matthews.

# Contents

# Editor's Preface

The 1930s and 1940s presented a unique challenge to the United States when the Great Depression brought with it tremendous economic hardship and then World War II followed and required the country to mobilize for total war. By the time Germany attacked Poland in September 1939, the world had seen almost a decade of economic deprivation, and unemployment in the United States still stood at over seventeen percent with close to ten million Americans out of work.[1] The influx of commercial and military orders from war-torn Europe between 1939 and 1941 helped stimulate the U.S. economy, but it still fell below 1929 levels. Once the United States entered the war in December 1941, the economy rebounded more robustly, but it also offered other challenges. Over the next four years, approximately seventeen million American men and women would serve in the military in some capacity, and many more would assist in the war effort in other ways.

The Great Depression and the war affected people differently, but few escaped either unscathed. Americans who were at least in their twenties at the start of the Great Depression witnessed hardships few could have imagined previously. It had been nearly forty years since the Depression of 1893, when unemployment rates hovered around ten percent for five years, and that paled in comparison to the Great Depression of the 1930s. The people who weathered this economic storm ultimately provided the backbone of the labor force once the United States entered the war in late 1941. While some of them did serve in the military, most were too old for combat or possessed vital skills for the economy that precluded them from military service. Most served the country willingly by supporting the war effort at home.

Unlike the generations who preceded them, Americans under twenty in the early 1930s experienced their youth through the lens of the Great Depression. They bore witness to economic hardship through the suffering of their own families. They learned lessons about frugality and being satisfied with what little they had. They had to adapt and often work hard to help their families

1. *The Statistical History of the United States: From Colonial Times to the Present* (New York: Basic Books, 1976), 126.

survive. In many cases, they had to grow up more quickly than children from earlier generations and assume responsibilities that were not normal for their age.[2] The outbreak of war continued these lessons. American teenagers and young adults of the 1930s formed a truly unique generation, as they had to face unprecedented economic struggles and withstand the worst of the fighting in World War II.

Thomas Pettit Faulkner came from this generation. He was born in March 1925 in Helena, Arkansas, and came of age during the Great Depression and the war. Tom's family endured significant economic losses during the depression and frequently moved from job to job. They got used to living without and being happy with what they had. Tom and his friends witnessed the start of the war in Europe in 1939 and knew that the United States could be drawn into it at any time, but it was not a pressing concern. As a sixteen-year-old at the start of his senior year of high school in Dallas, Texas, in August 1941, Tom worried much more about the upcoming football season and a breakup with his girlfriend than international events halfway across the world. That all changed in December 1941.

Tom and his family received the news that the Japanese had attacked Pearl Harbor and the country was going to war while he was lying in bed recovering from an injury he received in a football playoff game the day before. The country was going to war, and that meant dramatic changes for all Americans: especially for those young men in their late teens and twenties who were very likely looking at military service in their near future. With World War I having only occurred twenty years earlier, there was at least a general understanding of the human cost of going to war. Tom's generation was about to see that cost firsthand.

As a sixteen-year-old at the time of the Japanese attack, Tom did not have to worry about being drafted immediately. He knew he could finish his senior year, but after that, he would have to begin making some difficult decisions. He turned seventeen in March 1942 and graduated from high school a few months later. When he turned

2. Among the best works on the Great Depression are David M. Kennedy, *The American People and the Great Depression: Freedom from Fear* (New York: Oxford University Press, 2003); Robert McElvaine, *The Great Depression: America, 1929–1941*, reprint edition (New York: Times Books, 1993); and Amity Shlaes, *The Forgotten Man: A New History of the Great Depression*, reprint edition (New York: Harper Perennial, 2008).

eighteen the next year, he knew he would be eligible for the draft.[3] For Tom and his friends, it was not a question of whether they would have to serve in the military, but when that service would begin. None of them shirked from their duty, but they did decide to wait until they were at least eighteen to make a final decision about what they would do.

Tom and several of his friends decided to enroll in college immediately after graduating from high school in hopes of completing at least a year of college before having to enter the military. Most of them went to Texas A&M in the summer of 1942 to complete their first semester early and stayed through the fall in order to finish one year of classes. Tom transferred to Southern Methodist University (SMU), near his home, for the spring semester and began the enlistment process for the Army Air Forces (AAF) preferring to serve in an airplane than in the infantry. He hoped he would be able to finish at least a semester at SMU, but the AAF called him into service immediately after his eighteenth birthday in March. There was one clear benefit of having completed one year of college, however. The AAF enrolled him in a pilot training program that would make him an officer, albeit a very young one, if he completed it successfully.

Over the next nine months, he went through Preflight, Primary, Basic, and Advanced training before he earned his pilot wings (See Appendix A). He then trained as a B-24 Liberator pilot in Liberal, Kansas, and was assigned his own crew in the spring of 1944 for training in Nevada. Upon completion of their training, Tom and his crew flew a new B-24 from the United States to Italy where they were assigned to the 737th Bomb Squadron, 454th Bomb Group of the Fifteenth Air Force in September 1944.

By this point, the war had been going on for five years in Europe. Germany had conquered most of Europe in 1939 and 1940, and Italy joined it as an ally in June 1940. German forces continued their expansion in 1941: they pushed Great Britain to the brink of defeat, threatened the Suez Canal, and conquered roughly one-third of the Soviet Union. At the peak of its power in 1941, Germany seemed invincible; however, some of its weaknesses soon became apparent. For all its conquests, it failed to defeat either the

3. For the best study of the draft, see George Q. Flynn, *The Draft, 1940–1973* (Lawrence: University Press of Kansas, 1993).

Soviet Union or Great Britain, and in December 1941, declared war on the United States after the Japanese attack on Pearl Harbor. While its conquests looked impressive on a map at the start of 1942, Germany now faced three powerful enemies in the United States, Great Britain, and the Soviet Union. Individually, each country may not have been strong enough to defeat Germany, but together, they formed an imposing coalition.[4]

Although it still maintained very capable fighting forces, Germany began to lose ground in 1942. Its population and resource reserves were more limited than those possessed by the Grand Alliance of the United States, Great Britain, and the Soviet Union. By itself, the United States produced more military equipment and weapons than almost all other countries combined.[5] When considered within the context of an alliance, the potential power of the United States, Great Britain, the Soviet Union, and their other allies was immense. Germany, on the other hand, enjoyed less economic power, and its strongest ally, Italy, was much weaker than the other great powers in the war. Italians never supported the war effort like their leader, Benito Mussolini, wanted and did not add as much to the alliance with Germany as Adolf Hitler had hoped.[6] German and Italian forces suffered serious defeats in late 1942, and by the spring of 1943, the tide of the war had definitely turned. The war was far from over, but there was growing optimism among the allies that they would ultimately be victorious.

German and Italian forces had conquered all of Europe, and even at the start of 1943, they maintained large armies long distances from their homelands. For the allies to win the war, they had to recapture thousands of square miles of territory and destroy both Germany and Italy's ability to keep up the fight—no easy task. Great Britain and the United States had the responsibility to defeat German and Italian forces in North Africa before they could cross the Mediterranean Sea and the English Channel to attack southern and western Europe. Accomplishing this would require

4. The best one volume history of World War II is Gerhard L. Weinberg, *A World at Arms: A Global History of World War II* (New York: Cambridge University Press, 1994). I have drawn most of the general information on the war from this volume.

5. See Williamson Murray and Allan R. Millett, *A War to Be Won: Fighting the Second World War* (Cambridge, MA: Belknap Press of Harvard University Press, 2000), 533–540; and Alan M. Winkler, *Home Front U.S.A.: American During World War II*, 2nd ed. (Wheeling, IL: Harlan Davidson, Inc., 2000), 26.

6. See Weinberg, *A World at Arms*, 483–85.

unprecedented amphibious operations and prodigious numbers of troops and equipment. The Soviet Union faced German and other Axis forces on the largest front in the European theater, stretching from the Baltic to the Black Sea. Having defeated German forces at Stalingrad by February 1943, the Soviet Union had the task of driving them out of its territory along the Eastern Front.[7]

In the summer of 1943, American, British, and Russian forces began a series of operations to push back German and Italian Axis forces. After its stunning defeat at Stalingrad in February, Germany regrouped and launched several operations later in 1943, particularly against Kursk on the Eastern Front in July. However, the Russians were able to stop the Germans there, then launch a counterattack that began Germany's long retreat back to its border. In North Africa, British, American, and other Allied forces launched Operation Torch in November 1942. After months of fighting in very difficult conditions, Axis forces surrendered there in May the following year. In July, American and British forces invaded and captured Sicily. In early September, they attacked mainland Italy and captured the lower third of the country below the German defensive positions along the Gustav line. They also forced Italy to surrender and ultimately switch sides.[8] This was a critical victory, as the allies planned to build a base of operations around Foggia, Italy, for the new Fifteenth Air Force that would include crucial new airfields alongside existing ones.[9]

Tom Faulkner's role in the war was undefined at the start of 1943. Early that year, he had just transferred to SMU and was not officially in the military, although he had begun the enlistment process. What he did not know was that in addition to the Soviet Union's assault on German forces along the Eastern Front and joint American and British amphibious strikes in the Mediterranean, the United States and Great Britain were in the process of expanding the air war against Germany. Codenamed Pointblank, the operation called for U.S. and British long-range bombers to launch strategic bombing missions deep behind enemy lines

7. The best single account on the Eastern Front is David M. Glantz and Jonathan M. House, *When Titans Clashed: How the Red Army Stopped Hitler*, revised and expanded edition (Lawrence: University Press of Kansas, 2015).

8. Weinberg, *A World at Arms*, 597–601.

9. Barrett Tillman, *Forgotten Fifteenth: The Daring Airmen Who Crippled Hitler's War Machine* (Washington D.C.: Regnery History, 2014), 5.

against German infrastructure, industry, and transportation. To achieve their audacious goals of taking the war to the German heartland, they needed more long-range aircraft, pilots, and aircrews.[10] Tom signed his enlistment papers just as the British and Americans were ratcheting up these operational air attacks in Europe.

The strategic air campaign began well before the official implementation of Operation Pointblank. During the 1930s, both the United States and Great Britain recognized the potential importance of long-range bombers in future wars; more so than any other country. They devoted substantial resources toward the creation of strategic bombing forces.[11] The British ultimately developed the four-engine Lancaster and Halifax bombers, while the United States developed the B-17 and B-24. Toward the end of the war, the United States introduced the most advanced strategic bomber of the era, the B-29. Each of these bombers was far superior to the long-range bombers of any other country. In fact, neither Germany, Italy, nor Japan developed an effective four-engine bomber. While they built many quality fighter planes and shorter-range bombers, the Axis countries were at an extreme disadvantage to the allies in strategic bombing throughout the war.

The United States developed an efficient system for training pilots and aircrews, while also expanding production of both the B-17 and B-24. The United States ultimately produced over 12,000 B-17s and 18,000 B-24s.[12] The British produced over 13,000 Halifax and Lancaster bombers altogether.[13] Production in other countries was negligible. For training, the United States introduced a series of roughly nine-week training segments—Preflight, Primary, Basic, and Advanced. Every month it would start new groups of pilot

10. For the best accounts of U.S. strategic bombing doctrine in World War II, see Conrad C. Crane, *American Airpower Strategy in World War II: Bombs, Cities, and Civilians* (Lawrence: University Press of Kansas, 1993); Michael S. Sherry, *The Rise of American Airpower: The Creation of Armageddon* (New Haven, CT: Yale University Press, 1987); and Ronald Schaffer, *Wings of Judgement: American Bombing in World War II* (New York: Oxford University Press, 1985).

11. See Crane, *American Airpower Strategy in World War II*, 12–27; and Robin Neillands, *The Bomber War: The Allied Air Offensive Against Germany* (New York: The Overlook Press, 2001), 20–33.

12. "World War II Bomber Production Numbers," Airplanes of the Past, accessed on September 4, 2017, http://www.airplanesofthepast.com/wwii-bomber-production-numbers.htm.

13. "Aircraft of Bomber Command," Bomber Command Museum of Canada, accessed on September 4, 2017, http://www.bombercommandmuseum.ca/main_bombers.html.

trainees and those who completed Advanced training earned their pilots' wings as well as a promotion to second lieutenant. After Advanced training, the AAF sent the new pilots to Transition training where they specialized in their assigned aircraft. Tom trained as a B-24 pilot and upon completion of Transition training moved to Operational training with his assigned crew. After the completion of Operational training, the AAF assigned the newly trained crews to commands where needed.

As a pilot of a four-engine bomber, Tom could have ended up assigned to a command in either the Pacific or the European theaters of operation. In fact, Tom did not find out his destination until after he took off from an airfield in San Francisco and headed out over the Pacific Ocean. At that point, he and his crew were allowed to open their sealed orders. Since they were taking off from California, they assumed they were destined for some base across the Pacific. To their surprise, however, their orders sent them to Italy to join the Fifteenth Air Force.

The AAF operated two strategic bombing commands in the European theater—the Eighth Air Force in Great Britain and the Fifteenth Air Force in Italy. The Eighth Air Force started flying missions in the summer of 1942 from bases in eastern England. Together with the British Royal Air Force Bomber Command, the aircrews of the Eighth Air Force launched attacks against targets in German-occupied Western Europe and against Germany itself.[14] The AAF formed the Fifteenth Air Force in late 1943, and it operated from bases in Italy.[15] Both the Eighth and Fifteenth Air Forces flew B-17s and B-24s against targets in Germany and in German-held territory.

The AAF hoped adding operations by the Fifteenth Air Force from Italy would increase the firepower it could place on a target. Poor weather in England often limited the number of missions, and there was some thought that the weather in south central Italy would permit more. A further benefit was that missions from Italy could reach targets in Axis-held territory that were previously

14. For two excellent histories of the Eighth Air Force, see Roger A. Freeman, *The Mighty Eighth: Units, Men and Machines (A History of the US 8th Army Air Force)* (Garden City, NY: Doubleday and Company, 1970); and Gerald Astor, *The Mighty Eighth: The Air War in Europe as Told by the Men Who Fought It* (New York: A Dell Book, 1997).

15. Kevin A. Mahoney, *Fifteenth Air Force Against the Axis: Combat Missions over Europe During World War II* (Lanham, MD: Scarecrow Press, 2013), 1–4.

out of the Eighth Air Force's range.[16] This was particularly true for targets in central and Eastern Europe, including Austria, Hungary, Romania, and Yugoslavia. With the two American air forces in operation by 1944 and in conjunction with bombers from the RAF Bomber Command, the allies could bring unprecedented firepower against key infrastructure, industrial, and transportation targets in Germany and other occupied areas.

The Fifteenth Air Force's operations in 1944 and 1945 proved critical to the war effort. It focused its attacks against German oil production in Romania, airplane factories, and key infrastructure targets—railroad marshalling yards, bridges, and supply depots—in Germany, Austria, and Hungary. From its airfields in Italy, the Fifteenth Air Force could reach oil fields and refineries that provided seventy-six percent of Germany's fuel supply.[17] After repeated attacks by the Fifteenth Air Force over the spring and summer of 1944, Germany's fuel production had fallen to critical levels that undermined training, limited transportation, and severely hampered military operations. Fifteenth Air Force Commander General Ira Eaker claimed that as a result of the air attacks, "Germany's petroleum availability was reduced to less than 25%." He added the inability of the Germans to move forces easily and the "inelasticity of German defense" was a result of strategic air attacks.[18]

The lack of fuel as well as the destruction of transportation targets severely limited Germany's ability to meet its military and civilian needs.[19] Gerhard Weinberg argues that by the middle of 1944, German "planes were often destroyed on the ground because they lacked fuel."[20] Williamson Murray and Allan Millett note that in the first five months of 1944, the Luftwaffe lost 2,262 fighter pilots when they had only 2,395 fighter pilots available at the beginning of the year. Germany rushed to replace these losses, and its pilot trainees were receiving less than eighty hours of operational flight training. This was problematic when compared to the

16. Tillman, *Forgotten Fifteenth*, 5.

17. Robert S. Ehlers, Jr. *The Mediterranean Air War: Airpower and Allied Victory in World War II* (Lawrence: University Press of Kansas, 2015), 360.

18. "The Effect of Allied Strategic Bombing on the Present Status of the War," Library of Congress, Washington, D.C. [hereafter LOC], Ira Eaker Papers, Box 1:29, Folder 6 – Press Conferences, April 1944-February, 1945, Eaker Press Conference, 2/2/45, 20.

19. Glantz and House, *When Titans Clashed*, 358.

20. Weinberg, *A World at Arms*, 750.

225 hours required of American and British pilots.[21] Particularly on the Eastern Front, Germans found it virtually impossible to make needed defensive movements to counter Soviet advances.[22] While not decisive, the Fifteenth Air Force proved to be a critical component of the Allied effort to defeat Germany.

The Fifteenth Air Force opened its headquarters in Foggia, Italy, in November 1943 and began refurbishing airfields in the area to handle long-range B-24s and B-17s. Most of the airfields had smaller runways that were better suited for fighter planes and smaller bombers. It also built new airfields in the Italian countryside within a thirty-mile radius of Foggia. Altogether, twenty-one different bomb groups flew from these airfields, fifteen operating B-24s and six using B-17s.[23] Tom and his crew joined the 737th Bomb Squadron that was part of the 454th Bomb Group. His squadron flew out of San Giovanni Airfield, which was about five miles west of the small town of Cerignola. The town was about twenty-three miles southeast of Foggia. The 454th shared the airfield with the 455th Bomb Group, but they seldom interacted outside of missions because they were on opposite sides of the runways.

The 737th arrived at Cerignola during the winter of 1944 and began flying missions in February. To say the conditions were rudimentary would be an understatement. The AAF's engineers built two parallel runways, an operations tower, and gravel pads for the airplanes in late 1943, but did little else to prepare the area for occupation. When the men of the 737th arrived in late January 1944, they had to live in pup tents until more permanent housing could be arranged. They built most of their furniture from materials they could scrape together. In the end, the men put up groups of six-man tents that were set on poorly constructed concrete and plaster pads. The four officers of each crew shared one tent, while the six enlisted men shared another. By the time Tom and his crew arrived in early September, the crew tents were in place, but other parts of the infrastructure, like the Officers' Club and Enlisted Men's Club, were still not ready.[24]

21. Millett and Murray, *A War to Be Won*, 325.
22. Ehlers, *The Mediterranean Air War*, 373–74 and 377–81.
23. See ibid., 358; and Tillman, *Forgotten Fifteenth*, 6.
24. For an overview of the construction of the base at San Giovanni, see Joseph Chalker, *The Flight of the Liberators* (Rochester, NY: The Du Bois Press, 1946), 29–33.

Tom and his crew lived at San Giovanni for six months. During that time, Tom flew twenty-eight official missions (See Appendix B). Not unexpectedly, their first missions were a bit overwhelming. While Tom and his crew benefitted from solid training, the military could only do so much to prepare someone for actual combat. Everyone had to experience it for themselves and then learn to adjust. Most crews, like Tom's, did so with relatively few difficulties. Due to the unique rotation system used by the AAF and heavy losses to German flak and fighters, there was a great deal of turnover of crews, and new crews quickly became experienced ones. The AAF used different systems over the course of the war to determine when a crew would rotate home. Soon after Tom arrived at San Giovanni, it settled on a number of thirty-five missions. If a crew reached that number, it would return home.[25] Each month new crews arrived and old crews left. Since Tom flew ten missions in his first month, he quickly became one of the more experienced pilots in the squadron.

Looking back almost seven decades after the war, Tom decided to write his memoir in large part for his family to have a record of his experiences. They had heard some of his stories, but like most men who served in the military, he had not talked about the war much. Rather, he returned home and began to move on. He wanted to complete his education and make his mark as a civilian. He had also seen the realities of war and did not want to relive them; however, the war never truly let him go, and he never could put it completely behind him. His last mission particularly tormented him: German flak severely damaged his plane, and he was forced to land in the neutral Switzerland, which did not allow combatants who crossed its borders to return to the war. After a brief stay as internees in Switzerland, Tom and his crew were released to Allied forces and, per international law, required to return to the United States. Despite having little choice and potentially saving the lives of his crew by landing his bomber, Tom carried a tremendous guilt and uncertainty for seventy years. He doubted if he had done the right thing. His worries became so severe he suffered recurrent health problems spurred on by stress. It has only been in the past few years, after new information became known about his actions on his last mission, that he realized his doubts and worries were

25. Mahoney, *Fifteenth Air Force Against the Axis*, 265.

unnecessary. He had done what he should have and was ultimately recognized for his bravery and level-headedness under extremely stressful circumstances.

This memoir represents part of Tom's healing process. He would not feel comfortable being called a hero, and in many ways, he was no different from most in his generation. The country needed him to serve, and he did so without reservation. He enlisted in the AAF, spent eighteen months in training, and flew twenty-eight missions as a B-24 pilot all before he turned twenty. While it cannot be proven, he very well could have been America's youngest B-24 pilot in the war. Tom served with distinction and deserves the greatest respect like so many others from his generation.

World War II pilot memoirs are pretty common, but even if every other pilot had written one, there would still be a place for that one pilot who had not. Every person's experience was unique in some way. Tom was exceptionally young, and he became a second lieutenant at the age of eighteen during a time when youngsters often had responsibilities well beyond their age. On each of his bombing missions, he commanded crews of nine to twelve men. He also flew his missions out of Italy, an often-forgotten theater of the war. Barring a few exceptions, the exploits of the Eighth Air Force are much better known than those of the Fifteenth, as they have been the subject of movies and documentaries. Tom's memoir corrects this lack of emphasis to some degree, and it reveals what normal American young men faced during those years of profound turbulence. We are better off for their sacrifices.

# Acknowledgments from Tom Faulkner

When reading a book by two contributors, I always wonder who did what. In this case, let me hasten to say that, while the footnotes and technical data surrounding my wartime experiences were gathered and recorded by David Snead, he did not stop there. David completely reorganized my original book, *Combat Missions from Italy*, that I had self-published four years ago. His changes marked a significant improvement. He deleted parts of that first book that were not "tangential." He changed the structure to a more logical order while still leaving my words as written without alteration in what I said and how I said it. While we have not yet met personally, we communicated almost exclusively by email for well over a year. After seeing the final product, I certainly agree that David was right about what should go and what should stay and the order in which everything, new and old, is presented, So, thank you, David Snead. It has been a most pleasurable ride.

The small diary in which I recorded the events of each mission before turning out the light above my bunk remained dormant, lost away for sixty-five years. After Dan Matthews entered my life in 2013 and quickly uncovered the reasons for my ongoing sore throats, which ceased immediately, I resurrected the small diary and began writing about my wartime experience with enthusiasm. We were constantly in touch. His research and acquisition of information is reflected on many pages of this book.

The invisible signature of my wife, Ann, is also reflected throughout. For two years Ann taught English classes to mostly WWII veterans, who crowded SMU after the war on the G.I. Bill. Her last act as their teacher was grading final exam papers on our honeymoon. Her oversight in punctuation and grammar, and showing unbelievable patience in the writing and rewriting process, along with her affection and understanding was beyond the call.

Charley Cleaver, of Dallas, and Dan Matthews's good friend, whom I have known since his birth, is responsible for Dan becoming involved. I suspect both of them were behind the scenes of the DFC award ceremony that was held at the Ft. Worth Air Base, as well as the later ceremony at Love Field on March 18, 2015, when my name was added to the Honor Roll of hundreds of WWII airmen listed on the side of the *Witchcraft*, the last standing B-24, owned by the Collings Foundation of Stow, Massachusetts. There happened to be space left on the top line of a long list of hundreds of airmen. On that same line, mysteriously appeared the name, William Knauer, my copilot on that twenty-eighth mission, as well as the only aircraft identification number shown, 42-75458, the number of the plane Knauer and I were flying when we were shot down over Augsburg, Germany. Very strange. This was followed by my flying in the cockpit of the *Witchcraft* as their guest.

My son, Tom, Jr. was someone I could count on for assistance in all phases at any time, but specifically, I imposed upon him and his professional background in improving the quality of each and every photograph. Tom is an excellent writer and his advice has been invaluable.

I thank my daughter, Linda, also an accomplished writer, for her suggestions and editing.

Dani Egger, of Bern, Switzerland, who at Dan Matthews's request, completed research into Swiss records at Dubendorf Airport in Zurich to establish the extent of damage to our Liberator, and also translating their findings from German to English.

My self-published version of this book reached a few airmen of my squadron or their families. As a result, I have been in touch with them and what a delight it has been.

737[th] Bomb Squadron pilot, Sumner Williams, the one called "Willie," was my very good friend. I have had the pleasure of being in touch with his wife, Jane, daughters, Gina and Betsy, and son, David, all of whom have contributed to this memoir.

Fellow 737[th] Bomb Squadron pilot, Conrad Leslie, helped in my recollection of certain events and I have enjoyed reading his fascinating personal diary. He is a former member of the Chicago Board of Trade and now, at age ninety-five, Les is still writing, offering help to others based upon his financial background.

Erik Goldstein is curator of the Williamsburg Museum. He is also author of *Ray's Story* about his Uncle Ray, who was killed as a member of pilot Ted Schindler's crew during their tragic mission to destroy a Brenner Pass bridge. Erik and his family visited Ann and me here at the Tradition and shared information he had discovered while writing his book.

Bert Early was my best friend during my cadet days. His wife, Betsy and son, Mark, now a Dallas resident, also dined with us last year and I learned of Bert's post war success as an attorney who became Executive Director of the prestigious American Bar Association in Chicago.

General John F. Nichols, Texas Adjutant General and Commander of the Texas Military Forces, who called a special assembly of his airman at the Ft. Worth Air Base and presided over the ceremony to award the DFC to me on September 19, 2013, I offer my thanks, and also to Lt. Col. James T. Castleman, in charge of its preparation.

Steve Blow, writer for *The Dallas Morning News*, spent two hours with me and wrote a review headlined, "Pilot's War Wound Finally Heals," appearing the same day as the DFC ceremony.

I'm sure I've left contributing people out, and if so, I apologize and plead guilty by reason of being ninety-three years old.

# Acknowledgments by David L. Snead

Writing and editing a memoir requires many hands. Tom and I could not have completed this project without the help of many different people.

I could not have done the research for the memoir without the College of Arts and Sciences and the History Department at Liberty University. They graciously financed research trips and the printing of more historical documents than they probably realize. Sam Smith, Carey Roberts, and Roger Schultz have been devoted supporters of my research since I arrived at Liberty. They kept me going at times when I did not feel I could go anymore. Ruth Ronk and, more recently, Rachel Allison have served the History Department with dedication over the years, including assisting me with many requests. My colleagues in the department, Michael Davis, Donna Donald, Ben Esswein, Chris Jones, Herbert Pieper, Rob Ritchie, and Chris Smith, are wonderful to work with and are always there to offer assistance. Rob Ritchie, in particular, has been my go to source on Air Force history.

I would be remiss to not thank the many students that I have been privileged to teach over my years at Liberty. They are a constant source of wonder as their curiosity leads them to examine the most fascinating subjects. They truly are an inspiration to me. I need to thank two students in particular. Both Caitlin Curtis and Alex Bhalla helped me at different stages in this project and without their assistance my progress would have been slowed considerably.

I used materials from various archives and museums as I explored Tom Faulkner's training and military experiences. I owe a special thanks to Lynn Gamma and Tammy Horton at the Air Force Historical Research Agency, Jeff Flannery at the Library of Congress, and Matthew Heichelbech, Kaitlyn Crain Enriquez, David Langbart, and Paul Brown at the National Archives in College Park.

As can be seen at various points in the memoir, Dan Matthews's role has been critical to understanding Tom's twenty-eighth and final mission. After hearing of Tom's concerns about his actions on that mission from a mutual friend, Dan took it upon himself to investigate exactly what happened. He found Air Force documents as well as materials from Swiss historians that allow an almost complete view of the events on Tom's last mission. His efforts led to Tom receiving a well-deserved Distinguished Flying Cross. Dan shared the documents he found with me and helped me understand the intricacies of that mission. I am deeply grateful for his assistance.

I thanked my current students earlier, but it is always nice to remember former ones. Alex Mendoza, who worked with me while he was a graduate student and I was a young professor at Texas Tech University, has carved out an outstanding career at the University of North Texas as a prominent Civil War and Latino historian. Besides being a gifted historian, he is an excellent mapmaker. I have come to depend on him for producing maps that make complicated situations understandable.

Throughout the editing of the memoir, the University of North Texas Press, and particularly, Ron Chrisman have been wonderful to work with. Ron placed confidence in me when he approached me about editing Tom's memoir and has been a source of constant encouragement. I am also grateful that he asked two distinguished historians, Barrett Tillman and Robert Ehlers, to review the memoir on different occasions. Their comments have made the final edition that much better.

I have had the unique pleasure over the past couple of years to get to know Tom and his family, Ann, Linda, and Tom, Jr. They have been incredibly helpful from the beginning. Tom, Jr., in particular, has played an invaluable role collecting pictures and preparing them for publication.

Anyone who knows me will quickly realize how much I value my family. My mother and father-in-law, D.C. and Carolyn Hughes, have encouraged me for over thirty years. My mother, Marilyn Snead, remains an inspiration, and I thank her for passing along her love for history. My children, Reagan, Delaney, and Darel have always brought tremendous joy to my life. On this project, they have provided even more. I have been able to use them as reviewers of different sections of the memoir to get their impressions and advice. They have shown a keen eye and helped clarify several passages. Last, but definitely not least, is my wife, Lori. She has stuck with me many years as I worked on one project or another. She has been my companion on research trips, the chief reviewer of my writing, and a friend in times of happiness as well in times of need. She has put up with my research travels, long hours, and preoccupation with studying history with constant love and support. To her, I owe the greatest thanks.

# Introduction

If there was anyone responsible for my joining the Air Force, it was Warner Marsh. He was my best friend from the time we were in junior high. He was every boy's idol at Highland Park High School. With black hair, brown eyes, and dark skin, his looks were also outstanding. He received all the accolades—president of the student body, captain of the football team, major in the ROTC, and honor student. His attitude, morals, and values were bedrock. He was a great communicator and public speaker, and his confidence was tempered with humility. I would have followed him anywhere.

One afternoon in the summer of 1942, sitting in Warner's room with four other high school classmates during our freshman year at Texas A&M, the six of us talked about what we planned to do in the military. We knew that if we did not sign up with a branch of our choice soon, we would be drafted, probably to the infantry.[1] Four of them, Bill Wells, Bob Anderson, and Charlie

1. Congress passed the Selective Service and Training Act in September 1940 and required all men ages 18 to 64 to register. From the pool of registered men, the government inducted 10 million men. For a copy of the legislation, see "Selective Service and Training Act of 1940," *World Affairs* 103, no. 3 (September 1940): 179–86.

Hall, all members of our high school football team, plus Bob Phelps, the lone basketball star, all preferred the Marines. Warner, however, worshiped his father, who had been a fighter pilot in France in World War I. In high school, Warner proudly wore to class a moth-eaten old mustard-colored, knit wool, sleeveless sweater that his father had actually worn in combat. Without hesitation, Warner said he wanted to be a fighter pilot. That was good enough for me. While none of us enlisted right away, we knew we would before long.[2] I actually began the enlistment process in early January 1943, two months before my eighteenth birthday.[3]

Little did I know where that would lead, but just over a year and a half later, I wound up in Italy as the airplane commander of a B-24 Liberator, a four-engine heavy bomber. As a nineteen year old from North Texas, I was just as concerned as during my cadet days about what my reactions would be to that first mission, but that is the challenge, wonder, and reality of war, you are not asked what you want to do, or how you feel about it, you are told. Ready or not, I would be flying missions for the Air Force from our base in southern Italy and be responsible for my crew of nine other men.

In September 1944, my crew and I joined the 737th Bomb Squadron at San Giovanni Airfield near the Adriatic Sea.[4] Over the next six months, we would fly missions against targets in Austria, Germany, Hungary, Italy, and Yugoslavia. My first mission was on September 17, 1944, and this is what I recorded in my diary that night after I returned to our base.

2. Military recruiters frequently visited high schools and colleges to recruit prospective military personnel. See Charles A. Watry, *Washout!: The Aviation Cadet Story* (Carlsbad, CA: California Aero Press, 1983), 9–10.

3. Faulkner applied to the Army Air Forces Enlisted Reserve for an appointment as an Aviation Cadet (deferred plan) on January 10, 1943, and was examined by the Aviation Cadet Examining Board in Dallas, Texas. He was officially enlisted on February 20, 1943. See Application for Appointment As Aviation Cadet, January 10, 1943, in author's possession; Aviation Cadet Examining Board District Recruiting and Induction Office, Dallas, Texas, February 10, 1943, in author's possession; and Thomas Pettit Faulkner, Air Force Reserve Enlistment Record Enlisted Reserve Forces, February 20, 1943, in author's possession.

4. The Fifteenth Air Force consisted of five Bomb Wings: the 5th, 47th, 49th, 55th, and 304th; each Bomb Wing had four Bomb Groups; and each Bomb Group had four Bomb Squadrons. Faulkner was in the 737th Bomb Squadron, 454th Bomb Group, 304th Bomb Wing, Fifteenth Air Force. See "The Fifteenth Air Force," accessed on June 27, 2017, http://www.15thaf.org/index.htm.

## Mission 1 • September 17, 1944[5]
## Target: Marshalling Yards[6]
## Budapest, Hungary[7]

*I'll never forget that first one. I flew as copilot with a crew I had never seen before. The first pilot, named Sales, was a tall, thin red-headed fellow with a big red mustache.*[8] *I got a bang out of my first briefing. Just like I expected. The Chaplain said a prayer first thing. Then they lifted the screen on the wall. It showed a large map for today's target. A long red tape stretched from our airfield (5 miles from Cerignola), around the hump on the southeast side of the Italian coast, then northeast across the Adriatic, over Yugoslavia and into Hungary.*[9] *We were then briefed for weather, possible fighter opposition, flak (estimated number of anti-aircraft guns in the target area), emergency procedures, initial point of the target (that point from which the Group turns to begin the bomb run—usually a small town ten or fifteen miles from the target). We were then driven out to the planes in open trucks. By then, it was daylight. Under the wing we put on our clothing for flight, a new experience for me. It all seemed to weigh a ton, what with my long-johns, khaki flying coveralls, heated*

5. Forty B-24s participated in the attack on the Kobanya Marshalling Yards in Budapest. They were escorted by thirty-eight P-38s. Mahoney, *Fifteenth Air Force Against the Axis*, 236.

6. Railroad marshalling yards were a priority target for the Fifteenth Air Force during the summer and fall of 1944. Its leaders recognized that damaging the German transportation network on top of earlier attacks on Germany's main sources of oil would limit the Wehrmacht's ability to maneuver in order to meet Allied offensives both in Western Europe and on the Eastern Front. See Ehlers, *The Mediterranean Air War*, 377–85.

7. During World War II, Hungary allied with Germany against the Soviet Union because of longstanding grievances with the latter. It did declare war on the United States and Great Britain as well, but it made sure to tell those countries that its only disputes were with the Soviet Union. Furthermore, through most of the war, Hungary remained unoccupied and relatively free to makes its own policies. Because of this, it decided not to impede Allied planes that crossed its territory on bombing missions. However, this changed in March 1944 when Germany occupied Hungary and began attacking Allied planes. From that point forward, Allied forces, primarily from the Fifteenth Air Force, attacked various Hungarian targets, including Faulkner's first mission against Budapest. See Cecil D. Eby, *Hungary at War: Civilians and Soldiers in World War II* (University Park, PA: The Pennsylvania State University Press, 1998), 157–8.

8. Robert N. Sales served in the 737th Bomb Squadron and later reached the rank of captain. See "Robert Sales," 454th Bombardment Group, accessed on June 27, 2017, http://www.454bg.org/737th-squadron.cfm?LN=S. See also, "737th Bomb Squadron Crews," accessed on June 27, 2017, http://www.454thbombgroup.it/737th%20Squadron%20Crews.pdf.

9. Cerignola is a small city in Italy with a population of around 58,000 people. See "Cerignola," Encyclopedia Britannica, accessed on June 27, 2017, https://www.britannica.com/place/Cerignola. For some wartime pictures of Cerignola, see "Cerignola," 461st Bombardment Group (H), accessed on June 27, 2017, http://www.461st.org/Cerignola/Cerignola.htm.

*suit, heavy wool-lined, leather boots, yellow Mae West, parachute harness and oxygen mask—which wouldn't be hooked up until reaching high altitude—flak vest, which weighs at least fifteen pounds, and steel flak helmet (which is worn only during the bomb run).*[10] *Before takeoff, Sales and his crew circled around for a few seconds of silent prayer under the left wing. I thought this a good idea and decided to have my crew do this also.*

*We were number 8 ship in a ten-ship box.*[11] *Our squadron would fly in formation with two other ten-ship squadrons from our bomb group* (See Appendix C).[12] *All the way to the target, I was wondering if I would get terribly frightened. Before I knew it, we were on the bomb run. The nose gunner said over the intercom in a calm, deliberate voice, "Flak at 12:00 o'clock." I had never seen flak, and it looked perfectly harmless to me. I had been piloting the plane, but Sales took the wheel from me for the bomb run. I got a good look at the flak bursting around us at a few hundred yards, not truly realizing how dangerous it was.*[13] *After the bombardier—who, by the way, was Runyan,*[14] *the only*

10. For a thorough description of the clothing and extra protective gear that pilots and their crews wore, see Alfred Asch, Hugh R. Graff, and Thomas A. Ramey, *The Story of the Four Hundred and Fifty-Fifth Bombardment Group (H) WW II: Flight of the Vulgar Vultures* (Appleton, WI: Graphic Communications Center, 1991), 55.

11. American bombers flew in a combat box that allowed for "increased forward firepower and mutually protecting fields of fire." Stephen McFarland and Wesley Phillips Newton, *To Command the Sky: The Battle for Air Superiority Over Germany, 1942–1944* (Washington, D.C.: Smithsonian Institution Press, 1991), 92–3. Curtis LeMay, the commander of the 305th Bombardment Group in the Eighth Air Force early in the war and later the overall commander of U.S. strategic bombing missions in the Pacific, described his efforts to create the right flying formation. He explained:

> There must be a master formation, a combination of formations, which would present a maximum opportunity for perfect bombing results, and still constitute itself as an aggregation in which the maximum defensive effort could be maintained. In other words, destructive firepower of our 50-caliber machine guns, firing from different positions on planes, and from those airplanes' different positions in the formation, would constitute an effective deterrent against enemy fighter attack. … This was the evolution of the Lead-High-Low, the wedge-shaped combat box.

Curtis E. LeMay with MacKinlay Kantor, *Mission with LeMay: My Story* (Garden City, NY: Doubleday & Company, 1965), 232–34. For a description of the actual features of the box, see Robert J. Mrazek, *To Kingdom Come: An Epic Saga of Survival in the Air War Over Germany* (New York: NAL Caliber, 2011), 82–3.

12. Faulkner flew in the second box, or Box B. Headquarters 454th Bombardment Group (H), Operations Order #244, September 17, 1944, Mission #133, Air Force Historical Research Agency, Reel B0601 – 454 Records, 651.

13. The 455th Bomb Group flew this mission as well. Its historian described the flak as moderate. Asch, Graff, and Ramey, *The Story of the Four Hundred and Fifty-Fifth Bombardment Group (H) WW II*, 126. The official report noted that the flak was "moderate, inaccurate, [but] heavy at Budapest." Confirmed Mission Report, September 17, 1944, Mission #119, Air Force Historical Research Agency, Reel B0601 – 454 Records, 653.

14. Faulkner's bombardier was Howard W. Runyan.

*member of my crew aboard—shouted, "Bombs away," we made a sharp left turn, still in formation, and seemed to dive and pick up much air speed. This suited me fine, as I was anxious to get the hell home. All during the run, there was a faint sound in my earphones of a brass band playing some German tune—probably a Hungarian radio station whose music had filtered through to our earphones. It all seemed sort of weird, knowing that down below, people were probably being killed, sirens were blowing, and guns were blasting away at us. All the way home, we throttled back and took it easy.*

I flew twenty-eight missions over the next six months while stationed in Italy, and because this one proved relatively uneventful, I was lulled into the false complacency that combat was not nearly as scary as I had imagined. Later missions would confront my crew and me with a myriad of totally unexpected situations that would reduce the Budapest mission into the milk-run category when compared to what was in store.

For a guy who, three years previously, was beginning his senior year in high school with his most significant worry being whether or not he would make the football team, my experiences were now life changing. I graduated from high school, spent nine months in college, trained for about eighteen months learning how to fly a four-engine bomber and command a crew of men, and then spent six months on a combat tour over the skies of Europe. I ultimately flew my last and most trying mission just days before my twentieth birthday. Thankfully, I lived to record my experiences, but I could have easily been like the ones who did not, like my best friend, Warner Marsh.

# Chapter 1

# Early Life to Enlistment

I was born in a red brick bungalow on Oakland Avenue, a main thoroughfare on the outskirts of Helena, Arkansas, on March 3, 1925. The house sat high above a terraced front lawn that dropped sharply to the street. My father, the most fastidious man I ever knew, somehow enjoyed raising chickens as a hobby. They clucked away in a small backyard cut short by a towering orange cliff behind our house that was overgrown with dark green Kudzu vines.

Helena, a small town on the west side of the Mississippi River and about sixty miles south of Memphis, was the quintessential southern town. During the decades following the Civil War, Helena, surrounded by thriving cotton plantations and lumber mills, prospered and expanded upon its traditions of southern hospitality, lavish entertainment, and easy living. Words and phrases of those living in the heart of the fertile Mississippi Delta were spoken with the same deep southern drawl of those in neighboring Mississippi and Alabama.

My parents were married in June of 1917 during World War I. My father, James Miles Faulkner, was twenty-three and on leave from the Medical Corps. My mother, Louise Pettit, was seventeen.[1]

1. For more information on Faulkner's family, see Dallas Tabor Herndon, *Centennial History of Arkansas*, Vol. 3 (Chicago, IL: S. J. Clarke Publishing Company, 1922), 374.

Louise Pettit Faulkner, Tom's Mother, 1917

Tom with His Dad, James Miles Faulkner, 1942

Louis Pettit Faulkner, Tom's Mother, c. 1945

She was a beauty then and remained so all her life. With full make-up and coiffed hair, even at the age of 93, she still looked good. After arriving at Dallas's Baylor hospital in February 1993, and sensing she might be in trouble, she turned to my wife and said, "Ann, call my bridge partners and tell them I may not be there tomorrow." She died two hours later.

My earliest memory is at the age of four throwing rocks down to the street at passing automobiles. I swear I can still recall that sickening sound of the shattered glass windshield as I watched the car skid to a tire-screeching halt. The driver looked up, saw me, and jumped out, furious. I ran and hid behind some bushes and watched him storm up the long, steep row of concrete steps. He banged on the front door and demanded retribution from my father. My father was a stern disciplinarian, and I expected the worst, but was relieved to receive nothing but a stern lecture.

My father and my godfather, Warren Brown, were partners in the Brown-Faulkner Ford Motor Company dealership in Helena, where they sold more tractors than cars. Helena was a small town and everyone knew everyone else. To help boost sales, my godfather persuaded my mother to drive around town each year, smiling and waving at everyone to call attention to the newly arrived Ford models.

My mother, from Hot Springs, and my father would join large parties on the Mississippi paddleboats, dancing to the music of the all-black band led by W. C. Handy. The well-known Handy, still acknowledged today as the Father of the Blues, would lead his band as the boat pulled away from the Helena docks at dusk, roamed up and down the Mississippi River, and, after a night of dancing and revelry, returned to dock at dawn. Handy wrote many songs still popular today, including "The St. Louis Blues," and he frequently joined his good friend, Louis Armstrong, in New Orleans.[2]

The word "babysitter" would have been foreign to my parents. Until the roof fell in financially in 1929, I had a nurse, Rebecca Leech. She was black, and my family called her "Beeka." My parents hired her when I was born, and she was then 17. According to my mother, Beeka and I would sit on the front steps every day, side by side,

2. For more information on Handy, see Larry Nager, "W.C. Handy," Memphis Music Hall of Fame, accessed on June 9, 2017, http://memphismusichalloffame.com/inductee/wchandy/.

Rebecca "Beeka" Leech and Tom, c. 1927

looking down at the cars passing by on Oakland Avenue, while wobbling our knees and sucking our thumbs.

During the prosperity of the late twenties, we moved further out to a new, larger house in Waverly Woods, a new suburban section of about fifty homes on land cut out of a dense forest. The house sat on a promontory with two other houses. Inside a circular drive, they looked out from different angles over the curved street to the surrounding heavily wooded areas.

I loved Waverly Woods. My older brother, Jimmy, and I would play in the forest of tall trees and underbrush that stretched behind our house. I would wander through, searching for "Jack in the Pulpit," and watch the haze develop and float above the ground as the older boys laid down smoke screens with newspaper-fired torches tied to the top of fence posts while playing war games.[3] In wonder, I watched my father empty the lily pad-covered goldfish pond on the side of the house by sucking on a garden hose to set the draining in motion. I found a small tin star the size of a fingernail on the front lawn (probably from in a square of chewing tobacco) and was certain it had fallen from the sky. I would lie on my back on the grass and stare at the moving clouds. As a boy,

3. Jack in the Pulpit is a type of flower. Its official name is *Arisaema triphyllum*. See "Plant Database – *Arisaema Triphyllum*," Lady Bird Johnson Wildflower Center, accessed on June 9, 2017, http://www.wildflower.org/plants/result.php?id_plant=artr.

Tom with His Brother, Jimmy, c. 1929

I received a book with drawings of Charles Lindbergh, our national hero, and his *Spirit of St. Louis* flying machine. It was just three years after his historic flight to Paris, and he was still the most talked about man in America.[4]

Inside our house on the sun porch overlooking the fishpond, I would watch the turntable spin on the upright Victrola and listen to the records, fascinated by the image of the dog, cocking his head into the speaker horn. Our tall, mahogany radio with its oval top sat on a table against the wall. In the late afternoons, we all listened, along with one-third of the nation, to "Amos and Andy," which began every sequence with the familiar voice of its announcer with his distinctive introduction, "Here they ah."[5]

My father drove us all to Chicago during the summer of 1929 in a new, dark Lincoln sedan. Mother and Dad rode in front, while Beeka, who spent much more time with me than my mother did, would sit between Jimmy and me to maintain peace. At least that was the plan. The Chicago trip was a long and arduous disaster, made more difficult by my constant demands, always with the underlying threat of loud bawling. As we cruised over the two-lane highways, I would stand up behind my parents, calling for immediate responses to my thirst, my hunger, and my urgent need for the bathroom. For diversion, I would turn back and renew the ongoing tussles with my brother, all of this interspersed with the same question, repeated every few miles, "How much further is it?" On a long trip, a restless child is in total control.

At the Chicago hotel, my father learned that the New York Yankees were in town to play the Chicago White Sox and that Babe Ruth was on the roof and available for autographs. He took Jimmy and me up to the top deck to see him. Under an open sky above, we watched a small crowd of men, encircling, taking photographs, and laughing with the Babe as he stood alone, his back to the waist-high red brick barrier.[6]

4. For more details on Charles Lindbergh and his status as an American hero, see A. Scott Berg, *Lindbergh* (New York: Putnam, 1998).

5. "The Amos 'n Andy Show," IMDb.com, accessed on June 9, 2017, http://www.imdb.com/title/tt0043175/.

6. The New York Yankees and the Chicago White Sox played two series of games in Chicago during the summer of 1929. The first was from July 10–13 and the second from August 18–21. 1929 MLB Schedule, Sports Reference, accessed on February 4, 2018, https://www.baseball-reference.com/leagues/MLB/1929-schedule.shtml.

These glorious and prosperous times would come to an abrupt and unexpected halt. Suddenly, especially sudden for my brother and me, as we were never consulted about such matters, we began spending much of our time in Hot Springs in my grandmother's red brick cottage on Hobson Street. My father returned to Chicago, this time on the train, alone, looking for a job because his Ford dealership had gone bankrupt. The stock market crash in October 1929 snatched a life of comfort and optimism from my parents and thrust them, and virtually everyone else, into a bleak, uncertain future. The onset of the Depression caused tremendous changes for my family. Twenty years later, George Wagoner, a Yale graduate and my colleague at the Aetna Casualty Group, would tell me of his father's jumping from the window of a Wall Street skyscraper to his death so that he and his mother could survive on his father's life insurance. My own father, having no luck finding employment, told me of his looking down on a busy LaSalle Street from the open window of the Chicago skyscraper with the same resolution of his problems in mind.

I do not recall there ever being any gnashing of teeth or signs of panic on the part of my parents, even though this wrenching experience must have caused many hidden tears. As traumatic as it was, I believe the blow was softened because they shared the tidal wave of economic loss with many others around them, somehow lessening the pain individually. In the same way, I later watched airmen accept the sudden loss of their close friends with an unnatural equanimity, simply because of knowing they may be next. My father lost not only his business but his new home in Waverly Woods, for which he paid $18,000—a huge sum in the late 1920s.

Until recently, I had never felt my generation was special and assumed that we simply responded as any other American generation would have if faced with the challenges of Adolf Hitler and Japan's treachery.[7] But, now I wonder. This depression became a way of life, tenaciously hovering over our nation year after year for a decade. Could it be, that living a life of constant economic strain, experiencing years of struggle and deprivation during the worst and longest depression in our country's history, helped to fortify our young men and steel them with a discipline and strength to

7. Tom Brokaw popularized the idea of the greatest generation. See Tom Brokaw, *The Greatest Generation* (New York: Random House, 1998).

withstand adversity and hardship, as opposed to a life of comfort and ease during the relatively prosperous years since the war? For those reasons, perhaps it is possible that our generation was better prepared for what was to come than others.

It was during these stressful times, still a child, that I actually met popular humorist Will Rogers.[8] In February 1931, his plane landed on a grassy field just outside Helena. Rogers was the most beloved man in America and was often referred to as President Number Two. He and his pilot, the well-known record-breaking air racer, Captain Frank Hawks, touched down at 7:30 that morning in a single engine, biplane with two open cockpits. They were on a mission. The worst depression in history was now ravaging the nation. To meet the threat of starvation, daily breadlines were common in all cities. The government had closed Helena's First National Bank, which my grandfather had been president of before he died. My father's automobile dealership was bankrupt. National unemployment would reach twenty-five percent.[9]

President Herbert Hoover asked Rogers to make a tour of the nation to boost morale and instill hope.[10] Somehow, little Helena, Arkansas was on Roger's itinerary. Rogers arrived at the large, metal-clad Legion Auditorium at 8:20 a.m. The Helena Boys Band stopped playing when Rogers ran down the aisle and leaped up to the stage. The overflowing crowd cheered wildly as Rogers brought continuous laughter for over an hour with his unique brand of homespun humor. When finished, he jumped down and rushed back outside. Over two hundred cars, mostly all-black Ford Model A's and Model T's, followed him in single file along the narrow two-lane road back to the grass field to watch him take off. A collection taken at the rally raised $1,800 to buy food for Helena's hungry and needy.[11]

8. For a brief description of Will Rogers's life and career, see Cary Reed, "Remembering Will Rogers: 80 Years On, How The 'Cowboy Philosopher' Popularized Political Humor," August 15, 2015, NewsHour Production, accessed on June 8, 2017, http://www.pbs.org/newshour/rundown/remembering-will-rogers-80-years-cowboy-philosopher-popularized-political-humor/.

9. For a history of the Great Depression, see Kennedy, *Freedom from Fear*.

10. For President Herbert Hoover's use of Will Rogers, see Ben Yagoda, "'Bacon, Beans and Limousines' --Will Rogers (October 18, 1931)," Library of Congress, accessed on June 8, 2017, https://www.loc.gov/programs/static/national-recording-preservation-board/documents/WillRogersSpeech.pdf.

11. Rogers visited Helena on February 12, 1931. See Will Rogers and M. Jane Johansson, *The Papers of Will Rogers: The Final Years, August 1928-August 1935* (Norman: University of Oklahoma Press, 2006), 22. For Rogers's visit to Helena, see "Helena-West Helena (Phillips County)," *The Encyclopedia of Arkansas History and Culture*, Central Arkansas Library System, accessed on June 8, 2017, http://www.encyclopediaofarkansas.net/.

My father must have been involved with the reception committee because he was the last person to speak with Rogers. I remember standing at my father's knees, looking up at them as they talked by the airplane. Suddenly they both looked down at me, and Rogers leaned over and held out his hand as my father said, "Tom Pettit, this is Mr. Will Rogers," (children in Helena were addressed by their first and middle names). I have always remembered that kind face and friendly smile. I watched the plane turn for take-off and was almost knocked down by the prop-wash from its loud engine. For years I would hold up my hand and brag, "This is the hand that shook the hand of Will Rogers."

Over the next few years, we moved frequently. My father found employment with an insurance company in Chicago, and we moved for short stints to Oklahoma City, then Dallas, then to Houston, and finally back to Dallas, always finding time to revisit Arkansas.

I hated those trips to Helena to see our relatives and the hordes of my parents' friends. While my mother looked forward to these returns to her days of glory, to the place where she was loved and revered, these visits to me were—*anathema*. As a young boy, I found that Helena was no longer my happy home of play and fun, but a place where I was loath to return, a place where I was now looked upon by my mother's aggressive and kissy friends as a choice, enticing morsel. With my hair plastered down and dressed in clean, starched clothes, worn only for these tortuous occasions, I hardly recognized the pristine image in the mirror.

On sighting my mother, these young southern matrons would run and engulf her with shrill-voiced glee while I cringed at her knees, dreading the inevitable. With great anticipation in their eager eyes, they would turn to look down at me, a defenseless and inviting victim, quaking and dreading. Like sweet-scented vultures, they would pounce with the buzzing enthusiasm of bees swarming an isolated flower. At an early age, I learned the stark fear of a defenseless wildebeest, surrounded by attacking jackals. Seeking satisfaction of some primordial maternal urge, they would swoop me up and pass me from one to the other, squeezing me and anointing my face with multiple kisses. *Yuk!* This was agony. I was expected not only to endure these humiliations, but to enjoy them with a smile. It was impossible even to grin, but I somehow managed to bear it. As the years and visits grew further and further apart, the cooing and cuddling diminished, and as I grew up, Helena, once again, became a pleasant place to visit.

My grandmother's home in Hot Springs became our summer sanctuary. A city of 35,000, Hot Springs, Arkansas is like no other in the United States, and is much the same today as it was then. The stately cream-colored Arlington Hotel loomed above the end of Central Avenue and looked down upon eight large and individually distinctive bathhouses. They sat back from the street with manicured green lawns in front and they lined the north side of that busy thoroughfare. Abruptly behind them rose the towering North Mountain with its narrow, serpentine concrete road spiraling to the top. Across from the bathhouses were restaurants, auction houses, and shops. Until medical science gradually sliced into the popularity of "taking the baths" by providing alternatives to Hot Springs's therapeutic waters, well-known personalities from all segments of America were lured to this unique and attractive city. Many professional baseball teams, including the New York Yankees, Brooklyn Dodgers and Chicago Cubs, located their training camps in Hot Springs until the mid-1920s. For years, gambling was wide open, attracting tourists, celebrities, and even Chicago gangsters, like Al Capone, whom my grandmother had seen one evening at Belvedere, the popular local nightclub, where patrons dressed formally, dined lavishly, and gambled legally.[12]

My grandfather, Thomas J. Pettit, owned hotels in Hot Springs and Helena. He died in 1929 when I was four, leaving my mother's mother several small rent houses. We called her "Maywee" because my brother, at age two, could not pronounce "Mary." Maywee was a real character. She had been pretty as a young girl and when older, sitting in the back seat between Jimmy, age 11 and me at 6, patted her knees, smiled proudly at us, and said, "Don't you two think these are the most gorgeous legs you ever saw?" Actually, she was slightly bowlegged.

She had a heart condition, and I overheard my parents whispering she may have taken too many nitro glycerin pills. I knew about nitro glycerin from a gangster movie, and until they straightened me out the next day, I worried that she might explode.

12. See "History," Hot Springs National Park, Arkansas, accessed on June 9, 2017, http://www.hotsprings.org/pages/history/.

Tom, Jim Faulkner, and "Maywee," their Grandmother, c. 1943

My grandmother had built a new two-story house near the base of the Ouachita Mountains on Central Avenue. I would look forward to our visits every year when I would search for crystals around the nearby cliffs and towering trees. Although my brother, older by almost six years, and I shared the indignities of simply not being an adult, we still seemed to be at odds with each other about most things and, when facing a conflict with our parents, to my chagrin, Jimmy would often side with them. I simply could not count on him for support or understanding, and I was largely alone, isolated in an adult world while coping with my boyish interests. In growing up, we were, of course, largely influenced by our experiences at school, listening to the radio, our parent's daily prompting, and the occasional inclusion in after-dinner conversations, frequently with visiting guests. Sometimes we were allowed to sit and listen, but never to offer any comment or opinion.

On one of these occasions, when I was about nine or ten, I listened with wide-eyed but controlled excitement to my grandmother's guests, the Maniers, who operated the Lamar Bathhouse, one of the eight stately structures on Central Avenue.[13] She told us about a visiting foreigner who was using their facilities. "I'll call him," she said, jumping to her feet, "and see if he'll join us." We all watched and listened. After a brief conversation, she announced in an excited voice, "He's coming, but says he must bring his patient." As she described him, I realized with amazement that I was actually going to see, *in person*, a genuine Hindu from India. I identified immediately with him. I knew about India, the orient, and many mysterious sounding places like Katmandu, Baku, and Kuala Lampur, and their dark and sinister characters, some of whom supposedly possessed supernatural powers. These areas had always entranced me because of my vast knowledge of Chan Du, the magician, and Fu Manchu, the evil criminal genius, not to mention Ming the Merciless of the Flash Gordon Sunday comics.[14]

13. For a description of the Lamar Bathhouse in Hot Springs, see "Lamar Bathhouse," National Park Service, U.S. Department of the Interior, accessed on June 9, 2017, https://www.nps.gov/hosp/learn/historyculture/lamar-bathhouse.htm.

14. Chan Du, Fu Manchu, and Ming the Merciless were all fictional characters in popular culture in the 1920s and 1930s. For examples, see *Chandu the Magician*, directed by William C. Menzies and Marcel Varnel, Fox Film Corporation, 1932; *The Return of Dr. Fu Manchu*, directed by Rowland V. Lee, Paramount Pictures, 1930; and "Flash Gordon," King Features Syndicate, accessed on June 9, 2017, http://flashgordon.com/history/.

I am sure my mouth dropped open at hearing the slow, steady chant coming from the entrance hall as I stepped around to watch the man in black, the Hindu, slowly *backing* through the front door into the entrance hall. He was leaning over, arms and fingers outstretched but not touching his elderly, stooped patient, who was hunched over, following, slowly, one step at a time, in rhythm to the deep-voiced cadence of his mentor's strange sounding words. He backed into the living room, his patient still following in labored, staccato steps, until seated. The Hindu raised up, turned slowly, stood erect, and spoke, his dark, piercing eyes darting from one to the other. "Good evening," he said, "I am Doctor Mundavi." He was tall with broad shoulders and had a neat, black mustache and goatee. He wore a black suit, white shirt, and a black bow tie. His head was wrapped in a large, white turban with a red stone. He explained that his patient was partially paralyzed, but was responding to his hypnotic treatments, and added, with a nod to the Maniers, "And, of course, the daily healing waters at the Lamar."

For the next hour, he explained and demonstrated the benefits of hypnotism. He raised up the flesh of my mother's wrist and pierced through it with a long needle without any bleeding or pain. But I was to be his star example for the evening. He sat and motioned for me to come to him. My heart was racing as he felt my shoulders and my arms, turned me around, and said, "This boy will become very strong and live a long life." He sat me on his knee and asked me to look into his eyes. I will never forget those eyes. They were dark, piercing, and frightening. After what seemed an eternity, he said, "Your eyelids are heavy now and you will hear only my voice." I closed my eyes as he asked me to hold my arm out and hold it stiff. He then asked my brother to step over and try to bend it. Jimmy tried but could not. Then he asked me to stand and hold my body rigid. "Tighter, tighter," he said, until my body felt like a board. He ordered me to fall back, and he then placed my head on the edge of a dining room chair and my heels on another. "I weigh over 200 pounds," he said, as he lowered himself and sat on my prone body, then lifted his feet from the floor.

My mother later said she almost fainted.

My father's new job with an insurance adjusting company was in Dallas, Texas—a big city to us, with 250,000 people. Mother, Dad, Jimmy, and I spent the first night at the Baker

Hotel and ate in the basement cafeteria. We ran into old friends from Helena. They told Mother and Dad about a house for rent across the street from them; so, we moved into the 3400 block of Dartmouth in Highland Park. I entered the second grade at Armstrong Grade School. It was 1932 and the older boys and girls were talking about an election coming up. I would be hearing a lot about Franklin D. Roosevelt.

At least one school-age boy occupied most homes on Dartmouth, making it a great place to grow up. The street, with shallow curbs and sidewalks on each side, was our playground. We played touch football, baseball, soccer, and hockey. There was hardly any traffic, and we would take to the sidewalks when a car came by.

During those days in Highland Park, I sold magazines door to door. *Liberty* and *Colliers* cost 5 cents, while *Saturday Evening Post* was 10 cents. I never had a paper route, but Dallas news organizations printed and distributed *four* daily newspapers, the *Dallas Times Herald, The Dallas Journal*, *The Dallas Dispatch*, and today's sole survivor, *The Dallas Morning News*. The *Journal* and *Dispatch* loved to put out extras. Their delivery boys would roam up and down the neighborhood streets yelling, "Extra! Extra! read all about it." I recall several headlines—"Trotsky Murdered in Mexico," "Bonny and Clyde Rob Local Bank," and "Hindenburg Zeppelin Explodes in New Jersey."

Prices were astounding by today's standards. A penny would actually buy things. Three cents would buy a newspaper, a quart of milk, a loaf of bread, or a ride anywhere in Dallas on the streetcar. I paid ten cents for a movie ticket and a nickel for a bag of popcorn or large candy bar. A brand-new Ford sedan cost $495. My father was offered a membership in the exclusive Dallas Country Club. Although several friends belonged and my parents wanted to join, they felt obliged to decline because the membership was $900 (today it is $165,000) and my brother was approaching college age.

During this time, I could not believe my luck when my parents agreed to pay the $10 fee for me to try out for the new Mustang Midgets football team. This led to some unique experiences because of my coach. My hometown college team, the Southern Methodist University Mustangs, was undefeated and considered the number one team in the nation. They ultimately played Stanford in the

1936 Rose Bowl.[15] I was ten years old and in the fourth grade at Armstrong. SMU, on whose field we practiced, was only blocks away from our house on Dartmouth. Our coach, Jack Morrison, had been a SMU star. We played opponents at halftime of SMU's home games. The Mustangs' home stadium was always packed, and the crowds would roar for the Mustang Midgets.

I collected and kept in my room everything I could get my hands on. I sent off for books on self-defense, card tricks, hypnotism, and how to be popular with the girls. Cereal box tops provided free memberships to secret clubs, including a pin or a ring to prove it. One of my favorites was becoming a member of the Roscoe Turner Flying Corps. Roscoe Turner was a record-breaking pilot, second only to the great Charles Lindbergh. I received a signed photograph of this handsome daredevil of the sky with his debonair mustache, helmet, goggles, and white scarf along with a decoder ring, which designated me a member of his secret and exclusive flying group.[16]

I also collected old coins, Indian cards, marbles, spinning tops, college pennants, fossils, and arrowheads. I collected Big-Little books and amassed a foot-high stack of comic books, including *Superman*, *Batman*, and *The Green Hornet*, all filled with enticing novelty advertisements and invitations to a world crammed full of wonder. I became a magician, a mind reader, and a ventriloquist. However, I never seemed to master the art of throwing my voice across the room, as one ad promised. I became a Melvin Purvis Junior G-man, and I followed Charles Atlas muscle-building advice on how to handle a bully kicking sand in my face on the beach in front of my girl.[17]

After I graduated from high-school and went off to Texas A&M, my parents moved to Maple Terrace, a nice apartment-hotel. Alas,

15. SMU was the top-ranked football team through most of the 1935 season and was 12–0 when it went to the Rose Bowl. It lost to Stanford 7–0. See "1936 Rose Bowl – Stanford 7, SMU 0," Southern Methodist University Athletics, accessed on June 9, 2017, http://www.smumustangs.com/news/2009/12/23/1936_ROSE_BOWL_STANFORD_7_SMU_0.aspx?path=football.

16. Roscoe Turner flew several times through Dallas and was well known in the area. For a description of Turner and his fan club, "Roscoe Turner Flying Corps", see "Roscoe Turner," Davis Monthan Aviation Field Register, Delta Mike Airfield, accessed on June 9, 2017, https://dmairfield.com/people/turner_ro/.

17. Melvin Purvis was a well-known FBI agent because he led the operation that ultimately cornered and killed bank robber John Dillinger in 1934. See "Melvin Purvis, G-Man," The Outlaw Journals, accessed on June 9, 2017, http://www.babyfacenelsonjournal.com/melvin-purvis.html. Charles Atlas was a legendary strong man who was known as "The World's Most Perfectly Developed Male." See "Charles Atlas," The Official Website of Charles Atlas, accessed on June 9, 2017, https://www.charlesatlas.com/about.html.

all of my numerous collections were discarded. I understood. I knew that our home could not be turned into a museum, but I recently discovered that an original of the first Superman magazine and other comic magazines like those mentioned above, all of which I had kept neatly stacked in my closet, are now worth up to $1,000,000 *each. Ouch!*[18] I still have a copy of the letter I wrote to a novelty supplier ordering a "skull and crossbones" ring, and I still have the ring. The letter (which appears in the Afterword of this book) refers to seeing the ad in my "third addition" of Superman magazine. I am sure I also possessed the first and second editions. *Wow!*

Older, and reaching high-school age, I wanted to be suave, sophisticated and debonair, not realizing that some people just are not born with the capacity or characteristics ever to approach such attributes. I admired the detectives and adventurers I saw at the movies and tried to mimic their mannerisms and behaviors. I secretly smoked a Meerschaum pipe that replaced the Indian water pipe I had smoked in the closet while in junior high, and when I was sixteen and a senior, I graduated to a trim and more sophisticated briarwood model, the kind that Philo Vance and Bulldog Drummond smoked.[19] I would practice imitating the movie stars—I was not too bad. I did Lionel Barrymore reciting Poe's *The Raven* before my English class—not too good. However, I could (and still can) do a good Clark Gable—"I'm leaving you, Scarlett"—and a credible Cary Grant. Since I was sometimes known as the class clown, I just could not pull off the debonair look, pipe or no pipe, and though from time to time for the rest of my life, I would try, I never learned to be a cool and smooth jitter-bugger.

Although my parents were pillars of St. John's Episcopal Church in Helena, their moving around so often during the dogged and desperate days of the Depression seemed to have thrown their religious compass completely off course. Until leaving Helena, they were diligently following in the footsteps of my British ancestors

18. A first edition of the Superman comic book from 1938 in pristine condition sold for $3.2 million in 2014. Marc Graser, "First Superman Comicbook Sells for $3.2 Million," August 25, 2014, *Variety*, accessed on June 9, 2017, http://variety.com/2014/biz/news/first-superman-comicbook-sells-for-3-2-million-1201289733/.

19. Philo Vance and Hugh "Bulldog" Drummond were fictional characters from novels and films in the 1920s and 1930s. See "Philo Vance (Character)," IMDb.com, accessed on June 9, 2017, http://www.imdb.com/character/ch0036592/; and "Captain Hugh "Bulldog" Drummond (Character)," IMDb.com, accessed on June 9, 2017, http://www.imdb.com/character/ch0034942/.

who belonged to the Anglican Church of England at the time of their sailing for America. They landed in New York City in 1857 with their four children, including the four-year-old little boy who would become my grandfather. They remained in New York for four years, having another child, before moving on to Helena.

Yet, with all this religious background, I do not recall my mother and father ever attending any other church, or my brother or me ever going to a regular Sunday School class, anywhere, after leaving Helena. Although baptized as an infant at St. John's, I had never been officially confirmed as a Christian.

This did not seem to dawn on my parents until many years later when I was at home on my final leave during World War II before moving on to Tonopah, Nevada, for combat training with a B-24 crew. My mother quickly made arrangements for me to be confirmed at St. Matthew's Episcopal Cathedral on Sunday afternoon, March 28, 1943, since I would be leaving the next day. I have no idea how it is that Dean Moore (who four and a half years later would officiate at my marriage to Ann Harrison) agreed to confirm me without having ever even seen me. This was fortunate, because he would have learned that I had no knowledge of the Prayer Book or the rituals or beliefs of the Episcopal Church. I believe my mother, never one to accept no, must have convinced him to go through with the ceremony, suggesting that if I were killed in the war he would be responsible for jeopardizing my otherwise clear path to heaven.

However, I felt very much a Christian, so confident that I remember feeling that the education I missed in the Episcopal Church was actually unnecessary because of my having attended YMCA Camp Crockett in Granbury, Texas, for two months each summer for five years. Because of that background and the camp's focus on spiritual as well as physical development, I felt no inadequacy insofar as my belief in God, and my relationship with Christ or the hereafter. Many years later, in my forties, I would go through the Confirmation class with my wife, Ann, at the Episcopal Church of the Incarnation in Dallas. I was on the Vestry for two terms, serving one as Junior Warden.

I am forever indebted to Bobby Singleton for my learning about Camp Crockett. Bobby lived next door to us on Dartmouth and was six years older. He became my idol. He possessed an enthusiasm

Tom, Jim Faulkner, and Bobby Singleton, 1942

I had never seen before. He stood for everything good. To me, he was the All-American boy. When I was nine, he told my parents about YMCA Camp Crockett where he was going to be a cabin leader the following summer. The cost would be only $60 for two months. That summer, 1934, I loved every minute of those two months. Repeating this process for the next four summers, I would get to know boys from all over Dallas that would be lifelong friends. My parents did not send me there for any religious development, but all my life I have been aware of the influence that took root during those five extended summers at Camp Crockett.

Like all the other campers, I had a great respect for our camp director, H. Grady Spruce. One of Dallas's high schools now bears his name. He was our summertime father and conducted a devotional service each morning. We sat on a circle of benches under tall trees outdoors near the wide creek in which we swam. Accompanied by an organ, we would sing traditional hymns like "The Old Rugged Cross," "In the Garden," and "When the Roll is Called Up Yonder." Then Mr. Spruce would talk about how young boys should handle temptation and conduct themselves. He spoke in a manner that reached our hearts with the same basic theme—be strong and pure, and clean in mind, body and spirit. All of us—about 80 boys from age 9 to 17—would listen intently.

After supper in the mess hall at night, we would walk to a distant knoll where all 80 campers would sit on benches around a campfire in a large circle. We would sing songs like "John Jacob Jingleheimer Schmidt" and "The Dear Old Crockett Spirit." Then the *Arrowhead* editor, a camper, would read his nightly newsletter, usually revelations such as which cabin was short-sheeted by the scoundrels from a rival cabin, or comments about a camper receiving a perfumed letter, or other indignities or embarrassments, all resulting in hoots and shouts with glee and laughter.

The summer before my senior year in high school, Mr. Spruce invited me to become a counselor at Camp Crockett. I had always wanted to do just that; but I was now faced with other choices.[20] I wanted to try out for the football team, which required me to attend the football summer camp. Also, I wanted to take two summer school courses, allowing me to relax and take just three courses my senior year. Further, because of the war in Europe, I wanted to attend a month-long ROTC session at Camp Wisdom, the military base near Wichita Falls. To fulfill these other interests, I could not fit in a sixth year at Camp Crockett.

I almost could not believe how well things were going that summer. I was aware of being supremely happy and content with everything in my life, and looking forward with great anticipation to the start of a great senior year. Was I ever wrong! The foundation began to crack early on, and a few weeks later the roof would collapse around me—and my life would rush rapidly south.

During my sophomore and junior years in high school, I had dated only one girl, and it was a crushing blow to me when she called me over to her house one summer afternoon just before school started and told me she wanted to date other boys. She added it would be best if we stopped going out altogether.

I tried to handle this unexpected setback and focus on football camp. The camp started in late August, the last week before school began, and we stayed in cabins overnight for several days across the Trinity River near the Ft. Worth highway. Wow! Football camp was the hottest, windiest, dustiest most gruesome experience I had ever had. We endured long, sweaty scrimmages in the morning and in the afternoon with the temperature hovering around 100 degrees at times. We knocked each other all over the hard,

20. Faulkner did not see Singleton again after he left for Italy in 1944 until 2007 when the two of them were among twenty Highland Park graduates of World War II who were featured in an hour-long documentary titled "Heroes Among Us." It consisted of clips from interviews with each of them along with scenes from the war years.

Tom in ROTC Uniform as a High School Sophomore in 1939

weed-covered field. While this, along with losing my girl, was not a great beginning of the school year, it was child's play compared to what was in store.

At 165 pounds and six-feet-one, I made the team as the starting right tackle. This was a good size at that time. Bob Anderson, who would later become my roommate at Texas A&M, was our left tackle. My best friend, Warner Marsh, was the left guard. My senior football season could not have started any better, and while I did not know it at the time, we had two future football stars on our team.

Bobby Layne, our backup quarterback, would go on to become All-State at Highland Park the following year and later become an All-American at the University of Texas. As a sophomore, Doak Walker was a substitute halfback on our team and would lead Highland Park to the state finals two years later. He became a three-time All-American at SMU and also won the 1948 Heisman Trophy as the number one football player in America. To accommodate the overflowing crowds when he played, SMU moved all future games from Ownby Stadium to the Cotton Bowl, which kept

Front row, left to right: Kenneth Crowe, Charlie Hall, Roger Evans, Don Arnold, Bill Erck; Standing: Tom Faulkner, Warner Marsh, Relative of Warner's (unknown), Bill Henry, Bill Jones

Highland Park Football Team, 1941 (63 – Bill Wells, 66 – Warner Marsh, 70 – Bob Anderson, 76 – Tom Faulkner, 77 – Bill Henry, 83 – Charlie Hall, 93 – Bobby Layne)

expanding each year, and became known as "The House That Doak Built." Doak and Bobby, always fast friends, would later become All-Pro selections with the Detroit Lions and eventually be selected to both the College Football Hall of Fame and the National Football League Hall of Fame.[21]

Highland Park High School would produce two other highly regarded and nationally known athletes who are also very good friends, Clayton Kershaw, the Los Angeles Dodgers All-Star baseball pitcher who has won the Cy Young award, and All-American and All-Pro football quarterback Matthew Stafford with the Detroit Lions. Kershaw is at this writing the highest paid player in professional baseball and Stafford is currently the highest paid player in professional football. As renowned as Bobby and Doak both were, they never reached that highly elite status.

Because of the war in Europe, high school ROTC programs had become popular. I had been a cadet since my sophomore year and was not surprised when promoted to the rank of captain. However, I *was* surprised when the four company commanders were announced and I, along with Warner Marsh, Steve Schneider, and Bill Wells, were chosen. I was in charge of Company C, which consisted of two platoons, fifty cadets for one hour of training each day.

Warner was also elected to lead the Student Council, the most prestigious office of all, and chosen as captain of the football team, and Steve Schneider was elected as one of the six cheerleaders. Steve was one of my best friends at the time, and we remained so for the rest of our lives. Surprisingly, I was elected vice president of the senior class. I say 'surprisingly' because in all my years of attending Highland Park schools, this was the first, and only time I had ever been elected to a major class office.

So far, so good. Everything went swimmingly for the first six weeks. Our football team lived up to expectations and won all but one game. Known as the Highland Park Scots, and referred to since the Twenties as "the silk stocking" boys because of pricy Highland

21. For descriptions of Bobby Layne and Doak Walker's careers, see "About Doak Walker," Southern Methodist University, accessed on September 10, 2016, https://www.smu.edu/DoakWalkerAward/AboutUs/AboutDoakWalker; "Halfback Doak Walker," Pro Football Hall of Fame, accessed on September 10, 2016, http://www.profootballhof.com/players/doak-walker/; "Quarterback Bobby Layne," Pro Football Hall of Fame, accessed on September 10, 2016, http://www.profootballhof.com/players/bobby-layne/; and "Layne, Robert Lawrence," Texas State Historical Association, accessed on September 10, 2016, https://tshaonline.org/handbook/online/articles/fla87.

Park houses, we had a good team and were projected to reach the state playoffs. The newspapers covered our team's progress and a picture of me blocking a dummy appeared in the sports section of the *Dallas Times Herald*, prompting one of my wiseacre friends to ask which one was the dummy.

I probably should have known things were going too well. I had not realized that by taking only three courses my senior year, I had left myself with no margin for error. My math course was not hard, but I failed to give it proper attention and had a failing score on the first six weeks report card. The summer-school decision to lighten my study load to just three courses as a senior had backfired. All extra-curricular activities required passing three courses. Neither the math teacher nor I were aware of the dire consequences that quickly followed.

First, I was forced to endure the humiliation of having to attend a special meeting of the entire 400 member senior class to elect another vice president. I watched as nominations were made and Steve Schneider was elected as the new vice president to replace me. Second, I had to resign as captain of my ROTC company—hardly the example I wanted to set for the fifty boys in my company. Third, and worst of all, I was declared ineligible to remain on the football team and would not even be allowed to practice with the squad.

The following few weeks were embarrassing and among the most painful of my life. I brought my math grade in line, and three weeks later, I was reinstated as commander of Company C. I was also cleared to return to the football team, but I was badly injured in practice the first day back. I had missed so many workouts that I knew nothing of how to handle a trap play, and the pulling guard on the offense kept pounding my left thigh, play after play. It swelled up so much that I almost could not get the uniform pants off. I ended up being away from football for two more weeks. However, our team eventually won our district championship, and I returned to join them for the state playoffs.

On a bright Saturday afternoon on December 6 at SMU's Ownby Stadium and before a crowd of 20,000, we upset Paris High School, the favorite that year to win the state championship. The next day, December 7, 1941, I was still in bed nursing a back injury from the game, when Kenneth Crowe, a long-time friend, came by to tell us about Japan bombing Pearl Harbor in Hawaii. The following Saturday,

Warner Marsh, 1942

back at Ownby Stadium, our playoff run came to an end. Sunset High School of Dallas defeated us in the state quarterfinals, 7 to 0.

The shocking Japanese attack stunned us with the reality that our country was suddenly at war. The summer of 1942 was approaching; graduation was upon us; and our high school days

Kenneth Crowe and Tom, 1937

were almost over. There was a strange, new atmosphere. A patriotic fervor had developed in the nation. A new outlook, mixed with an unfamiliar shade of uncertainty, permeated every action, decision, and thought. By the time the excitement of graduation activities arrived six months later, our reactions had adjusted and blended in, and our new normal was influenced largely by ongoing wartime news reports. Yet, since the war was far away, the usual graduation festivities would not change, and Warner Marsh and I signed up to try out for the senior play.

Peggy Harrison taught drama in the English Department and directed our senior play. She was single, a delightful and attractive person, in her mid-thirties who spoke with a hint of a British accent. The play was set in nineteenth century Austria. Warner was miscast as the old Field Marshall, and I played a young officer with designs on his daughter. My début on stage was a disaster. Ms. Harrison should not have had to deal with clumsy teenagers, and fortunately, within a few years, she would become the head of the drama department at SMU.

My grand entrance from the left wing called for me to enter with a flourish, brandishing my sword, shouting at Warner and others on stage. On opening night, I wore a Cossack type uniform with a tall major domo headpiece for the first time. On cue, I entered, sword drawn and shouting as I ducked under the doorway, but not quite enough. I knocked my tall, furry hat off, and it bounced to the floor. I quickly stooped to pick it up, not realizing the hat had knocked over a burning candelabra on the table. I rose, replaced the hat to my head, and began repeating my shouted remarks and again swinging the sword. "The table!" someone interrupted in a frantic stage whisper, "Tommy, Tommy, the table!" I glanced back to see that the candelabra had set fire to the crepe paper decorations on the table. As Warner and the other actors on stage watched in dismay, along with others from the wings, I again had to turn my back to the audience while patting out the flickering flames. Then, holding tight to my wobbly hat, I turned back again, brandishing my sword, and repeated my opening shouts for the third time, but no one was listening, as my lively lines were literally lost in the loud and lusty laughter that lingered in the large assembly hall. I did not mind that so much, although this was not supposed to be a comedy, and I felt badly about fouling up the first act of Ms. Harrison's otherwise serious senior play.

As graduation approached, my classmates and I all knew we had decisions to make. While none of us had previously heard of Pearl Harbor, we knew the Japanese attack would change our lives drastically. At seventeen, we were ripe for the draft; so, a large number of us skipped our summer vacation and enrolled immediately at Texas A&M, at that time an all-boys' military school.[22]

22. For a brief history of Texas A&M, see "History of the University," accessed on September 10, 2016, http://www.tamu.edu/about/history.html.

Bob Anderson, my old football teammate, and I roomed together on the third floor in Dorm 17. Bill Wells, also a lineman on the team, and Bob Phelps, a Highland Park basketball star, were roommates on the first floor. Warner and Charlie Hall, our high-school fullback, roomed together on the second floor. Texas A&M was the perfect fit for us. Although we attended regular freshmen classes, the focus was on military matters.

If Warner had not been the super person he was—had he not possessed the character of a more mature person, even in high school—he probably would have stopped speaking to me and the other four Highland Park graduates residing with him in Dorm 17 in the fall 1942. We let him down drastically on a November night, but being who he was, Warner never blamed us for anything. It was as if it never happened—never the slightest grudge. We had all come back to Dallas for a long weekend because the A&M football team was playing SMU. The university declared the game a "Corps Trip," which meant no classes for four days. It was a big rivalry game and was one we would never miss.

Bob Anderson was at the wheel of his dad's new Dodge sedan on that Thursday night before the Saturday game. The six of us were just riding around, not looking for trouble, when we drove by the SMU campus. Stacked in the center of the large practice field adjoining Ownby Stadium was a towering pile of logs and lumber that would provide the bonfire celebration at the big SMU student pep-rally the next night.

I do not recall who thought of it, but the temptation for all of us was too great. We had to do it. It was dark. There were no lights. We would be lauded as heroes back at A&M for prematurely setting ablaze the SMU bonfire, thus dampening their pep-rally. Bob drove to a gas station and each of us filled a can with gasoline. Bob turned off the car's lights and slowly, quietly eased his big sedan over the curb and onto the open field and stopped next to the giant pile of wood. We all jumped out and quickly encircled the huge stack, cans and matches at the ready, when all hell broke loose! A horde of cars, with blaring horns and blinding headlights, all packed with SMU fraternity boys, roared down on us from behind the stadium just as we were in the act of spreading the gasoline. It was a trap! "Let's go! Let's go!" we all yelled, tossing the cans aside and piling into the car. We looked back. Warner was still at the base of the tall structure, determined to carry out our plan, ignoring our pleas and frantically shaking the gas on to the wooden pile.

"Come on, Warner, come on," we yelled, but it was too late. Bob sped away just as the SMU fraternity boys had jumped out of their cars and pounced on Warner. Layden Stroud, a friend to all of us from our high school football team, told me years later that he was the one who had caught Warner as he bolted from the stack of wood. "Nice tackle, Layden," Warner had told him, as they got up off the ground.

They had captured Warner, and we had driven off, leaving him to face unknown punishment. We drove around in silence, trying to decide whether to go back and share in his captivity. We never did. It was not easy to explain to Mr. and Mrs. Marsh what we had done. We did not know what had happened to Warner until the next day. Layden and some other SMU students had let him out at his house after midnight. They had cut Warner's hair to his scalp in irregular patches, and they had painted half his scalp red and the other half blue, SMU's colors. Warner was a handsome guy, but he did not look so good at the Saturday game.

The rest of us felt like the cowards that we were until we returned to the campus the following Monday. All our upperclassmen were delighted at our efforts to ruin SMU's pep-rally and Warner was celebrated as a campus hero. Now, with his red and blue scalp, and easily recognized by all students, he was admired and lauded for his bravery under fire. Warner was a campus-wide A&M celebrity. I can see him now, shaking that gas can, so determined—awkwardly trying to douse that stack of wood, ignoring our frantic pleas. He would not give up. That was Warner Marsh.

In January 1943, after completing our freshmen year at Texas A&M, Warner, Bob, and I transferred to SMU, hoping we would be able to complete at least one semester before being called up. I knew that that was not likely as I would be turning 18 in March, and, having enlisted in the AAF, I could be called at any time.

For the brief time we were at SMU, we thought we were in heaven. A&M had been a strict, hard-nosed military school with a harsh class-system. The sharp contrast between A&M and SMU during fraternity rush week was palpable. SMU fraternities wined and dined us, and treated us like kings. Warner, Bob, and I would glance at each other in wonder and smile during those bizarre days, shocked at our sudden and delightful change of treatment by upperclassmen. We pledged Kappa Alpha, but we never joined since the military called all three of us before initiation day. I was the first to go and received a notice from the AAF while still seventeen. I reported to the downtown post office for a physical examination and written tests.[23] Bob Anderson reported to the Marine Corps and Warner left for the AAF only weeks after I left.

Aside from building all sorts of World War I model airplanes—German Messerschmitt tri-wing fighters, English Sopwith Camels, and American Spads—and hanging them from my bedroom ceiling as a boy, I had no knowledge of airplanes.[24] Until Warner declared he was joining the Air Force, I had not given the subject of enlistment much thought and was, at seventeen, uncomfortable even thinking about it. It was not as much fear of flying or even combat as it was apprehension of the unknown, new faces, new places, being all alone. The farthest I had ever been away from home was going to college at Texas A&M, less than 200 miles away. I had never been inside an airplane and had only been close to one once, and that was during my brief encounter with Will Rogers twelve years earlier. Having just turned 18 and less than a year out of high school, my life was about to change in ways that I could never have imagined.

23. "Brochure – Aviation Cadet Training for the Army Air Forces (1943)," Kendall King Holt Collections, Civil Air Patrol National History Program, accessed on October 4, 2016, http://history.cap.gov/file/1432. Charles Watry recalls that once applicants passed the written and physical exams, "they were given a letter to the commander of the local armed forces induction station. Then they went to their local draft board, where they volunteered for induction. … Our first assigned duty was to return home and wait for a call to active duty." Watry, *Washout!*, 11–12.

24. The Smithsonian National Air and Space Museum in Washington, D.C. has a wonderful exhibit on the influence of flight on popular culture where it shows a model bedroom of a young boy with model airplanes hanging from the ceiling and airplane magazines and books on a desk. It gives an excellent representation of what Faulkner's bedroom would have looked like. For a description of this aspect of popular culture, including a look at model airplanes, see "Culture – Barron Hilton's Pioneers of Flight Gallery," Smithsonian National Air and Space Museum, accessed on June 25, 2017, http://pioneersofflight.si.edu/culture.

# Chapter 2

# Flight Training and Move to Italy

For a brief time in early 1943, the Air Force needed more pilots and reduced the requirement of two years of college education for pilot trainees to only one year, provided that they also passed a comprehensive written examination.[1] This relaxed rule was soon reversed, but I believe that it was during that brief window that Warner and I were allowed to enter the pilot training program with only one year of college. I was called up right after my eighteenth birthday and sent to the San Antonio Aviation Classification Center (SAACC). Nine months later, I received pilots' wings and a commission as a second lieutenant.[2] Because of that sequence of events, I was one of the youngest, and I have always wondered, maybe even *the* youngest pilot to have flown the B-24 Liberator,

1. The U.S. Army Air Forces entered World War II requiring applicants for pilot training to be at least twenty years old and to have completed two years of college. Because of the ever-increasing need for pilots, it lowered the minimum age to eighteen and lowered the required amount of college to one year. Ultimately, the one year of college was replaced with a written examination. Wesley Frank Craven and James Lea Cate, eds., *The American Air Forces in World War II*, Vol. VI – *Men and Planes* (Chicago: The University of Chicago Press, 1955), 28. See also Bruce Ashcroft, *We Wanted Wings: A History of the Aviation Cadet Program* (HQ AETC Office of History and Research, 2005), 32–3.

2. Faulkner was called to active duty on March 23, 1943, and officially inducted on March 29, 1943. See Armed Forces Induction Station, Dallas, Texas, Special Orders No. 88, March 29, 1943, in author's possession.

trained as Airplane Commander with a crew, gone directly into combat, and completed twenty-eight missions over German occupied territory while still nineteen.

How well I remember my father dropping me off at the curb of the downtown Dallas post office on his way to work. Before I opened the door to step out of the car during that special farewell with my dad, he wished me good luck and we shook hands. By his grim expression, I knew what he was thinking.

I now belonged to the federal government, and, with fifty-seven other AAF enlistees, I was taken to the local train station en route to SAACC where they would determine if I was suited for pilot training.[3] If not, I would then be sent to another base that the AAF judged was most appropriate for me—bombardier, navigator, radio operator, aircraft engineer, gunnery school, or to some non-combat or office duty.

I was lonesome, already homesick, and a little scared as I boarded the train and found a seat. I would have done almost anything to see a friendly face. It was years later that I discovered there were two others in that group that I knew very well. Kenneth Higgins and Lawrence McBride were in my class at Highland Park High School, and both were among those fifty-seven recruits. Kenneth and I had been good friends since grade school. Many years later, I learned that Lawrence completed his training and won his wings as a fighter pilot. Most, but not all, cadets wanted to be a pilot. Kenneth became a radio-operator by choice. How the three of us missed seeing each other on that train, I will never know.

The train dropped us off on the outskirts of San Antonio at the Classification Center, and we marched through the entrance of this military base with its rows upon rows of barracks and enormous training fields to begin our new lives. As we straggled through the narrow streets, still in our civilian clothes, we were hounded by jeers and catcalls of uniformed cadets yelling, "You'll be *sorrrry*," and similar warning jibes, all the way to our new barracks. We spent only a few days at the Classification Center, and while

3. For a list of the other new aviation cadets, see Armed Forces Induction Station, Dallas, Texas, Special Orders No. 88, March 29, 1943, in author's possession. The San Antonio Aviation Cadet Center was located at Lackland Air Force Base. See *Handbook of Texas Online*, Art Leatherwood, "Lackland Air Force Base," accessed September 25, 2016, http://www.tshaonline.org/handbook/online/articles/qbl01; and Thomas Manning, *A History of Military Aviation in San Antonio* (Washington, D.C.: Department of Defense, 2000).

Tom After Receiving His Wings, 1944

there, we quickly added new words and phrases to our vocabulary. The most prominent and most dreaded one was "washout." Men were "washed out" or shifted to new assignments for either health or performance reasons.[4]

Here we were given all sorts of physical exams, including testing for color-blindness, depth perception, and even a personal psychiatric exam.[5] Other cadets deluged me with all sorts of warnings about the psychiatrist questioning me about my sexual fantasies and my relationship with my mother. Others told me that my bitten-down fingernails would probably result in my being washed out. This was truly a new experience.

4. Most of the men who failed to make it through training "washed out" during Primary training. Roughly one quarter of the cadets failed to complete the Primary training as pilots. See Ashcroft, *We Wanted Wings*, 39. For an excellent account of the experience of being washed out, see Watry, *Washout*.

5. Another aviator remembered, "First came the physical examination which required the whole flight to line up without a stitch of clothing. Trying to hide behind a clipboard, which held our medical forms, was next to impossible .... Bend over, stand up, say ah-h-h, stand on one leg. It was probably our most humiliating moment of our lives." Eugene Fletcher, *Mister: The Training of an Aviation Cadet in World War II* (Seattle: University of Washington Press, 1992), 22.

I was surprised at how the other boys (that is what most all of them were, just boys) seemed so very different. They talked different, acted different, and some even looked different. It was a new world. I had only known Highland Park boys. These were country boys, city boys, Yankees, westerners, and boys from the Deep South, all with their defining accents. Although most of these young men wanted to earn pilots' wings, many would fail to qualify.[6]

After only a few days, those of us lucky enough to be selected for pilot training were marched from the Classification Center to barracks at nearby Preflight school. Much of the two-month period at Preflight was spent in rigid physical training with morning and afternoon group exercise sessions. With the instructor standing on an elevated platform, and in unison to his cadence, several hundred cadets at a time would struggle through pushups, side-straddle-hops, knee bends, running-in-place, and every other exercise imaginable until we were ready to drop. We ran obstacle courses and also a two-mile, winding, jogging trail; and we received a heavy dose of close-order drill instruction.[7]

The classroom work included learning to tap Morse code, identifying enemy aircraft, and even recognizing German and Japanese naval vessels flashing in silhouette at one-tenth of a second. One of the new areas of instruction was a real shocker of a movie. I had no idea what they were talking about. It was a movie, the likes of which I had never ever seen before. It showed unbelievably graphic pictures of the horrible consequences of various social diseases. It seemed as if the AAF wanted its men to avoid women—not even "your sister's best friend" could be trusted.[8]

6. Between July 1, 1939, and August 31, 1945, the Army Air Force graduated 193,440 pilots. During the same period, 124,000 failed to complete Primary, Basic, or Advanced Training. This number includes cadets who washed, died in training, or left for other reasons. See Craven and Cate, *The Army Air Forces in World War II*, Vol. VI, 577–78.

7. There were four preflight schools in the United States: Maxwell Field in Alabama, Ellington Field in Texas, Kelly Field in Texas, and Santa Ana Army base in California. Preflight was a nine-week training program that included training in mathematics, physics, the use of aeronautical maps and charts, enemy aircraft recognition, radio code instruction, and basic military discipline. Cadets also received physical training. See ibid., 559–61.

8. This story is common. George Gilkeson, a World War II veteran, later remembered, "Believe me, it wasn't very pretty. I saw big strapping men faint, and some became nauseated and ran from the room while viewing these movies. They were always shown … just before the men took off for a big weekend." Abigail Van Buren, "Vet Urges Release of Wartime Films on 'Social Disease,'" *Desert News*, January 27, 1992. For the video, see "WWII Army and Navy Venereal Disease/VD Scare Film," Periscope Film, accessed on October 4, 2016, https://www.youtube.com/watch?v=aro1HE1KB0w. For examples of the propaganda used by the U.S. military to discourage illicit sexual behavior, see "Venereal Disease Propaganda," Welcome to the Home of Psywarrior, accessed on October 4, 2016,

We were military cadets and introduced to the class system, patterned after West Point. It was nothing new to me as Texas A&M had been much tougher. We were underclassmen for the first month, living in double deck bunks on the first floor of the barracks and were subjected to the whims and orders of the upperclassmen, who lived on the second floor. In the barracks, we were singled out to do pushups, run in place and "brace" (chest way out, stomach way in) at stiff and rigid attention until relief would finally come with the words, "At ease."[9]

The head upperclassman would pass out the mail every day, calling out the cadets by name. He, along with the other upperclassmen, would ridicule any cadet with a perfumed envelope or the red imprint of lips on the back and assess special punishment. During the first week, with all cadets in the barracks gathered for mail call, I received a letter from Bob Anderson, now in the Marines. Bob had addressed the letter, which was called out loud by the upperclassman so all gathered around in the barracks could hear, to "*Tailspin Tommy Faulkner, America's Ace of the Airways*." *Tailspin Tommy* was a popular comic strip hero that started in the twenties. He was a barnstorming pilot of a single engine plane who found himself in one serious scrape after another, but always came out on top to the adoration and delight of his beautiful blond girlfriend.[10] Bob's letter was worth fifty pushups. Days later, Bob addressed another letter to *"'Big Tom' Faulkner, Gridiron Gladiator"*—another fifty. After that, from upstairs, they would yell, "Big Tom," whenever they wanted anything. To a degree, the name followed me through cadet training.

Thankfully, we were allowed to go into San Antonio on weekends. The first time I went with several others, Flemke, Foote, Fabian, Forshee, and Fitzgerald.[11] On this occasion, Flemke had too many beers and wound up flailing away in the downtown

---

http://www.psywarrior.com/PSYOPVD.html; and Mark Murrmann and Elizabeth Gettelman, "The Enemy in Your Pants: The Military's Decades-long War against STDs," *Mother Jones* (May/June 2010), accessed on October 4, 2016, http://www.motherjones.com/media/2010/05/us-military-std-posters.

9. For a picture of the brace position, see Flecher, *Mister*, 26.

10. Tailspin Tommy – Comic Strip, Pioneers in Aviation, accessed on May 22, 2017, https://av8rblog.wordpress.com/2013/05/22/tailspin-tommy-comic-strip/.

11. There is no additional information on Flemke. The others were Julius Fabian, James Fitzgerald, Erwin Foote, and William Forshee. See A.A.F. Pilot School (Basic), Special Orders No. 231, August 31, 1943, in author's possession; and Air Force Basic Flying School, AAF Pilot School (Basic), September 1, 1943, in author's possession.

Bob Anderson

Riverwalk canal. The cool water quickly sobered Flemke up after Fabian, Foote, and I pulled him out, soaking wet. Notice that all my cadet friends had one thing in common: the first letter of their last name. I ate, slept, and trained with the "F's". This was the case at every cadet base that followed. No "E's" or "G's"; pretty much just "F's". There was one exception. One of my best friends was an "E," Bert Early. He was from West Virginia and a real gentleman. After the war, he became a lawyer for a Huntington coal mining company, married, and had five children.[12] Bert came home on leave with me a couple of times. Mother and Dad loved him. After we received our wings, Bert was sent to a base near Dallas, and he would stay with them sometimes, even after I was overseas.

12. For a brief description of Early's career, see "Bert Early, former ABA executive director, dies at 91," August 8, 2013," *ABA Journal*, accessed on November 7, 2016, http://www.abajournal.com/news/article/bert_early_former_aba_executive_director_dies_at_91/.

Tom After Graduation from Advanced Training, 1944

Preflight school was followed by Primary, Basic, and finally, Advanced training schools, all at different fields in Texas, and each lasting two-and-a-half months.[13] We were designated Class 44-A,

13. For brief descriptions of each level of training, see Rebecca Hancock Cameron, *Training to Fly: Military Flight Training 1907–1945* (Washington D.C.: Air Force History and Museums Program, 1999), 390–408, and 566. For an excellent detailed description of each phase of training, see Flecher, *Mister*, 61–186.

Buzz French, Bert Early, and Tom in Uvalde, Texas, 1943

our class being the first class of the following year to graduate—January 1944—and after graduation from Advanced training, we were sent to airfields for combat training in one of many different types of bombers or fighters.[14]

During the nine months when I was a cadet, the attrition rate of those washing out diminished at each level. There were no wash-outs, that I recall, at Advanced training school. Until then, it was a constant threat. One of my friends, Buzz French, from Ohio, washed out in Primary. Prior to practicing a spin, he failed to circle and look down to clear the area below. He nearly collided with a plane flown by Julius Fabian and was washed out that afternoon and sent to navigation school. Another close friend from high school, Jimmy Long, after having a similar experience at another Primary field, was sent to bombardier school. Both graduated and became officers, but not pilots.

At Primary at Garner Air Field in Uvalde, Texas, we slept in comfortable beds, not in double deck bunks. We lived in long, one-story pink stucco buildings, six cadets to a room, close to our classrooms and the

14. For a list of U.S. Army training airfields in the United States during World War II, see Lou Thole, *Forgotten Fields of America: World War II Bases and Training Then and Now* (Missoula, MT: Pictorial Histories Publishing Co., Inc. 1996), 147–54.

flight-line.[15] We only had one exercise session per day. We attended classes on meteorology and learned about aeronautics, reciprocating aircraft engines, and other mechanical parts of an airplane. The food was great.

Life was drastically different at Primary! No significant class system existed at Garner Field. On the contrary, there seemed to be the relaxed atmosphere of a country club. A large swimming pool sat right in the middle of the one-story buildings, but there was not a lot of time to use it. Actually, this whole operation was conducted by civilians, from classroom teachers to flight instructors, cooks, and aircraft maintenance—all civilians. There was a military presence, but barely. My first experience sitting inside the cockpit of an airplane came here. I carried a parachute out to the flight line with three other students and met our instructor, Henry Hein.[16] He had a mustache, a German accent, and a lot of patience. He taught us to fly the single wing PT-19.[17] All pilots recall the excitement of that first flight with the instructor, as well as that first solo flight—all alone.

We were told in Primary training that the great majority of aircraft accidents were caused by "pilot error," something over 90 percent. Like automobile drivers, pilots also make mistakes, and, of course, there is the weather, which could be disastrous. One of my best friends in Basic and Advanced training was Bill Chaffin. Bill was tall, slightly heavy-set, with short, wavy blond hair. He was always happy and smiling. He was from LaRue, in east Texas and a nicer guy, I had never met. At some point, before leaving the United States, I learned that Bill Chaffin had been killed.[18] Bill had been sent to an airbase in Colorado to train with

15. Faulkner took Primary training at Garner Field in Uvalde, TX. See Willard Wiener, *Two Hundred Thousand Flyers: The Story of the Civilian-AAF Pilot Training Program* (Washington D.C.: Infantry Journal Inc., 1945), 185. See also Uvalde: Aviation Museum at Garner Field, accessed on November 5, 2016, http://txhillcountrytrail.com/plan-your-adventure/historic-sites-and-cities/sites/aviation-museum-garner-field.

16. There is no additional information on Henry Hein. He would have been one of thousands of civilian flight trainers for Primary training. See Cameron, *Training to Fly*, 390–1. Hein and other instructors rated Faulkner as Satisfactory, and Faulkner completed Primary Training at the end of August 1943. See Elementary Flying Training, 305$^{th}$ (P), Uvalde, Texas, August 31, 1943, in author's possession.

17. For a description of the PT-19, see Gordon Swansborough and Peter M. Bowers, *United States Military Aircraft Since 1909* (Washington D.C.: Smithsonian Institution Press, 1963), 307–9.

18. Bill Chaffin died, along with the rest of his crew, in a crash near Trinidad, Colorado, on June 29, 1944. See "2LT William W. Chaffin," accessed on November 5, 2016, http://www.findagrave.com/cgi-bin/fg.cgi?page=gr&GRid=70946308.

Tom (upper left) at Primary Training, 1943

his B-24 crew, and he crashed into a mountain during a storm on a practice mission. I thought of his parents and what a blow it must have been to them. Had he lived, we would have remained friends after the war.

Coincidentally, the little town of LaRue, Texas, Bill's birthplace, was actually named after a highly successful oilman who developed the area, and who was the great-grandfather of Bill LaRue, a later Phi Delta Theta fraternity brother of mine at Southern Methodist University, where we graduated after the war in 1948. Bill LaRue also became a B-24 pilot at a very early age. Until we compared notes and birthdays decades after the war, he had always been certain that he was the youngest pilot to have ever flown a B-24. But Bill had turned nineteen before his first B-24 flight.[19]

During Basic training at Waco Army Airfield, we flew the heavier and more advanced BT-13s.[20] There, because of a surprising but

19. Bill LaRue Obituary, *Dallas Morning News*, accessed on May 22, 2017, http://www.legacy.com/obituaries/dallasmorningnews/obituary.aspx?pid=177123272.

20. For a description of the B-13, see Swansborough and Bowers, *United States Military Aircraft Since 1909*, 589–90.

unfortunate tendency to black out completely while attempting certain acrobatic maneuvers, specifically loops, I had to promise my instructor, Lieutenant Junior Hendricks, I would never fly fighter planes and would request that I be sent only to multi-engine pilot training schools for Advanced training at the next level. Otherwise, he said, he would have to wash me out.[21] "You'd blackout in a turn in a P-38," he said. We tried repeatedly to overcome my problem. He would take me through one loop after another, explaining how I should tighten my neck muscles to prevent the blood from draining from my brain. I can still hear him laughing from his seat behind me each time I would regain consciousness, my head flopping around after he completed each loop. As it turned out, this was a real stroke of luck. All cadets wanted to be fighter pilots. But, because of my promise to Lt. Hendricks, I was one of the few to request multi-engine training. There was a glut of fighter pilots on hand at that time, and all graduates, except the few asking for bomber schools, like myself, were shipped out to be trained as multi-engine *copilots*. How's that for logic? And how's that for luck? At Blackland Army Airfield, also in Waco, where I was sent to Advanced school, we learned to fly small twin-engine aircraft, and I received my wings and commission as a second lieutenant on January 7, 1944.[22]

My mother invited my Uncle Tom Faulkner down from Helena, Arkansas to join my Dad and her at my graduation ceremony in Waco. Uncle Tom was a decorated captain who served in the Field Artillery in France in the First World War. We drove back to Dallas for a celebration dinner that evening and something happened that night that would change the lives of everyone around that table. Tora Tetley was one of Mother's best friends, and Mother invited Tora and her daughter, Suzanne, and son, Bob, to the dinner. Uncle Tom was a widower of three years. Tora Tetley's husband had been killed in an automobile accident four years before. As they left the dinner, Uncle Tom offered to take Tora home and, unknown to any

21. Hendricks was a 2nd Lt. See Thomas P. Faulkner, Basic Flying Training, November 3, 1943, in author's possession.

22. Blackland Army Airfield was located five miles west of Waco and operated from June 1942 to October 1945 as a military airfield. See *Handbook of Texas Online*, Art Leatherwood, "Blackland Army Air Field," accessed September 24, 2016, http://www.tshaonline.org/handbook/online/articles/qcb04. For Faulkner's appointment as a 2nd lieutenant, see Memorandum to Thomas Pettit Faulkner, Temporary Appointment, January 7, 1944, in author's possession.

of us, sparks were already flying. Uncle Tom and Tora sat in her driveway, talking until almost dawn, and hours later, three dozen red roses arrived at her front door. Uncle Tom proposed to Tora the next day. Tora, the soul of decorum, accepted three days later, but was so embarrassed that she did not tell her own children for weeks. They were married three months later.

Through their marriage, I acquired a new step-cousin. After the war, Bob Tetley would become my best friend, much more like a brother than a step-cousin. Bob, a true mathematical genius and an inveterate lover of all sports, and I would spend many years playing golf together. And today, "Uncle Bob" is as close to our family as any real uncle could ever possibly be.

The night after I received my wings, I had a date with Little Jane Carter, (as distinguished from Highland Park's taller Jane Carter). When I picked her up I really felt like a hot pilot, wearing my brand-new class A uniform and new trench coat, to take her to Louann's.[23] Louann's was a dance hall that was located on the well-travelled Greenville Avenue near Lovers Lane on the edge of Highland Park and University Park. The place was packed every night with uniformed soldiers, sailors, and their dates. Nothing fancy, just the simple fare of popcorn, soft drinks, and beer were served at tables surrounding the dance floor. A big jukebox sat at one end and provided big band music for couples dancing and jitterbugging to the great tunes of the late thirties and forties. I still love the songs of that time like "String of Pearls" and "Tuxedo Junction" by Glenn Miller, "Begin the Beguine" by Artie Shaw, and Tommy Dorsey's "I'll never Smile Again."

As Jane and I were getting ready to leave, word spread quickly that a nearby house was on fire. We all ran to join dozens of people standing outside the chain link fence surrounding the small, one-story house on the corner. The fire trucks had not arrived, but we could smell the smoke and I heard someone say they could hear crying inside. The gate of the fence was locked, and it was at least seven or eight feet high. I climbed over the fence and rushed to the front window. It was high off the ground and the windowsill was just below my eye level. Sure enough, I could hear not one,

23. Louann's was a popular dance hall near SMU in the middle of the twentieth century. Tom Peeler, "Remembering Louann's," *D Magazine* (February 1977), accessed on September 1, 2017, https://www.dmagazine.com/publications/d-magazine/1977/february/remembering-louanns/.

but two babies crying. The screen was tight and the windows were closed. I had nothing with which to cut the screen or break inside. I rushed around the house, looking for some kind of opening or place to break in. It was tight as a drum. An older man was standing on the back porch trying to force his way inside the back door. Like the front door, it was solid. I heard sirens in the distance and went back to the front window and tried to break the screen. The crying had stopped and I dreaded what had happened. I read the next day about the two babies that had died and ever since, I have wondered what I should have or could have done to save them. I still hear those babies crying and still wonder.

After a two-week leave at home in Dallas following the nine months of training as a cadet, I was sent to Liberal, Kansas, in late January for Transition training to become a four-engine B-24 Liberator pilot. I will never forget that first B-24 flight. The instructor was waiting for me and fellow student, Lt. McCarthy, on the flight-line with two graduating students. The instructor would be taking those two up for their last training flight before shipping out. Lt. McCarthy and I were his new students, and we would be paired together for all future training flights. But for today, we were just observers.

This was what all those nine months as a cadet were for. At Advanced training school in Waco, I had learned to fly a light, cloth-covered little twin-engine AT-17.[24] But here standing by a B-24, what a difference! We all ducked down into the bomb bay and then climbed up onto the flight deck. The plane seemed enormous, and I had never seen so many dials and switches and levers. How could I ever manage to figure it all out and still fly the plane? It had snowed heavily in Liberal, and a dark overcast hovered just above us. We would actually be going through those clouds. As they started the four engines, one at a time, with their loud, bellowing roar, I had this feeling of being completely overwhelmed and out of place.

McCarthy and I flanked the instructor as the three of us stood on the flight deck behind the student pilot and copilot. As the pilot taxied out to the runway, the copilot called off each item from pages of a long and complicated checklist. Turning onto the runway,

24. For a description of the AT-17, see Swansborough and Bowers, *United States Military Aircraft Since 1909*, 158–60.

the student pilot pushed the throttles forward and the engines roared as the giant aircraft lumbered ahead, slowly at first, picking up speed. The blast was so loud that it made any conversation impossible. I had been used to small, quiet little airplanes with quick responses. Now I felt as if I were flying in a gigantic winged hotel that responded slowly with ponderous movements.

The runway was bordered with piles of snow, and as we lifted off the wet concrete, I looked out to see the entire landscape blanketed in clean, stark white snow. The instructor, hunched over between the two pilots, reached down suddenly and yanked one of the four throttles back. We were not far off the ground. The plane lurched, and the instructor yelled.

"Which one is it? Which one? Which one?"

"Feather four!" the pilot shouted. "Feather four!"

The copilot quickly reached up to push the number four red feathering button above the windshield. When an engine fails on takeoff, the pilot can be in deep trouble. He has to act fast, first looking at his instruments to see which engine RPM was failing, but he can also tell by the feel of the sudden drag. If number four, the outside engine on the right, cuts out, for example, it causes more pull to the right than if number three, close to the fuselage, is lost. The number four propeller slowed and stopped, its blades slicing into the wind, feathered. This was an exercise for advanced students ready to move on to meet and to train with their crews.[25] The three propeller blades of each of the four B-24 engines are like wide paddles and an un-feathered engine, with a propeller windmilling, or worse, frozen in place, creates significant drag, adding to the problem of having lost the engine's power.

After the engine was restarted, we resumed climbing, but suddenly, we lost sight of the ground below. We were in the clouds, another new experience—flying blind and on instruments. Minutes later we emerged to a brilliant sunlight and bright blue sky, and as we continued to climb, I looked down on a sight I had never seen, or even imagined before. A beautiful blanket of unblemished, pure white clouds covered the earth and stretched flat to the horizon beneath us in all directions, and looked much like the clean,

25. For a description of feathering, see Interview with Lt. "Pep" Petrocine, 398th Bomb Group Pilot, 600th Squadron, Eighth Air Force, 398th Bomb Group Memorial Association, accessed on November 14, 2016, http://www.398th.org/History/Veterans/Voices/Transcriptions/Interview_Petrocine_Pep.html#PP_Feathering.

white, snow-covered Kansas landscape we had just left below. I had never given any thought to what it could be like above an overcast. I knew then that I must be the luckiest guy that ever lived. Daunting as it seemed, I could not wait to sit behind the wheel of that enormous, olive-colored monster.

Our instructor was a first lieutenant, of medium height, with dark, straight hair. The next day, McCarthy and I took turns in the pilot's seat, and over the weeks we gradually learned to fly what was called "the flying boxcar."[26] I admit—this airplane is not the slickest looking flying machine in the Army Air Forces, but to me, the Consolidated B-24 Liberator four-engine bomber was awesome and beautiful.

One of the requirements for all B-24 crew members was to experience the effect of high altitude inside the controlled conditions of an oxygen chamber.[27] The nearest oxygen chamber was located at Ellington Field in Houston. The day before taking off for Houston, it was cold and our instructor was wearing just his standard leather A-2 flight jacket. While he and I were standing on the flight-line, waiting for McCarthy, he explained to me that he had lost his heavy, fleece-lined jacket. He thought it might have been stolen and was upset because the quartermaster expected him to reimburse the government fifty dollars. He also told me that six or seven enlisted men would be flying to Ellington Field with us as they were also to go through the oxygen chamber experience. In the late afternoon of the next day, we all ducked under the bomb bay and climbed up inside for the overnight flight to Houston. The enlisted men sat as passengers in the large space behind the bomb bay.

On the flight down, McCarthy and I traded off in the pilot's seat while the instructor, as always, sat in the copilot's seat. We practiced instrument flying. I had already taken my turn at the wheel and McCarthy took over. With the student-pilot wearing green-tinted goggles and with the entire windshield covered with a transparent red plastic shield, the pilot is unable to see the horizon or anything else outside the cockpit. The instructor, however, has a clear vision outside through the red plastic shield. McCarthy was flying blind and relying solely on the dashboard instruments.

26. For nicknames like the "Flying Boxcar" for the B-24, see Consolidated B-24 Liberator, Warbird Alley, accessed on November 14, 2016, http://www.warbirdalley.com/b24.htm.

27. For an excellent description of the training in an oxygen chamber, see John Joseph Hibbets, *Take 'er Up Alone, Mister!* (New York: Whittlesey House, 1943), 222–8.

He would stay on course by following the beam. By listening to the Morse code signals in his earphones the pilot is able to maintain an exact course to the destination, regardless of wind or weather. When he strayed to the left of the beam, he heard a dah-dit (long tone-short tone) and if he drifted to the right, he heard a dit-dah (short tone-long tone). The further off course he got, the stronger the signal became. When the two signals merged into a constant tone, he was on course—thus, the expression, "on the beam." He knew he was over the field when the signal stopped, just for a few seconds, and he no longer heard any tone at all, the cone of silence.

I had moved to the radio desk behind the copilot's seat, listening for the silence of the tone over Ellington field. As we passed over the silent cone, I assumed that the instructor had decided to continue on beyond Houston to give McCarthy more instrument time. We plodded on and on, way out over the Gulf of Mexico, and finally, I realized we would be running out of fuel unless we turned back. I leaned down and asked the instructor if he knew we had passed over the cone of silence forty minutes before. He grabbed the wheel and spun the plane around back toward Ellington Field. They may have been talking, or the instructor may have gone to sleep and McCarthy simply missed the cone over the field. I had heard of planes mysteriously disappearing over the Gulf, and realized this was one way it could happen.

The next morning, we all entered the oxygen chamber, learned about the dangers of high altitude, the effects of anoxia, and how to use oxygen masks and the small yellow, portable tanks for movement about the plane. Afterwards, we walked back out to our B-24 with the enlisted men and climbed inside. My fleece-lined leather jacket was gone. It was not cold in Houston's warmer climate, and I explained to the instructor that I had left my coat hanging on the radio-desk chair. He immediately called for everyone to deplane to the tarmac, lined them up, and insisted that anyone who knew anything about the missing jacket should come forward. He finally concluded that it had to have been taken by someone on the base during the night. I could not get it out of my mind that the instructor may have taken it. He could have come back and entered the plane during the night without anyone knowing, but what could he have done with the coat? On the return flight, while McCarthy was taking his turn at the wheel, I dropped down to the narrow bomb bay catwalk and eased myself through the bomb bay to the rear, where the enlisted men were all sitting. I looked around and discovered a small space above the bomb bays, but the light was not good and I could see nothing but an irregular jumble of tubes, metal braces and colored wires all commingled together.

But there—there was something. I reached way in and touched it. The coat! It was rolled up in a tight ball. I pulled it out. The instructor seemed just as surprised and glad for me as McCarthy and the others. The jacket was one worn only by officers. None of the enlisted men would have any use for it. I was certain I knew who had taken it.

Life in Liberal was different. I was an officer now and treated with respect, not like being an Air Force cadet. I learned that I was, even at the age of eighteen, a bachelor because I was housed in what was called the BOQ, or the Bachelor Officers Quarters. Married officers lived elsewhere with their wives, but I never knew exactly where because bachelors rarely mingled with the married guys. We bachelors got to know each other pretty well. It was a relaxed atmosphere, without the tension associated with being a cadet and always anxious about each test hop. There was camaraderie, even harmless horseplay and jousting, which could lead to headlocks, hammerlocks, and twisted arms. I had gone against Jim Glasgow of California before when we were cadets together in Waco. We were good friends and although I was bigger than Jim, he would wrap me up like a pretzel in seconds every time—very depressing. I had another go at him in Liberal, but with the same quick and painful results, leaving me even more deflated until Jim finally admitted he had had a certain amount of experience in such activity. Before enlisting, Glasgow had been an officer with the Los Angeles Police Department!

We not only learned to fly the B-24, we learned everything about the plane itself. It seemed to me to have similarities to the human body. It had to be fed oil and gas; it had an oxygen system, an electrical system (nerves), a hydraulic system (muscles), and a system of cables extending to the tail and out to the ailerons (tendons), which controlled its movement. It even had a skeleton frame and was covered with a protective aluminum skin. The automatic pilot is the brain. After ten weeks in Liberal, Kansas, and right after my

Jim Glasgow with Tom in Liberal, Kansas, 1943

nineteenth birthday, I felt as if I knew the Liberator inside and out and felt comfortable and confident at its controls.[28]

28. For a brief description of the B-24, see Swansborough and Bowers, *United States Military Aircraft Since 1909*, 176–86. For more detailed technical histories of the B-24, see Michael O'Leary, *Consolidated B-24 Liberator* (Oxford, Great Britain: Osprey Press, 2002); and Larry Davis, *B-24 Liberator in Action* (Carrollton, TX: Squadron/Signal Publications, 1987).

The AAF next sent me to Tonopah, Nevada, and assigned me a crew for combat training.[29] The three other officers of our crew—copilot, navigator, and bombardier—were all second lieutenants, as was I. The six enlisted men were all corporals, and each one was trained in his specialty at different bases. The day I arrived in Tonopah, I met our navigator and bombardier. Later that day, we met with the six enlisted men in the open, on the concrete tarmac. We were advised that the copilot assigned to us, Lt. Eugene "Obie" O'Brien, had some kind of illness and was recovering in the base hospital.[30] I would not have a regular copilot or even meet O'Brien during the first month of our training. Instead, base officers would fly as my copilot, and I would have the benefit of their experience and advice. But, O'Brien was denied valuable training time. He had never been inside a multi-engine bomber, much less a four-engine Liberator. I do not recall what the illness was, but it was chronic and plagued him throughout his entire time with us, though not serious enough to pull him off the crew permanently. He was gone for more than half the time while we were stationed in Tonopah.

Our navigator, Arnold "Arnie" Nelson, hailed from Harrisburg, Pennsylvania, and had attended college there.[31] Probably only 20, Arnie was quiet and independent, smooth-faced, average height, studious, very agreeable, and pleasant—obviously from a good home. He and I were the only two on the crew who did not drink, smoke, or shave at that time. Nelson was the one I felt I had the most in common with, but he seemed self-sufficient, not especially outgoing, and we never became close friends. He was a good navigator and his skills would be severely tested in the months ahead.

Howard Runyan, our bombardier, was from Des Moines, Iowa.[32] He was scruffy looking, of medium height, with a rough complexion and short blond hair. Although usually in a jovial mood, Runyan was extremely outspoken, rendering strong opinions on every subject. Well aware of his reputation as something of a hard case, he unashamedly boasted of always looking out for "number one,"

29. For a history of Tonopah in World War II, see Tracy Henderson-Elder and Keith Myhrer, *The History of the World War II Tonopah Army Air Field, Nevada* (Nellis Air Force Base, Nevada: United States Air Force Air Combat Command, 2009).

30. O'Brien was a 2nd Lt., and his full name was Eugene R. O'Brien, Jr. See Headquarters Fifteenth Air Force, Special Orders No. 261, September 17, 1944, in author's possession.

31. Nelson's was a flight officer, and his full name was Arthur A. Nelson. See ibid.

32. Runyan was a 2nd Lt., and his full name was Howard W. Runyan. See ibid.

Arnold "Arnie" Nelson, Eugene "Obie" O'Brien, Tom, Howard Runyan

Howard Runyan, Jane McNab, Jean McNab, and Tom in Los Angeles, 1944

no pretense here. He was the opposite of the somewhat shy and usually quiet Nelson. Runyan used foul language, not prevalent among others in the crew, and was usually, while not unpleasant, totally unpredictable. After arriving at our base in Italy, for example, when we stepped into our tent for the first time, Runyan quickly sized up the situation and declared, "Hey, I'll take that one," pointing to the more private bunk in the far corner with a table and away from the light of the tent opening and its traffic.

Halfway through our Tonopah training, "Obie" O'Brien, our copilot, finally joined us. Obie was at least twenty-five, older than all others on the crew with the exception of McCorkle, the tail-gunner, who was thirty. Obie was from Brooklyn, but had no accent and was probably a college graduate. He was the only married officer among the four officers. He was tall, nice looking with brown hair, and wore a trim, debonair mustache. I was the youngest man on the crew. The age difference did not matter to me, nor anyone else as far as I know, except I suspect that it did matter to O'Brien. I would learn over the next few months that he was a man with a lot of ambition and pride, and I would understand if he was frustrated and resentful, being outranked by an airplane commander who had just turned nineteen. Early on, I sensed that he was not satisfied with his situation. Unquestionably, he, like so many other copilots, yearned to fly fighters and was not pleased at being stuck in a slow, ponderous four-engine bomber in which he had had no experience—and worse, playing second fiddle to a teenage first-pilot. Although he missed out on over half our Tonopah training flights, by the time we departed for San Francisco, he appeared to be ready and fit.

As time passed, it would appear to me that while the four officers of other crews seemed, from a distance, at least, to have much in common, with almost a fraternity-brother relationship, the officer corps of our crew was, by comparison, something of a mixed bag—O'Brien was several years older and married; Runyan was independent and totally self-serving; Nelson was serious-minded and somewhat withdrawn; and I was a teenager, at the helm. Still, each of the four of us responded to a common cause, which totally consumed our attention, and as a team, brought us closer together.

The age difference played no part in my relationship with the six enlisted men, some of whom were several years older, with the tail-gunner being eleven years my senior. There was a good rapport between the six enlisted men and the four officers. They were relaxed and quick to find levity in everything, and there was always a lot of good-natured kidding, laughing, and jibing back and forth between themselves. I liked every one of them. They contributed heavily to my having a great experience in Tonopah and in Italy. Notwithstanding what may have been a less than perfect relationship between the four officers, the whole experience was exciting, memorable, and it was just plain fun to be involved in this totally new life

Corporal Will Gorman, the crew chief and engineer, led the enlisted men.[33] Will was about five feet, nine inches tall. He was young, dedicated, efficient, and my right arm. In combat, he operated the top turret guns, but otherwise remained on the deck behind the pilots' seats. Will was eager, knowledgeable, and aware of his position's importance. As engineer, he was responsible for the mechanical functioning of the entire plane, an in-house mechanic while in flight, more familiar with the plane's working parts than anyone else. He was invaluable.

Corporal Willie Horvath, the nose gunner, was older, married with a child and one on the way.[34] There was lots of laughter with the enlisted men, and Horvath was almost always at the center. He originated the expression, "lotta laughs, guys, lotta laughs," a phrase that was repeated over and over from Tonopah to Newfoundland and the entire time in Italy. It became the crew's rallying cry, "Lots of laughs!" It was all part of our feeling that all was well—a refusal to admit to pressure or adversity, a reminder to keep our optimism, our spirits high while we were on an adventure of a lifetime. In combat, we were given our own plane, and we named her "*Lotta Laffs*."

Corporal Jim Hamilton, the radio operator, was from California.[35] His pull-down radio desk was located on the flight deck behind the copilot's seat. Jim also served as the waist gunner, behind the bomb bays in combat, manning the .50 caliber machine guns at the window on the left. Jim and his wife visited our home in Dallas in 2007 for a few days and we reminisced about our Italian experience. He reminded me of something I had actually forgotten—a spur-of-the-moment dip

33. Gorman's full name was William G. Gorman. See ibid.
34. Horvath's full name was William F. Horvath. See ibid.
35. Hamilton's full name was James W. Hamilton. See ibid.

Tom's Crew in Tonopah, 1943—Bottom (left to right)—Will Gorman, Jim Hamilton, Talmidge "Jonesie" Jones, Willie Horvath, Tony Barone, and Mac McCorkle; Top (left to right)—Tom Faulkner, Eugene "Obie" O'Brien, Arnold "Arnie" Nelson, Howard Runyan

down inside the Grand Canyon while on a practice mission. My son laughingly reminded me recently that if I did that today, I would be arrested.

Corporal Tony Barone, short, stocky, with wavy blond hair, was also from California. He operated the ball turret protecting the underside, the belly of the ship.[36] The ball turret was retractable but lowered for combat, so that his body actually swiveled around outside of the fuselage while cramped inside his small sphere.

Waist gunner Corporal Talmidge "Jonesie" Jones, a fellow Texan from Houston, manned the guns at the window behind the bomb bays on the right side.[37] Jonesie was quiet, unassuming, but participated very well as an amused audience for the more extroverted members of the crew.

36. Barone's full name was Anthony Barone. See ibid.
37. Jones's full name was Talmadge R. Jones. See ibid.

Corporal Mac McCorkle, tail-gunner, became ill soon after arrival in Italy and missed almost all of our missions.[38] McCorkle drank a lot and, being much older, did not seem to be as convivial as were the other five enlisted men. In combat, in his absence, the squadron assigned other tail-gunners to take his place.

In training at Tonopah, the crew was together constantly during the day except for meals, when the four officers would depart for the Officers' Mess and the enlisted men to their mess hall. The six enlisted men became a close-knit group. Their relationship with us was as with all crews. They called us "Lieutenant," while we called them by their first name. They addressed us with respect, sometimes ending or beginning a statement or question with "Sir." I often wondered how this existed so well—young men of the same age thrown together, seemingly accepting without question the marked difference in status, with rank alone determining everyone's behavior with each other. It seemed to me that, while equality was absent in the military, this kind of division of authority was absolutely necessary. This has to be why West Point, the Naval Academy, and Texas A&M seemed to accept, actually support, the value of a class system, which granted older students authority over new arrivals for at least their freshman year. Like anything else, the "bullying" and "hazing" tactics called for maturity and responsibility in upperclassmen and acceptance of authority by underclassmen. I could see the purpose of being subservient at Texas A&M and being called Fish Faulkner and Fish Anderson (fish being the "lowest form of life"), while addressing the upperclassmen by their last names as "Mister."

Midway through our crew training in Tonopah, we were all given a three-day pass. Arnie Nelson (navigator), Howard Runyan (bombardier), Jim Hamilton (radio operator), Will Gorman (engineer), and I decided to rent a car and drive to Los Angeles. It was a tough drive over the Sierra Mountains on a narrow two-lane road. I had written a letter to Dorothy Maloney, a high-school classmate whose stage name was now Dorothy Malone, and she had sent a simple post card reply, "Tommy, I'd just LOVE to see you." This resulted in no end of razzing, especially from Runyan. I had made a big deal of the fact that Dorothy was a big-time movie star. I believe she had been in a couple of Boston Blackie films and other B movies.

38. McCorkle's full name was James C. McCorkle. See ibid.

Dorothy would later become famous, winning an Oscar in 1956 for Best Supporting Actress in *Written on the Wind* and be paired with almost every leading man in Hollywood.[39]

We drove by the Studio Club, where young starlets lived. Dorothy was on location and we would not see her, but she left passes for us to enter Warner Brothers, her studio. First, we visited the set of *Tall in the Saddle*, and watched John Wayne and Ella Raines act out a scene. When finished, they both came up to us. I did not have pen or paper, so John Wayne tore off the back cover of his movie script, signed his name at the top, and gave it to me. The other stars we met all signed their names beneath his. Ella cursed like a sailor. Above her autograph she wrote, "The best of what you like???" We also talked to screen star, Pat O'Brien, who starred in *Knute Rockne, All American*, along with Ronald Reagan, who played George Gipp (the Gipper). We spent several minutes with song-and-dance man, George Murphy, who later became a U.S. senator for California.[40] They were obviously going out of their way to be courteous to servicemen, particularly George Murphy. I had the feeling he felt "on stage," wanting to show a genuine interest in us and say the things that servicemen would appreciate.

That night, Runyan and I discovered two beautiful identical twin girls at a pool table in the basement of the Ambassador Hotel where we stayed.[41] They referred to themselves as "starlets." We had dinner dates with them for two nights. They were the McNab twins, Jean and Jane. They were pretty, with enough hair to stuff a mattress. In Italy, we learned that the McNab twins had dated other Air Force officers and were very well known in Hollywood. While lying on my cot in Italy one day, reading the *Stars and Stripes*, I ran across a small article about one of the twins. The headline read, "*Starlet Sues Hollywood Canteen*." It reported that Jean McNab, my date with the big hair, had fallen to the floor at the large dance emporium where Hollywood stars and starlets volunteered

39. For a description of Dorothy Malone and her career, see Dorothy Malone Biography, IMDb.com, accessed on November 8, 2016, http://www.imdb.com/name/nm0540416/bio.

40. For information on Pat O'Brien's career, see Pat O'Brien, IMDb.com, accessed on November 8, 2016, http://www.imdb.com/name/nm0002285/?ref_=nv_sr_1. For information on George Murphy's career, see George Murphy, IMDb.com, accessed on November 8, 2016, http://www.imdb.com/name/nm0614278/?ref_=fn_al_nm_1.

41. For a brief history of the Ambassador Hotel in Los Angeles, see The Ambassador Hotel, Los Angeles: Every Spoke, But It's History, TheAmbassadorHotel.com, accessed on November 9, 2016, http://www.theambassadorhotel.com/.

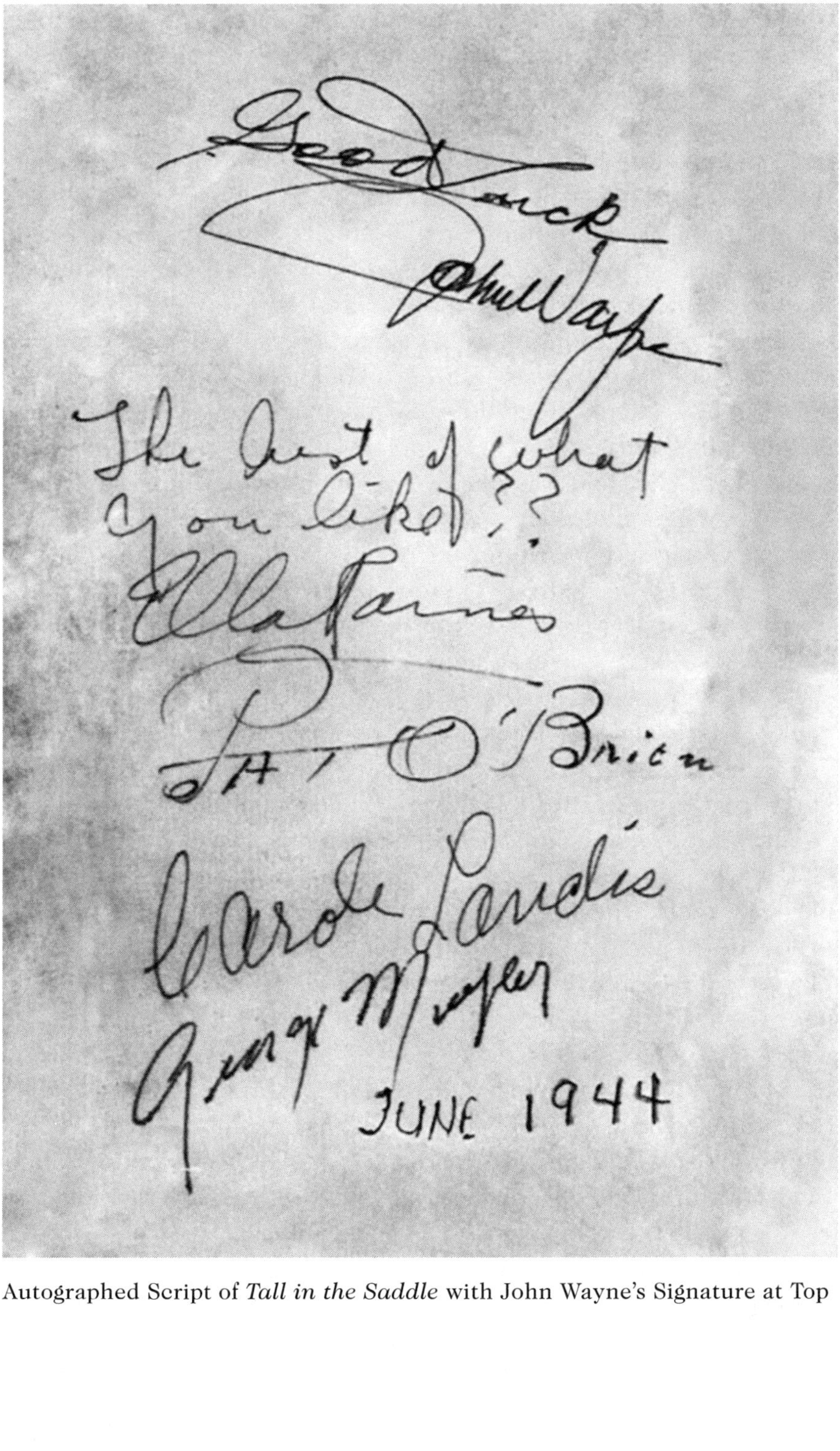


Autographed Script of *Tall in the Saddle* with John Wayne's Signature at Top

to entertain servicemen. She had broken her ankle while dancing with a Marine and was suing the canteen for damages.[42] Maybe she should have sued the Marine.

I will never forget the nightmarish trip back to Tonopah. First, Runyan left all of our gasoline rationing stamps on the dresser at the Ambassador. Not being aware of this until after we had filled the gas tank of our rented car half way back to Tonopah, I sped away before the owner of the gas station could ask for the stamps. It was completely dark on a moonless night as we wove our way through the high mountains between Los Angeles and Tonopah. While speeding down a steep hill, the headlights suddenly shorted out. What a shock! I could see nothing. Pitch dark, we were engulfed in blackness! What a helpless feeling as I slammed on the brakes. The road was narrow and winding. It could have been ugly. The lights flickered back on, but would go off intermittently with several more terrifying blackouts occurring before we left the mountains and finally reached Tonopah—more terrifying, we speculated, than the missions we would later be flying.

How fortunate we were that we survived that trip and then later, the combat missions. Many of my good friends failed to make it back. I think my1942 Highland Park High School class lost more young men to the war than any other class. Many of them were flyers, and some of those who were killed did not die as a result of enemy action. Handsome, well-liked John Scogin, not long married to Pat Cheney, was killed at a California base while landing his plane just after the war was over.[43] Popular George Jackson, with a Bob Hope personality, had been the colonel of the ROTC and played center on our football team. He was killed on Okinawa right after the war while performing a loop in a Marine Corsair. George was not an experienced Corsair pilot. He flew twin engine B-25s for the Marines and somehow obtained permission to take up a Corsair. Something went wrong. He may not have had enough instruction, or he may have begun the loop too low. George was just killing time, waiting to come home to be discharged. His older brother,

42. The McNab twins had small parts in a few movies in the 1940s. See Jean McNab, IMDb.com, accessed on November 9, 2016, http://www.imdb.com/name/nm0573520/; and Jane McNab, IMDb.com, accessed on November 9, 2016, http://www.imdb.com/name/nm0573519/?ref_=fn_al_nm_1.

43. For a brief story on John Scogin's death, see *Abilene Reporter-News*, July 22, 1950, 3. There is no additional information on Pat Cheney.

Earl Jackson, was a paratrooper transport pilot in England.[44] On D-day, Earl hauled paratroopers in a C-47 and pulled gliders full of troops over the English Channel to drop them off over France. Earl made it home and lived well into his eighties.

George Jackson was a clown and always upbeat. Before graduation at Highland Park High, he suggested that the two of us perform an act for the Senior Day stage production for the student body. George wrote the entire skit. Wearing straw boaters, striped coats, and white pants, and sporting walking sticks, we tried to mimic a Hope and Crosby vaudeville routine, telling jokes, singing and even attempting a dance act together with the canes. It was a lot of fun and went over very well. Some of the parents were there. My mother said she almost fell in the aisle, laughing so hard. I realized what entertainers feel. It was very compelling. For three nights I remember not being able to fall asleep thinking about it, laughing.

But George's fatal accident in the Corsair on Okinawa was not unusual. More American pilots were killed during the war in noncombat activity than by enemy fire.[45] At that age there is just not a well-developed sense of mature judgment. A teenage pilot is confronted with his own natural love of excitement, of daring and adventure, the lure of speed, and the temptation to propel his loud, powerful machine through the sky as fast as it will take him. The thrill of the moment sometimes seems to overcome the instinct for self-preservation and the fear of injury or even death. This fearlessness and a sense of being immortal carry them through life-threatening situations. Recognition of this recklessness played its part in the Air Force going to meticulous extremes to train and prepare its pilots and flight crews for any eventuality. I always felt that American pilots were furnished the very best equipment and the best possible instruction in the classroom and in flight, with safety of the pilot and crew always paramount.

I personally broke the rules only once, and because of the near-fatal results, I was never again tempted. We were in Tonopah and were sent out to the bombing range to practice low-level bombing.

44. Earl Jackson died in 2005. See Earl Norwood Jackson, *Dallas Morning News*, accessed on November 9, 2016, http://www.legacy.com/obituaries/dallasmorningnews/obituary.aspx?n=earl-norwood-jackson&pid=3149488. The obituary does mention George Jackson's death in Okinawa.

45. While it is difficult to determine how many airmen died in accidents, there were over 1,000 aircraft accidents alone in Florida during the war. See Robert Widner, *Aircraft Accidents in Florida: From Pearl Harbor to Hiroshima* (Lulu.com, 2009).

The area assigned to us was a half-hour away. Nelson steered us to the target area, and I dropped down to 500 feet and waited for Runyan to give me instructions.

"Tom," he said, lamely, over the intercom, "I forgot the bombsight."

"What? Forgot the bombsight!"

I could not believe it. How can a bombardier forget his bombsight? This occurred just days after he had left our vacation gas rationing coupons on the hotel dresser in Los Angeles. There was not enough time to go back, land, taxi in to pick up a bombsight, and return to the area. We would have to come back the next day, and I was furious. Already at a low level, I pushed the throttles forward, turned the B-24 into a steep bank, nosed the plane down to pick up more speed and leveled off just a few feet above the desert ground. I suddenly realized looming in front of us and also on the left and the right, were steep, high mountains, too close for any attempt to pull up and over. I had flown into a cul-de-sac. I banked the plane in a steep turn to the right and then quickly back to the left just inside the circular base of the mountains and emerged from the cup. I was not mad at Runyan anymore, but I was mad as hell at myself. I would never again pull a stunt like that. Pilot seats are no place for bad tempers, especially with nine other men on board. I have often thought about that incident. Had we crashed into the mountain, no one would have ever known it was because of a pilot's momentary, foolish impulse. There were numerous crashes like this during the war where the cause was never determined. I imagine a lot resulted from this kind of rash behavior.

On August 11, 1944, all ten of us packed up and boarded the train in Tonopah, bound for Hamilton Field in San Francisco.[46] Hamilton Field was a staging area for B-24 crews who would fly new B-24s overseas. There were twenty or twenty-five other B-24 crews there from Tonopah and other bases. On the way we had a four-hour layover in Reno, Nevada. The officers and enlisted men separated, and we four officers headed for Harrah's, the famous gambling spot. I put a dime down on the Chucaluck cage and won.[47] I could tell

46. For a history of Hamilton Field, see Historic California Posts, Camps, Stations and Airfields: Hamilton Air Force Base (Air Forces Station, San Rafael; Hamilton Field, Hamilton Army Airfield), accessed on November 13, 2016, http://www.militarymuseum.org/HamiltonAFB.html.

47. Chuck-a-luck is a game played with three dice and is also called Birdcage. See Chuck-a-Luck, accessed on November 13, 2016, http://casinogambling.about.com/od/Othercasinogames/a/How-To-Play-Chuck-A-Luck.htm.

that the girl in charge of the game was new. Whether her greenness or my luck prevailed, I was not sure. But I kept doubling up and walked out with fifty dollars—yes, ten cents to fifty dollars.

San Francisco was the most exciting place I had ever been. After sweltering in Tonopah for three months, we found it strange when warm August afternoons would turn into delightfully chilly evenings. The ten of us had arrived there for several days of orientation, physicals, immunization shots, and a lot of time off to go into San Francisco before flying off with a brand-new B-24 to an unknown destination. Up to now, this was the most important event of my life. We did not know it at the time, but it was an honor for our crew to have been selected to fly a plane to our combat destination. All other crews that I knew of had transferred overseas by boat. We wondered where we would be flying our new B-24. These were awesome times, and every day would bring a new development or unexpected experience.

By a lucky coincidence, my brother, Jim, a navy lieutenant J/G, was a gunnery officer assigned to a ship docked in San Francisco. I had not been in contact with Jim before, but our mother, knowing of our whereabouts at all times, put us in touch with each other. Because of the age difference between us, we had never been close, but now, in San Francisco, both of us older and also officers in the military, we began to appreciate each other with new respect. After the war, Jim married Mary Munger, and they had four delightful children, two sons and two daughters. Beginning with that brief time in San Francisco, our relationship with each other changed from being somewhat adversarial as young boys to his becoming my best friend—and remained so until his untimely death at the age of fifty from a sudden and massive heart attack.

At the Stage Door Canteen in San Francisco, where servicemen could mingle with movie stars and meet local girls, Jim had met a Mrs. Zellerbach. She had taken a liking to Jim and introduced him to a pretty young friend of their family. Mrs. Zellerbach's husband was the head of the large, Fortune 500 paper manufacturing company, Crown-Zellerbach.[48] I met Mrs. Zellerbach when Jim and

48. For a history of Crown-Zellerbach, see Crown Zellerbach Corp., Lehman Brothers Collection – Contemporary Business Archives, Harvard Business School, Baker Library, Historical Collections, accessed on November 14, 2016, http://www.library.hbs.edu/hc/lehman/company.html?company=crown_zellerbach_corp.

Jim Faulkner in Navy, c. 1944

I picked up a relative of hers—my date—at the Zellerbach mansion in nearby Burlingame. Jim looked great in his dress blues. Never a hardy person, the navy seemed to agree with him. He would be promoted to a full lieutenant (same as a captain in the Air Force) right after I left San Francisco.

The girls were both pretty and were dressed in black. We took them to dinner at a small nightclub. Jim was always at home in any social setting, one of many such traits that were somehow left out of me (giving rise to his constant razzing me when we were young boys that I was adopted—or that I was switched by mistake with his real brother at birth). Since I knew nothing about ordering a drink, I asked for the same thing my date ordered. The waiter gave me a strange look and brought us each a Pink Lady. It looked and tasted like a milkshake, but I loved milkshakes, and had another and maybe even something else, my second experience with too much alcohol. The first had been a beer-bash with roommate Bob Anderson, Warner Marsh, and other freshmen at Texas A&M when my bed became like a storm-racked raft, and I fell off of my upper-deck bunk to the maroon-painted concrete floor.

The second night, I was more careful when the four of us joined a young married couple at the Copacabana, a large, popular nightclub on Powell Street with a great orchestra.[49]

The next morning at Hamilton Field, all crews reported for roll call. For me personally, this would turn out to be one of the most significant (and most unfortunate) mornings of the war. For here, I was confronted with making a decision that would affect my relationship with my copilot from this day on. Each of about twenty-five crews lined up in a single file, with the pilot in front, followed by the copilot, navigator, bombardier, and the enlisted men down the ten-man lineup. The adjutant called for an unexpected verbal report of attendance from each pilot. I had to make a quick decision. O'Brien was not there. His wife had traveled all the way from Brooklyn to see him before he was to fly overseas. I remember meeting her briefly. She was pretty, well-shaped, with blond hair and, like Obie, older than I by several years. They had three days together. He was, of course, with her, but his pass called for a return to the base the night before.

What should I do about Obie's not being there? I had about ten seconds to decide. As the other pilots were calling out, "All present and accounted for," I made what I immediately felt was one of the saddest decisions of my life. I had no idea of what kind of trouble either of us would be in—him for being AWOL or me if caught lying. I yelled to the adjutant that our copilot was absent. I had no time to wonder whether the guards at the gate would report him absent or when he would actually return.

Two hours later, I was standing by my double-deck bunk on the second floor of our barracks when Obie came storming up the stairs. He was livid, his fists clenched, his face red with anger. He stopped in front of me, glaring and furious and said, "You son-of-a-bitch!" I said, "Obie, I'm sorry. I'm really sorry." He wheeled around and left.

I would not have been surprised if he had swung on me. He was that angry. Our relationship after that became simply a polite acceptance of two guys forced to live and work together. I have worried about it ever since. I never knew the nature of his punishment,

49. The Copacabana Night Club opened in 1941. For its history, see Joaquin Garay, The Virtual Museum of San Francisco, accessed on November 14, 2016, http://www.sfmuseum.net/war/garay.html.

but I have no doubt but that it involved a sacrifice of precious time with his wife. That incident and the traumatic events that occurred on my twenty-eighth mission, hounded me for many decades.

The time had finally come! What a thrill it was to climb up through the bomb bay and step up into the cockpit of a beautiful, brand new silver Liberator, sit in the pilot's seat, and prepare for takeoff. The plane had just arrived from the Ford Motor plant in Michigan. It smelled exactly like a new automobile. As the wheels left the ground to the strange and distinctive purr of new engines, we immediately found ourselves over water. Hamilton Field's runway ended at San Francisco Bay. The Golden Gate Bridge loomed into view with puffs of white clouds clinging to its massive structure. We had no idea where we would be landing.

I opened the sealed orders in flight as we headed west out over the Pacific Ocean, assuming we were on our way to a Pacific base. I read the orders, banked the plane around and pointed it in the opposite direction, still climbing, I handed the instructions to navigator Arnie Nelson and asked him for a heading. We were going back across the United States and then over the Atlantic Ocean to Europe. Our flight path would take us close enough to New York City that we would fly over Manhattan Island on a hazy day and look down on the skyscrapers and the Statue of Liberty. Our destination was Bari, Italy, and Nelson would be responsible for getting us there. As it turned out, however, this trip took much longer than we expected.

The formal relationship that existed between the officers and enlisted men relaxed, actually was dropped almost entirely while we were stranded for ten days in Newfoundland.[50] First, an engine problem was discovered at the base in Newfoundland after we landed, and while a replacement part was being flown from the United States, we were left with nothing but time on our hands at a remote foreign airbase, encircled by a forest of aspen trees, and totally away from civilization. I strolled into the woods bordering the airfield, peeled a foot-wide piece of paper-like bark off an aspen tree and wrote a letter on the parchment to my parents.

50. Faulkner and his crew were following the mid-Atlantic transit route which left from Newfoundland for the Azores then to North Africa. From there, planes could be delivered anywhere around the Mediterranean. See Wesley Frank Craven and James Lea Cate, eds., *The American Air Forces in World War II*, Vol. 1—*Plans and Operations, January 1939 to August 1945* (Chicago, IL: The University of Chicago Press, 1948), 312.

The war was far away. The enlisted men began playing poker and invited us to join in. All ten of us took turns, sitting in at different times. At first, we played every poker game imaginable, starting with five-card stud, but finally evolved into just one special poker game that we played exclusively for days—and nights. We labeled it "Seven Card High-low Split the Shit." When the new engine part arrived, we were all anxious to takeoff, but the weather turned bad. We were still stranded, and the poker game continued. Each day we replayed the game into the early morning hours of the next day, almost without stop. There was a benefit. Rank seemed to disappear and the ten of us came to know each other well during those ten days.

We finally took off, discovering once again ocean waters at the end of the runway as in San Francisco, heading for the Azores, depending on Nelson to find those small islands, actually his first big test at navigation. We landed, refueled, and took off immediately for Marrakech.[51] The sun was beginning to set, and there was a cloud cover as we approached the coast of western Morocco. This was not good. I dreaded the prospect of having to make an instrument landing—not my specialty. For hours, pilots spend time in Link trainers learning how to navigate and land safely in socked-in situations, but I never felt proficient at it. I had cracked up several times in the Link trainer before getting it right. Now I was facing the prospect of the real thing. If the overcast was less than 500 feet, we could be in real trouble. By that time, we had little gas, and going north to Casablanca, the nearest airport, was out of the question. But, we were lucky. The clouds parted, and I could see the field below through the haze. What a relief!

Marrakech was the first experience any of us had ever had in a foreign land. We spent the next morning looking around. On one side of the large, open plaza-like area was the Kasbah, which we were warned against entering.[52] I bought two curved daggers inside metal scabbards with Arabic engraving which now hang on my daughter's living room wall. The Arab boy who I bought them from said they were made mostly from melted coins.

51. For a description of Marrakech, Morocco in World War II. See 1940's Morocco: World War Two, accessed on November 14, 2016, http://marocmama.com/1940s-morocco-world-war-two/.

52. The Kasbah is a fortified citadel.

Having flown from half a world away, we finally landed at our destination, Bari, Italy, and parked the plane on a grass field.[53] We were on our own for the afternoon and evening, and all ten of us foraged into town. I remember a lot of white one-story stone buildings and nearby stone residences. We wandered around. A long line of G.I.s stretched from the front door to the street of a one-story house. It was a house of ill repute.[54]

That evening we ate in Bari and went to a bar. My dad drank Scotch whiskey and sometimes, a martini. I had tasted both and did not care for either, so I would stick with wine. I had tried Port in Marrakech. The shelves of the small Bari bar were lined with all shapes, sizes, and colors of bottles, and one I had heard of, Vermouth. So I ordered a glass—another, maybe another. I cannot seem to remember. I do recall never having been as sick in my life. I spent a horrible night with the most sickening nausea imaginable. I can still remember that awful taste in my mouth. We were lying on the grass, side by side, under the wing of our B-24, trying to sleep. I am sure that in my agony, I kept the others awake most of the night.

We did acquire an unexpected bonus before reaching our final destination in Italy. Back in San Francisco, on the day we climbed into our new B-24 with all our gear, the enlisted men called on the intercom from the rear to report that a huge crate was sitting in the center of their aft section. I had no idea of what it could be and neither did they, but it was too late to deal with, so we took off without finding out what was inside or what we were do with it. The AAF would never fail to provide instructions on eventualities such as this, but somehow, we missed out on the purpose of this huge box. Each day during our flight to Italy, we all became more curious, so somewhere en route, we decided to break open the mysterious crate. Inside, the enlisted men found 1,000 small boxes of K-rations.

On landing at the field in Bari, we were told we could not keep our new plane, which was disappointing to hear, but no great surprise. However, as to the K-rations, in the absence of instructions for their disposition, we unloaded the crate before boarding the plane that would take us to our assigned airbase, and we divided the 1,000 boxes of K-rations between the ten of us. No one ever asked us about

53. Bari Airfield was the headquarters of the 15th Air Force from December 1943 to September 1945. See Tillman, *Forgotten Fifteenth*, 6–7.

54. Prostitution was common near the airfields and bases. See Chalker, *The Flight of the Liberators*, 37.

them, and we never knew their actual purpose. By the time we left Italy, I can say that not one box of K-rations was left. The contents of each box varied, and although these K-rations were generally much maligned because there was always something inside not to like, there were a few nice delicacies, such as a tin of American cheese, a chocolate bar, and always two cigarettes. Of course, most of us who did not smoke would try out the free samples of cigarettes. I am sure the tobacco companies reaped huge profits over the following decades from the thousands of American servicemen who became addicted to cigarettes, including myself, because of these free samples inside the World War II K-rations.

# Chapter 3

# Flying with the Fifteenth Air Force

My home from September 1944 to March 1945 was San Giovanni Airfield. Our flight from the United States in a new B-24 ended in Bari, Italy. From there, we were flown to San Giovanni Air Field, five miles west of Cerignola, Italy, to join the Fifteenth Air Force. I flew my first mission over Budapest, on September 17 and participated in twenty-seven more missions before I returned home the following March. Nothing could have prepared me for what I ultimately experienced. While the training provided by the AAF had been excellent, until I began flying missions and actually faced the reality that someone was trying to kill me, I had not understood what it meant to fly in combat. After six months, I had logged over 800 hours of flying time—the great bulk of it on combat missions.

After landing at San Giovanni and being taken to our tent to unload our gear where we would be living for the next six months, I was told to report to the squadron headquarters. It was a small stone building across from a little larger frame structure which housed a seldom used barber shop, a canteen or PX of sorts which sold mostly beer and candy bars, and the post office, all of them open for very limited hours each day. The stone mess hall,

Officer's Tent at San Giovanni Airfield

Mess Hall at San Giovanni Airfield

not much larger than the headquarters, was also in the grouping of buildings.

Waiting for me at headquarters were the squadron officers, Captain Arthur Pitts, Captain Eugene Goosen, and Captain Billy Jacobs, who was also from north Texas.[1] They were in charge

1. For information on Arthur Pitts, see "737th Bomb Squadron Crews – Arthur S. Pitts," Aircraft and Airmen from the 454th Bombardment Group in Italy during World War II, accessed on July 14, 2017, http://www.454thbombgroup.it/737th%20Squadron%20Crews.pdf;

of squadron operations, but each occasionally would lead the squadron on missions. They interviewed me for twenty minutes or so, trying to learn about my flying background. I had the feeling that they would have liked for me to speak up for myself, maybe giving me an opportunity to take a quick leadership role, but I was not comfortable under the microscope and not knowing what was in store for me or my crew, I did not take the bait, if, in fact, there was any there.

After this introductory conference, I returned to join my three tent-mates and to check on the enlisted men. The other officers of our tent, Runyan, O'Brien, and Nelson, were now settled in place, one in each corner with plenty of room. On entering our tent that first day, we discovered four canvas cots on cross-legged wood frames, one in each corner, each with a rubber air mattress, flat and unfolded, and two army blankets. That was all—no sheets, no pillows, no towels, no washrags, no soap, and no toothpaste. At least the cots had been unfolded and set up in place, but we each had to blow up our rubber air mattresses. Per orders, all first pilots like me had their cots located in the front left corner by the entrance. The remaining six members of the crew, Barone, Gorman, Hamilton, Horvath, Jones, and McCorkle, slept in a separate tent about ninety feet away. The two tents were the same size, and the enlisted men seemed a bit crowded.

Since we had spent the previous night sleeping on the grass under the wing of our B-24 in Bari, the cots looked pretty good. After getting used to the very narrow air mattress wrapped in a scratchy army blanket for a bottom sheet, another scratchy army blanket for a top sheet, and my bundled-up clothing for a pillow, I never slept better. Even after the clothes became dirty, I still bundled up the soiled ones for a pillow throughout my time at San Giovanni. There was nothing else. This, plus the lack of bathing, contributed to my acquiring a dark, dirty ring around my neck. I did not think that ring would ever wash off. Even back in Dallas

---

and 454th Bombardment Group (H) AAF – History for the Month of December, n.d. Air Force Historical Research Agency, Reel B0601 – 454 Records, 1052; for Eugene Goosen, see "737th Bomb Squadron Crews – Eugene C. Goosen," Aircraft and Airmen from the 454th Bombardment Group in Italy during World War II, accessed on July 14, 2017, http://www.454thbombgroup.it/737th%20Squadron%20Crews.pdf; and for Billy Jacobs, see "Obituary for Billy Joe Jacobs, 1920–2014," *Reno Gazette Journal*, accessed on May 16, 2017, http://www.legacy.com/obituaries/rgj/obituary.aspx?pid=171244606, and Chalker, *The Flight of the Liberators*, 123.

on leave, I still had that dark ring, but it gradually faded after weeks of scrubbing.

We each had a B-4 bag and a duffle bag, and we got by on very few clothes. Long underwear for flights, a few khaki shirts, a couple of pairs of khaki pants, and an olive flight suit, which we always wore in flight and sometimes on the ground. We had our Class A uniforms, but of course, unlike our more fortunate Eighth Air Force counterparts in England, we had no occasion to wear them except for a one-time Medal Day event for the entire group in a nearby open field, or for rest camp for a week on the Isle of Capri. When necessary, depending on the weather, we would wear our brown leather A-2 jacket or our heavy sheepskin jacket.

One thing I liked about the Air Force was their uniforms. We usually wore the Air Force A-2 leather jacket during routine duty or in flight, and we wore either the traditional cloth campaign cap with the point in front or the more formal hat with the leather visor. Because pre-war Air Corps pilots found they could not place earphones on their head if they were wearing the hat with the visor because of its round, stiff grommet, the grommet disappeared, and the hat looked better, resulting in a more casual, jaunty appearance. To attest to that, style conscious General Douglas MacArthur removed the grommet from his hat. During the summer time, officers could wear light tan uniforms. In Italy, with little regulation about clothing, I had a light green, cloth Eisenhower jacket made by an Italian tailor.[2]

After the war, this jacket, which I really liked, along with my summer tans and Class A olive uniform were all kept in the storage room over our garage for many years. But each article of my uniform gradually disappeared when my son, Tommy, at the age of fifteen, discovered that these various Air Force uniform parts, enhanced his attire while performing as the leader of his high-school rock band, *The Coconuts*.

I had hoped that our living conditions would improve over the course of our time in Italy, but they did not. With the onset of cold weather, they got worse. Since we did not have easy access

2. The origin of the Eisenhower jacket came from its namesake, Dwight Eisenhower, during World War II as he was looking for a wool jacket that looked better, was more comfortable, and was also more practical. See Timothy Rives, "The Ike Jacket," November 11, 2014, The National Archives Pieces of History, accessed on November 8, 2016, https://prologue.blogs.archives.gov/2014/11/11/the-ike-jacket/.

to bathing, we seldom bathed. We only had infrequent chances to take a shower, and even when we did, we often decided it was not worth the effort. The "showers" were located two miles away and were not exactly modern plumbing. If we chose to take a shower, an open truck hauled us to a large, grassy field, where two showers had been set up for use of the entire group of over 1,000 men. The showers were in the open with no curtain or even a fence. There was not even a showerhead, just a pipe from a water tank above. Of course, there was no heat for the water; so, standing buck naked in an open field during the fall and winter to take a shower was not appealing. I can remember showering only once during our entire six months at San Giovanni.

To make matters worse, we seldom washed our clothes. On rare occasions, an unreliable Italian laborer provided a laundry service for us, but since there was no place to go that called for us to look even halfway decent, we seldom used our formal uniforms. We definitely were not the freshest smelling bunch, but since we all were basically equally unclean, no one seemed to notice.

We did have access to electric lights, and I managed to hook up a bare and very dim light bulb above my cot. One of my letters home that my mother showed me years after the war reminded me that in order to read or write at night, I also had to light a kerosene lamp. Letter writing was the norm for most airmen, and servicemen in general, as this was our only way of communicating with our families. When we arrived at San Giovanni, we were told not to write home about our missions or about anything that would benefit the enemy. Further, and to my surprise, the first pilot, as airplane commander, was charged with the responsibility of reading all the outgoing mail of his crew's enlisted men and censoring anything that was even remotely revealing about our military activities. I was fully prepared to delete military matters, but the letters to wives and girlfriends were personal and sometimes *very* personal, and as the youngest member on our crew, I received a quick and astonishing education in areas somewhat foreign to me to that point.[3]

3. The military tried to limit information that soldiers shared in their letters and had officers censor their subordinates' mail. See War Department Pamphlet, No. 21-1 – When You Are Overseas These Facts Are Vital, July 29, 1943, accessed on August 7, 2017, http://penelope.uchicago.edu/Thayer/E/Gazetteer/Places/America/United_States/_Topics/history/_Texts/US_Government/War_Department/Pamphlets/21_dash_1/pamphlet*.html.

While at San Giovanni, I also discovered some other military truisms. While there is an old saying that an army operates on its stomach, I found that the military also operates on its watches. Every aviation cadet received a round, black wristwatch along with his clothing. There would be no excuse for not being "on time" in a disciplined AAF. Of course, everyone is regulated by "time," but much more so in the military, up to and including the synchronizing of our watches at all mission briefings. There was no a.m. or p.m. A military twenty-four clock does away with references to the civilian second half of the day, calling it like it is. Two p.m. is fourteen hundred hours.

### Mission 2 • September 18, 1944[4]
### Target: Railroad Bridge[5]
### Budapest, Hungary

*This was the first mission I flew as pilot with my own crew, except for a replacement copilot named Rutz[6] (my copilot, O'Brien, who came with us from San Francisco, was still being treated for an ailment). Rutz was a good pilot. We were assigned to a fairly new ship, a "J" model, number 664.[7] We flew wing-man most of the time. We had a lot of laughs on this trip. I really enjoyed it. The flak this time over Budapest was much worse.[8] We were hit in a few places in the nose. Holes about the size of a quarter. I would see the stuff popping all around us. All ships got back okay. After the mission we all had coffee and doughnuts at Group headquarters, and later, the boys talked about their experiences until late that night. A good bunch of fellas and a good crew.*

4. One hundred forty-nine B-24s, escorted by thirty-seven P-38s and thirty-six P-51s, attacked railroad bridges in Budapest. Mahoney, *Fifteenth Air Force Against the Axis*, 343.

5. Railroad bridges were critical targets for the Fifteenth Air Force as successful attacks against them would disrupt Germany's ability to move troops and supplies. Gerhard Weinberg asserts that "the Allied bombing of the German oil industry and the transportation system inflicted critical damage on Germany's whole industrial and military system in 1944." Weinberg, *A World at Arms*, 773.

6. "737th Bomb Squadron Crews – Jack H. Rutz," Aircraft and Airmen from the 454th Bombardment Group in Italy during World War II, accessed on August 4, 2017, http://www.454thbombgroup.it/737th%20Squadron%20Crews.pdf.

7. Headquarters 454th Bombardment Group (H), Operations Order #245 – Plan Able, September 18, 1944, Air Force Historical Research Agency, Reel B0601 – 454 Records, 646.

8. The flak was heaviest around Budapest. Confirming Mission Report, 454th Bomb Gp (H), Mission #120, September 18, 1944, Air Force Historical Research Agency, Reel B0601 – 454 Records, 648. Don Miller explains that while flak was "a grossly inefficient defensive measure" because it required 8,500 rounds to down a single bomber, "it was a devastatingly effective psychological weapon" and ultimately shot down 5,400 American planes. Donald L. Miller, *Masters of the Air: America's Bomber Boys Who Fought the Air War Against Nazi Germany* (New York: Simon & Schuster, 2006), 316.

Destroyed Railroad Bridge Over Danube River, September 21, 1944 (National Archives)

The United States Joint Chiefs of Staff approved the creation of the Fifteenth Air Force in October 1943, and it became part of the Mediterranean Allied Air Command in December. After much debate, the British and U.S. Combined Chiefs of Staff decided to appoint General Ira Eaker, the former commander of the Eighth Air Force in Great Britain, as the head of Mediterranean Allied Air Forces.[9] Eaker commanded all British and American aircraft located in the Mediterranean area. General Nathan Twining led the Fifteenth Air Force in Italy and served as Eaker's chief subordinate.[10] Eaker and General Carl "Tooey" Spaatz, the new commander of the U.S. Strategic Air Forces in Europe, both answered directly to General Henry "Hap" Arnold at the Pentagon in Washington.[11] Together, these men directed the American strategic bombing campaign in Europe for the remainder of the war.[12]

The 454th Bomb Group Commander, Colonel Horace Aynesworth, or another senior officer, led our group over the target and on the return to San Giovanni.[13] Every bomb group would usually

9. Craven and Cate, eds., *The Army Air Forces in World War II*, Vol. I, 745–51.

10. For a good, brief description of Nathan Twining, see General Nathan F. Twining, U.S. Air Force, accessed on July 15, 2017, http://www.af.mil/About-Us/Biographies/Display/Article/105367/general-nathan-f-twining/.

11. For excellent biographies of Ira Eaker, Carl Spaatz, and Hap Arnold, see James Parton, *"Air Force Spoken Here": General Ira Eaker and the Command of the Air* (Maxwell Air Force Base, AL: Air University Press, 2000); David R. Mets, *Master of Airpower: General Carl A. Spaatz* (Novato, CA: Presidio Press, 1997); and Dik Alan Daso, *Hap Arnold and the Evolution of American Airpower* (Washington, D.C.: Smithsonian Institution Press, 2000).

12. For a detailed official study of the last two years of the American air war in Europe, see Wesley Frank Craven and James Lea Cate, eds., *The Army Air Forces in World War II*, Volume 3 – *Europe, Argument to V-E Day, January 1944 to May 1945* (Chicago: University of Chicago Press, 1951).

13. Horace D. Aynesworth was the commander of the 454th Bombardment Group

B-24 Over Smoke Enshrouded Budapest, 1944 (National Archives)

fly three or four squadrons for each mission. Each of the twenty-one combined B-24 and B-17 bomb groups in Italy were capable of flying up to forty planes at one time. Weather permitting, on any day, the Fifteenth Air Force could muster upwards of 1,000 heavy bombers to attack German targets from a small area of southern Italy. Though we would usually hit the target, we sometimes would damage only a portion of it. Rarely would we miss it altogether. There is no question that our 737th Bomb Squadron and our 454th Bomb Group, as part of the Fifteenth Air Force, contributed heavily to shortening and winning the war in Europe.

The Fifteenth Air Force used B-17s and B-24s as its long-range bombers.[14] Many arguments were held in officers' clubs and bars when B-17 pilots and B-24 pilots were brought together—proclaiming

---

from July 1943 to March 1945. See Chalker, *The Flight of the Liberator*, 10; and "Brigadier General Horace D. Aynesworth," accessed on July 17, 2017, http://www.af.mil/About-Us/Biographies/Display/Article/107799/brigadier-general-horace-d-aynesworth/.

14. There were over twenty different airfields around Foggia that were used by the Fifteenth Air Force. Tillman, *Forgotten Fifteenth*, 6.

the merits of the Flying Fortress and the Liberator, respectively. The Liberator was designed several years after the Flying Fortress. It was advertised as being able to fly faster, further, and with a greater bomb-load than the Fortress. B-17 pilots vociferously disagreed. Although we never came in contact with them in Italy, when we met elsewhere, they were ready to defend their plane at all times, as were we.[15]

I like to point out that Winston Churchill chose the B-24 over the B-17 and the larger four-engine British bombers for the long-distance flights he made from England to North Africa for conferences with his military officers and even for his meeting with Joseph Stalin and Franklin Roosevelt at Yalta in February 1945. He would fly at night to avoid German fighter planes, and frequently at high altitude, using an oxygen mask. The British fixed a bunk and a comfortable overstuffed chair for him in the center, behind the bomb bays, but it was loud and, at altitude, always freezing cold because the B-24 had no heat. He must have worn a heated suit, as did the crew. I have a hard time envisioning Churchill spending hours and hours in such extreme discomfort and enduring the constant, roaring blast of the four engines.[16] I have never heard or read of his complaining about these trips, but the long, cold and noisy flights had to have been extremely difficult for him.

Much was said about the "Davis wing" design of the Liberator, but I never understood what was so great or different about it.[17] Personally, I think the B-24 and B-17 were about equal. There was no marked difference in performance. I had to admit (not to them, of course) that the Fortress was certainly better looking, with its streamlined, graceful appearance. The B-24, also known by various demeaning names like ugly-duck and swoose-goose, was box-like and ungainly looking. Regardless, I loved flying it, even the super-stiff 664, "*Lotta Laffs*," that we flew on most

15. For a description of this rivalry, see Bowman, *The USAAF Handbook*, 241.

16. Winston Churchill's personal transport was a B-24 nicknamed, "Commando." Graham Chandler, "Travels with Churchill: A World War II Flight Engineer Dishes on the Most 'I' of the VIPs He flew With," *Air & Space Smithsonian*, July 2009, accessed on August 4, 2017, http://www.airspacemag.com/history-of-flight/travels-with-churchill-136166507/.

17. The Davis Wing was a unique design developed by David R. Davis in the late 1930s that offered twenty percent less drag than other wings at that time. Graeme Douglas, *Consolidated B-24 Liberator Owners' Workshop Manual: 1939 Onwards (all marks): An Insight into Owning, Servicing and Flying the American Second World War Heavy Bomber* (Somerset, U.K.: Haynes Publishing, 2016), 18.

Flak Damage to Tail of B-24 From Munich Raid, September 23, 1944 (National Archives)

missions, and which was assigned to me on my second mission, my first as first pilot.

The usual procedure for all incoming crews was for the first pilot to fly up to five missions as copilot with an experienced crew before being turned loose with his own men.[18] When we arrived, there was a shortage of crews but a real need to have a full squadron formation; so, my crew flew with me for the first time on this, my second mission. Surprisingly, we were assigned #664, a fairly new ship. It was a beautiful silver J Model and unpainted, unlike the camouflage olive-colored old *Dinah-Mite* and *Gentleman Jim* (D Models which I would fly on some missions).[19] The Air Force had decided that the olive camouflage (and the extra weight of the paint) of the D Models was not all that necessary, plus the silver aluminum skin created less drag, improving speed and fuel consumption.

We found out the night before if we were to fly the next day. The pilot's name would be posted at squadron headquarters along

18. When Faulkner arrived, the plan was for new pilots to fly five missions with experienced crews to help them acclimate to combat. However, he only flew as copilot for his first mission and then served as the plane commander for his remaining missions.

19. For descriptions of the development and evolution of the B-24, see Douglas, *Consolidated B-24 Liberator*; and Davis, *B-24 Liberator in Action*.

with the aircraft assigned his crew. We were not told anything else. Targets were always a closely guarded secret and revealed only at the mission briefing. Each mission would begin with an orderly awakening the pilot of each crew, always in the dark and usually around four a.m. The pilot was responsible for getting his officers to the briefing and the enlisted men to the flight line. I would awaken the officers and immediately walk to the enlisted men's tent to awaken them. There was always time to dress and have breakfast in the mess hall. Only the officers of each crew attended the target briefing. Enlisted men would be taken down to the flight line in trucks from the mess hall and dropped off at their assigned B-24.

Before every mission, each of us received a small, clear plastic packet escape kit. It included a colorful silk map of the German-controlled territory within our radius, a concentrated chocolate bar, a compass with a pocket-watch-like cover, and a small amount of German money.[20] Of course, we were always expected to carry with us our .45 caliber pistols. If we had to bail out, we were to avoid capture and especially German SS troops, whom, we were told, could be merciless in their treatment of American airmen.[21] We were expected to make our way back to friendly territory, and the escape kit would help. We carried it in a pocket on the right leg of the flight suit, and we had to return it upon arrival at the debriefing session at headquarters immediately after each mission.

Before takeoff, around sunrise, the flight procedure was always the same. We would wait in our planes for the sight of the green flare from the top of the two-story tower, signifying the start of the mission, and then the pilots would begin the Start Engines checklist. We would already have made an outside inspection of the aircraft; and the crew would have circled under the wing for

20. For a fuller description of the escape kit, see Asch, Graff, and Ramey, *The Story of the Four Hundred and Fifty-Fifth Bombardment Group (H) WW II*, 55.

21. Generally, the most anxious times for prisoners of war were immediately before and when they were actually captured. While Faulkner mentions the German S.S. as a big concern, angry civilians were generally as dangerous, if not more so. See Guests of the Third Reich: American POWs in Europe, National World War II Museum, New Orleans, accessed on August 7, 2017, http://guestsofthethirdreich.org/capture/. Because the commander of the Luftwaffe, General Herman Goering, believed in a shared kinship with airmen in general, captured American and British pilots were generally treated better than other prisoners. See William Paul Skelton, III, "American Ex-Prisoners of War," Veterans Health Initiative, Department of Veterans Affairs (2002), 6.

Tom and His Crew in Front of *Lotta Laffs* Before Second Mission, September 18, 1944

Tom in Front of *Gentleman Jim* Before Third Mission, September 20, 1944

Map of Europe with Tom's Missions

our moment of silent prayer and put on all the flight gear before ducking under the bomb bay and climbing up inside. We would always wear long underwear under our one-piece khaki flight suit. Next, we put on a light-weight heated suit and heated gloves, fleece lined boots and a jacket, a yellow Mae West life preserver around our necks, and the parachute harness last. Our choices of parachutes were the back-pack variety or the snap-on chest pack, always worn over the target.

Before the bomb run, we would put on our steel helmets, just like the infantry wore, along with a heavy, steel-ribbed flak jacket. We used a ribbon-like throat mike snapped around our necks for radio communication, and we donned our oxygen masks at 10,000 feet altitude.

The ground crew readied each B-24, sitting on its own round, gravel hard stand, and as we slept, they fueled and loaded the planes. The types of bombs varied by mission, depending on the target. We normally carried between 3,000 and 6,000 pounds of ordnance, ranging from 100-lb. fragmentation bombs to 2,000-lb. high explosive bombs.[22] The bombs were not armed before takeoff. Only after we were well on the way to the target, but before reaching an altitude requiring an oxygen mask, Runyan, our bombardier, would drop down to the bomb bay catwalk and arm the fuse for each bomb.

Once we boarded the plane, we would taxi out in the proper sequence based on our formation position to the gravel taxi way, and like ducklings following its mother, would slowly move in single file until reaching the end of the runway and our turn for takeoff. The group leader would takeoff first, followed in turn, by the other ships of the lead squadron at one-minute intervals, so that the prop-wash from the previous plane would have time to dissipate. Each pilot would position his plane to look down the long, narrow runway and quickly run through the takeoff section of the checklist, revving up and checking each engine one at a time, with the copilot reading each step aloud. With the pilot pushing hard on the brake pedals with his feet to hold the plane in place, he would push all four throttles all the way forward slowly until all four engines were blaring their deafening roar just outside the two pilots' windows, the plane, holding in place, vibrating and quivering, like a racehorse eager to bolt away. Releasing the brake pedals, the loud plane would slowly creep forward, gaining speed for the one-mile race to lift off before reaching the end of the runway, always close, and always a concern.

The squadron formation was referred to as a box, and each one was identified by the Morse Code letters. The lead squadron would be referred to at the briefing, in flight, and in reports following the mission, as Able or A box. Its seven to ten planes would rendezvous over the field at 3,000 feet and then head for nearby Cerignola where they would circle and wait for the other three squadrons at 5,000 feet. The second squadron, called Baker or B box, would then takeoff, repeating the process of Able box. It would then

22. For an overview of the ordnance used by the bombers, see Bowman, *The USAAF Handbook*, 186–91.

position itself to the right, and slightly behind Able box, where it would remain for the entire mission. The next squadron, Charlie or C box, would take its place on the other side of Able box. Dog or D box, would come up behind and below Able box, completing the diamond formation (See Appendix C).[23] With all planes in place for the mission, the 454th Bomb Group would proceed around the hump that protrudes into the Adriatic Sea and take its place in single file with the other groups for the mission, usually flying up the center of the Adriatic to avoid German anti-aircraft guns from the Yugoslavian coast on the right and the Italian coast on the left. Each group, following entrain, slowly gained altitude all the way. The groups would usually separate before reaching the Alps, each one heading toward its assigned target.

**Mission 3 • September 20, 1944[24]**
**Target: Marshalling Yard**
**Győr, Austria[25]**

*Gyor is not too far from Vienna, but the flak was light. We were number 10 in a ten-man squadron, or "tail-end-Charlie". I hate flying there. Would much rather fly on a wing, as we are tomorrow. Fonner is my copilot.[26] He's had 19 missions. We flew 664 again. I think they have assigned her to our crew. It would be nice to have our own ship.*

As the new boy on the block, I flew the tail-end-Charley position, last plane, number ten, in the squadron box on this mission. Over time, I gradually moved up. Toward the end of my tour, on one mission, I flew as number two, off the squadron lead ship's right wing, in position to take over the lead in the event he had to drop out for any reason. There were about twelve or thirteen crews in each of the four squadrons living on our side of San Giovanni Airfield. The first few months after we arrived in September, were warm and summer-like. We would fly frequently, two or even three

23. For a good overview of a formation, see Robert S. Capps, *Flying Colts: Liberator Pilot in Italy, Diary and History, World War II, 456th Bombardment Group (Heavy), 15th Air Force* (Alexandria, VA: Manor House Publications, 1997), 104.

24. Fifty-four B-24s, escorted by forty-five P-51s, struck the marshalling yard at Gyor. They destroyed more than one hundred railroad cars and damaged the railway lines. Mahoney, *Fifteenth Air Force Against the Axis*, 239.

25. Headquarters 454th Bombardment Group (H), Operations Order #245 – Plan Able, September 20, 1944, Air Force Historical Research Agency, Reel B0601 – 454 Records, 641.

26. "737th Bomb Squadron Crews – Edwin Fonner," Aircraft and Airmen from the 454th Bombardment Group in Italy during World War II, accessed on August 4, 2017, http://www.454thbombgroup.it/737th%20Squadron%20Crews.pdf.

Tom in Front of His Tent at San Giovanni Airfield

times a week. When the cold weather came, with its inclement flying conditions, we would be lucky to complete four missions a month.

The tents and small buildings of our 454th Bomb Group sat a safe distance back, but the four squadrons were each a separate community with their own headquarters, mess hall, and service buildings in four clusters over the length of the one-mile runways. Our bomb group shared San Giovanni with the 455th Bomb Group, which was located across the two parallel runways that separated the two groups.[27] The runways were gravel and covered at each end with smooth, steel matting upon which the planes would touch down on landing, preventing the gravel from chewing up the tires.

Our base was well down the east side of the Italian boot five miles west of Cerignola and only a few miles from the Adriatic Sea. Our airfield was one of eight B-24 Liberator airfields within a twenty-mile radius of Cerignola.[28] They were home base to fifteen B-24 Liberator Bomb Groups. Thirty miles to our north, near Foggia, six B-17 Flying Fortress Bomb Groups operated out of four airfields.[29] The headquarters of the Fifteenth Air Force was based in Foggia.

I visited Cerignola once with another pilot, Willie Williams, from Atlanta.[30] Willie had arrived at San Giovanni about the same time as I, and we became good friends. While we named our plane *Lotta Laffs*, Willie and his crew named their plane, *Willie the Wolf*. I never understood why. Willie was not the least bit a womanizer. After the war, Willie would obtain his Master's degree from Emory University in Atlanta, become a math professor at Furman University in South Carolina, build and direct a boy's camp at Cedar Mountain, North Carolina, which his family still operates, all while flying his own twin-engine Comanche. He visited me in Dallas in 1951.

27. For a brief history of the 455th Bomb Group, see "455th Bombardment Group (H)," 455th Bombardment Group Association, accessed on August 4, 2017, http://www.455th.org/index.htm. See also Asch, Graff, and Ramey, *The Story of the Four Hundred and Fifty-Fifth Bombardment Group (H) WWII*.

28. For a description of San Giovanni Airfield, see "San Giovanni Airfield," American Air Museum in Britain, accessed on August 4, 2017, http://www.americanairmuseum.com/place/152480.

29. For a description of the Foggia complex, see Tillman, *Forgotten Fifteenth*, 4–7 and 10–11; and James Holland, *Italy's Sorrow: A Year of War, 1944–1945* (New York: St. Martin's Press, 2008), 46.

30. "737th Bomb Squadron Crews – Summer M. Williams, Jr.," Aircraft and Airmen from the 454th Bombardment Group in Italy during World War II, accessed on August 4, 2017, http://www.454thbombgroup.it/737th%20Squadron%20Crews.pdf.

His real first name was Sumner, which I wish I had known. "Willie" never suited him at all. He had a reserved, scholarly demeanor, and I always felt that calling him "Willie" was like addressing Cary Grant as "Willie."

Cerignola was a drab, colorless, and lifeless town. There were no women anywhere, only old Italian men, mostly in black capes and black hats, standing stooped on street corners, giving us wary glances as we passed. Large posters of Stalin were plastered on several building walls. This bothered me, as they were leaning to communism. During the brief times we were in their presence, we always treated them with respect and friendship, but they did not reciprocate. While in Italy, I could not understand why they did not seem to like us; however, I should have realized that we were, after all, an occupying foreign enemy. How could they have liked us?[31] The only friendly faces were of small boys following us, pleading, "Shine, Mister? Shine?" They would have been happy with 10 cents; however, Willie and I both gave them a dollar for their work. In those days, that was a lot, especially to them.

**Mission 4 • September 21, 1944[32]**
**Target: Railroad Bridge**
**Kiskore, Hungary**

*Cinch mission—real milk run.*[33] *No flak. No fighters. Lots of P-38's all around us.*[34] *They're really a welcome sight over enemy territory. We had one close call. Right after bombs away, the formation cut power and I almost slid right into the ship in front—had to pull the nose up and out and had to jam the throttles forward. Two of the props ran away with a loud whine. Props are supposed to fly off at 3100 rpms. We had 3300 rpms, but Fonner, the copilot again for this mission, hit the feathering buttons and brought them both down okay.*

31. Benito Mussolini led Italy into the war as an ally of Germany, but Italians, in general, never enthusiastically supported it. After Italy's defeat in North Africa in May 1943 and Sicily a few months later, the Italian king reasserted his authority and ousted Mussolini from power. Italy ultimately switched sides in the war late that summer. See Weinberg, *A World at Arms*, 593–601.

32. Faulkner's plane was one of twenty B-24s that attacked the railroad bridge. Mahoney, *Fifteenth Air Force Against the Axis*, 240.

33. A milk run was simply a mission where there was little or no enemy opposition.

34. The P-38 "Lightning" was a twin-engine fighter plane in World War II. Its two-engine design made it one of the most unique fighter planes in the war. It was also one of the main Allied fighter escorts by 1944. For a full description of the P-38, see Michael O'Leary, *Lockheed P-38 Lightning* (Oxford, U.K.: Osprey Publishing, 1999).

*We were flying Dinah-Mite, an old B-24 D model, on her 75th mission—a good ole ship. We've had 664 on every other mission so far, and tomorrow we have her again. God, how I hate those stiff controls. Good ship otherwise. The ship we flew over from San Francisco (the new "J" model), only to be taken away from us, was in the lead box flying her first mission. Understandably, new crews don't get new planes. Her engine nacelles were painted a bright red. On the way to target we had to skirt a few thunderheads and even fly through a few clouds. It's a hell of a feeling to be flying in a tight 30 plane formation and have them all suddenly disappear.*

The original B-24D models, like *Dinah-Mite*, had flown out of North Africa to bomb the Ploiești oil fields in Romania.[35] While they had nose and tail guns, the newer B-24 silver J model had maneuverable nose, tail, and top turrets as well as a belly turret which meant that the gunners in these four turrets would actually sit inside a movable, clear plastic bubble and swivel around to follow and aim at their targets. A few of the newer, silver J models were equipped with PFF radar. Called "Mickey" ships, they were able to see through the clouds and navigate to and from the targets in bad weather, and most important, they could also see images of targets for bombing through overcasts. They usually required at least one or two radar specialists who became the eleventh or twelfth man on the crew.[36]

### Mission 5 • September 22, 1944[37]
### Target: Munich Aerodrome
### Munich, Germany[38]

35. Ploiești, Romania, was the center of much of the Axis oil production during the war and became the primary target of the Fifteenth Air Force in the spring and early summer 1944. See Tillman, *Forgotten Fifteenth*, 82–113 and 130–37; and Ambrose, *The Wild Blue*, 120–21.

36. The AAF introduced the H2X radar or Pathfinder (PFF) to both the Eighth and Fifteenth Air Forces in the spring of 1944. As the radar units became more plentiful and crews became more proficient with it, it allowed the air forces to make bombing runs that previously would have been canceled because of weather conditions. See Craven and Cate, *The Army Air Forces in World War II*, Vol. 3, 286, 290–91, and 306; and Mahoney, *Fifteenth Air Force Against the Axis*, 414–16.

37. For this mission, 150 B-17s and 107 B-24s were escorted by 102 P-51s and forty-two P-38s. Mahoney, *Fifteenth Air Force Against the Axis*, 240.

38. According to Allied Headquarters, Munich was "a bottleneck situated at one of the focal points in the German rail system." "Target Information Sheet – Munich," April 12, 1944, National Archives of the United States, Washington, D.C. [hereafter NA], Record Group [hereafter RG] 331 – Records of the Allied Operational and Occupation Headquarters, World War II, Box 114, Reel, 59D.

*For the Fifteenth Air Force, Munich is considered as one of the two toughest targets (along with Vienna). There are 240 flak guns there, but we would be in the range of only 56 of them.*[39] *Over the city, I could see one group was getting pounded. I never saw such flak. I kept more distance from the other ships over the target today and all went well except after "Bombs away." The lead ship made a sharp turn to the left and I saw flak puffs creeping toward our ship from the right. They stopped just in time. The last burst was too close. One more would have hit us.*[40] *Guess the good Lord was with us again. On the way up, we saw one crew bailing out over the Adriatic. Just found out today that we completely demolished the Gyor marshalling yards (3rd mission)—plus forty German planes on a nearby field. Tomorrow I'll have McComas as a copilot as O'Brien, our copilot, is still in the hospital.*[41] *He has no missions flown yet. They're loading 2000 pound bombs tonight—must be something big.*

Every part of the mission followed a precise schedule. We took off at prescribed times and flew at pre-determined altitudes. Our course, when possible, avoided concentrations of German anti-aircraft guns, and we always flew to the Initial Point (IP) to begin the target run. The IP was a specific point within fifteen miles of the target where the group would begin its final approach. Upon reaching the IP, the bombardier of the group's lead ship with the aid of the lead navigator, who also occupied the glassed-in nose of the ship, would identify the target and engage his bombsight. Once on the predetermined heading to the target, the lead pilot would relinquish all control of the ship to the Norden bombsight and its electronic signals to the automatic pilot. The bombsight would mechanically steer the lead aircraft, calculate speed, altitude, wind direction, and other factors, and then determine the precise instant when the bombs should automatically be released to hit the target, four to five miles below. The bombardiers of the ships

39. For the strong anti-aircraft defenses around Munich, see Edward B. Westermann, *Flak: German Anti-Aircraft Defenses, 1914– 1945* (Lawrence: University Press of Kansas, 2001), 276.

40. According to the official report on the mission, the flak was "intense, accurate, [and] heavy." Confirming Mission Report, 454th Bomb Gp (H), Mission #123, September 22, 1944, Air Force Historical Research Agency, Reel B0601 – 454 Records, 635.

41. "737th Bomb Squadron Crews – Stephen J. McComas," Aircraft and Airmen from the 454th Bombardment Group in Italy during World War II, accessed on August 4, 2017, http://www.454thbombgroup.it/737th%20Squadron%20Crews.pdf.

Destruction in Budapest after B-24 Bombing Attack, 1944 (National Archives)

following, seeing the bombs released, would instantly "toggle" their bombs loose manually and call out, "bombs away." With at least six five-hundred-pound bombs falling together from up to forty ships from each group, a large pattern of destruction would result.

On every mission, most of the ships were also given bales of chaff to drop when flying over the target. Chaff was nothing but the very same silver Christmas tree tinsel that we had tossed onto our Christmas trees every year since I was a boy. It was one of Winston Churchill's many ideas.[42] Its thin strips of silver metal would confuse German radar. The tinsel would float down among the bursts of flak over every target.[43]

42. Whether it was Churchill's idea or not, he did approve and encourage the use of chaff starting in the spring of 1943. Peter Huber, "Passive Countermeasures," *Frontline Defense* 8, no. 4 (2011), accessed on August 4, 2017, http://defence.frontline.online/article/2011/4/1907-Passive-Countermeasures.

43. Chaff, or window as it was often called, was a regular part of missions by 1944. During Faulkner's second mission on September 18, each aircraft was required to carry "three cartons of window" and dispense it "at a rate of six bundles every twenty seconds, starting three minutes before the IP, and continuing until clear of flak." Headquarters 454th Bombardment Group (H), Operations Order #245 – Plan Able, September 18, 1944, Air Force Historical Research Agency, Reel B0601 – 454 Records, 645.

Even though the pilot and copilot would share flying duties because missions into Germany would usually take up to eight hours, by the time we returned and reached sight of our field, we were always totally exhausted. Flying in formation required constant handling and adjustment while holding the wheel. The muscles in my arms and hands ached after every mission because of the ongoing strain of gripping the wheel. I wrote my parents during the war about a hard callus that developed across my left hand below the fingers. Half of our missions were flown in my favorite, "*Lotta Laffs*" (664). All B-24s are stiff, but "*Lotta Laffs*" had the reputation of being the stiffest of them all, and I still, even today, have a faint remnant of that callus below my ring finger.

On our return flights, we would still be flying in formation and would circle the field, peeling off one at a time for landing. It was always late in the day, and I recall the sun often being low and blinding as we struggled to keep our place in formation—not a good feeling when the plane you are trying to stay close to suddenly is blotted out by the sun for several seconds.

Even with these distractions, piloting a B-24 on a mission in a squadron formation box was the part of flying that I most enjoyed. I even came to enjoy flying tail-end-Charley, which most pilots did not like. As number ten in a ten-ship formation box, I found it the easiest slot of all. The ships are numbered from the lead, which is number one, to his right wingman, number two and left wingman, number three. Number four is below number one, completing a diamond shape. Then number five is on number four's right wing, with number six on his left and number seven below number four.

I had not always enjoyed formation flying. I remember how confused and flustered I was when first attempting to fly on the wing of another plane. It was in basic training in Waco as a cadet. What a disaster! I felt I had lost all control over that BT-13, like my first attempt to steer a bumper car at the Texas Centennial in 1936. When driving alongside another automobile, it is easy to keep the same distance and speed, but in a cockpit, another dimension is added—the vertical. Holding to both a horizontal and vertical position was maddening. My instructor, Lt. Junior Hendricks had said, "Okay, Tom, get ready. I'm going to bring us alongside the wing of that ship ahead." As he approached slowly, I thought to myself, this will be a cinch. No unexpected surprises would occur here, like those unfortunate blackouts during the loops a few days before. I felt that now, with instructor Hendricks watching me closely on every flight, I was on probation of sorts. Another bad performance and my dream of receiving pilot's wings would have quickly become a nightmare.

As he eased the BT-13 up beside the other plane, he said, "Okay, Tom, take over." I took the stick and almost immediately we soared above and away. I pushed the stick down to reach the original position as wingman, and we shot well below the other ship. I pulled back and again I over corrected. I was flying a machine with its own mind, a self-guided roller-coaster car. Up and down, up and down, we went. Gradually, with declining error, the exhausted bucking stallion grudgingly gave up, and I got the hang of it, much like my learning to ride a bike. From the back seat, I heard the same loud laughter as during the disastrous loops. I suspected that Lt. Hendricks had played a trick on me. What looked so simple and easy was quite the opposite, and he knew it. Having corrected my over-corrections, I concluded that an airplane is a sensitive animal and like a woman, requires delicate handling, particularly in formation flying. She expects constant attention and respect, responds to a soft touch, reacts badly to rough handling, and can never be taken for granted.

While I came to love formation flying during daylight, I hated it at night. It was a real challenge for me. We were told to keep an eye on the wingtip and tail-lights of the other plane, but on a pitch-black night, I still found it difficult holding to a steady position. Actually, I just did not like flying at night under any circumstances, not even our short cross-country, three-legged nighttime flights as a cadet. In Advanced Training, we flew all over east Texas. On one of these round trips I experienced one of the two occasions during the war in which I learned that self-preservation trumps all other instincts when confronted with a sudden and unexpected threat of imminent death. One such incident occurred on a dark and cold December night over east Texas. The other happened one year later in Italy at dusk, not far from our San Giovanni Airfield.

My copilot and I were between Tyler and Waco on the last leg of our trip. We were scheduled to graduate and receive our wings in a matter of days. We had learned in class all about the dangers of icing on wings. It can build up quickly on the leading edges.

San Giovanni Airfield (National Archives)

Ice distorts the wings lift and the added weight can bring a plane down. Our little AT-17 had no rubber deicer boots on the leading edge to break away accumulating ice, and we were warned to be on alert for this. The two of us had been talking ever since leaving Tyler, and even though we had encountered heavy mist and light rain, we had not even thought about the wings. Halfway home, at 7,000 feet, my copilot was resting, his eyes closed when I looked out at the wings. *They were covered with ice.* Before yelling at the copilot, I unsnapped my seat belt, ready to get up, then glanced back at the wings for another quick look. I alerted my copilot, and he agreed that the layer of ice was too thin to bring us down, but we had to drop to a lower altitude. We received immediate radio clearance. During those quick, split seconds, when my first reaction was to unsnap my seat belt, rather than alert my flying companion, I realized I must be careful to change my priorities when confronted by a sudden jolt of a perceived impending disaster.

Something similar happened again, midway through our Italian tour. By that time, I had faced all sorts of life-threatening events. I had watched men bail out of ships as flames gushed from their bomb bays, been grazed above my eye by flak, forced to make several three-engine landings, and spent two weeks in the hospital with an injured leg resulting from a crash landing. Over enemy territory, trouble was expected, but not so much within a few miles of San Giovanni Airfield. While still in formation, I happened to look back. There was a door separating the flight deck from the bomb bays. In the middle of the door was a one-foot, square glass window. Out of the corner of my eye, a glint of light caused me to turn and look back at that window. A bright orange glow! *My God! The bomb bays are on fire.* Again, my first impulse? I unsnapped that seat belt; however, before pushing the alarm bell on the center pedestal and using the intercom to order the crew to bail out, I turned again for one quick look. As I banked with the formation, the orange glow disappeared. I had reacted to the bright and blinding reflection of the sun sitting not far over the horizon.

Both of these incidents, ice on the wings in Texas and faux fire in the bomb bays in Italy, though quick and brief, were as frightening to me as any other wartime occurrence. But in both of these cases, I could only thank God that my instinct for self-preservation accompanied just enough of a delay to prevent me from making a complete jackass of myself.

Being tricked by a reflection and the weather are just two examples of strange events a combat pilot could encounter. One time on a practice mission in formation flying in Italy, a squadron above ours slowly angled over us from right to left. I was flying number four position, directly below our squadron lead ship. Looking up, I had no relationship to the horizon and suddenly I felt convinced our entire squadron was flying *backwards!* It was an extreme vertigo experience—so extreme, I had to ask the copilot to take over. It was a helpless feeling, but one I could not shake until I could actually see the horizon. It was the same effect as sitting inside a train, when the train on the next track moves and you are not sure whether your train or the other one is moving. It is much worse than that in the air. There may have been numerous tragic accidents when this happened to other pilots when there was no copilot to take over.[44]

**Mission 6 • September 23, 1944[45]**
**Target: Viaduct**
**Venzone, Italy**

*Aha! This was one to remember! We were briefed for a milk run, no flak, no fighters. I flew with a green copilot named*

44. Developing vertigo was a terrifying experience for pilots as they literally did not know what direction they were flying. Another pilot recalled, "my feelings were that we were still in a screaming dive" when in actuality he was flying straight and level. See James M. Davis, ed. David L. Snead, *In Hostile Skies: An American B-24 Pilot in World War II* (Denton: University of North Texas Press, 2006), 64–5.

45. While members of the squadron completed this mission, Faulkner had to turn his plane around before reaching the target because of mechanical issues. For a description of the mission see Mahoney, *Fifteenth Air Force Against the Axis*, 241.

*McComas. He hadn't been inside a B-24 in two months—a first pilot on his first mission. We flew 458, an old D model. Before takeoff the crew chief said to watch it closely as she was due a 100-hour inspection when we got back. We had the heaviest load we'd ever carried, one 2,000 pound bomb and four 1,000 pound bombs.*[46] *On takeoff she barely made it. We used up the entire length of the runway and into high grass. We hit a log or some unseen object which bounced us up a few feet. She didn't want to climb—almost took a power line with us. Then the number one engine dropped five inches M.P. (manifold pressure).*[47] *We lagged behind all the way to the target. I was afraid to give it any more power as the engines were already too hot. Before reaching the target I goosed it up a little more to get in formation. We went over the primary target in style, but there was an overcast so the group couldn't drop the bombs. The formation was circling back to the secondary target—another bridge—when Jim Hamilton, the waist gunner, reported No. 1 was trailing black and white smoke.*

*I reduced power on that engine, but she started vibrating and kicking. Even so, I checked the cylinder head temperature and was surprised to see it dropping rapidly. Then there was a loud whine. No. 1 had run away. I hit the feathering button, attempting to bring it down—no help. I finally feathered it and dropped out of formation. There was no way we could keep up without losing another engine. No. 3 was overheating, too. I called Arnie (Nelson, our Navigator) to give us a heading home—but quick. I reduced power on the three good engines and began a slow descent, but we lost speed and altitude too rapidly. I told Runyan, the bombardier, to salvo the bombs over the Adriatic as soon as possible. He did so and the ship lurched as they dropped and flew much better.*[48] *I told the crew to stand ready to throw all equipment overboard—flak suits, machine guns, ammunition, etc.—in case No. 3 should conk out. I dropped 8 degrees flaps and trimmed the dead engine high to hold altitude better. We flew down the coast and all went well. Coming in,*

46. The 1,000 and 2,000-pound bombs were high explosive weapons. See Bowman, *The USAAF Handbook*, 187–191.

47. The manifold pressure gauge measures the intake pressure of air going into the engine's cylinders.

48. It was standard operating procedure for planes returning early from a mission before dropping their bomb load to release the bombs over the Adriatic Sea. Once the bombardier armed the bombs in flight, it was very dangerous to try to land with them.

*we made a landing to the north and fortunately it was a fairly good one. There was a strong cross wind directly from the east. The crew was sweating it out, I know, but now I'm sure they have a lot more confidence in the B-24 and maybe even their pilot. Though we didn't drop our bombs on a target, we will get credit for the mission.*[49] *Tomorrow we get a day off. Thank heavens!! I'm dead!*

[Footnote added months later]: *Lieutenant McComas, the above-mentioned copilot, was killed while buzzing the Adriatic.*[50]

This takeoff highlighted one of the most dangerous parts of any mission, and one that terrified me. While we had a one-mile long runway, we often had to use all of it to get off the ground. When we had a particularly heavy load, it was even more of a problem. I always tried to use as much of the runway as I could to gain as much speed as possible before liftoff. With even a normal load of three tons of bombs, the results of running out of runway before lifting off could be catastrophic.

Landings could sometimes be equally scary. All fields I had ever landed on before had at least one runway at a diagonal to provide an optional direction. With our runways facing basically north and south, we had no relief if strong winds came from the east or west. Landing a B-24 in a strong crosswind on a narrow runway can be very tricky, especially if all planes were carrying a full bomb load, as was the case a few times when the group was forced to return to our base because of bad weather.

We were instructed never to land with a full bomb load, so on the few times we were forced to drop out and returned alone, we jettisoned the bombs in the Adriatic Sea. However, when the entire Group was forced to return home, unable to complete the mission because of bad weather, or some other reason, all planes would land with their full bomb load. We attempted missions during the winter months when we encountered weather so bad even after reaching the Alps that we had to return fully loaded. Another time, such as our later mission to Mestre, Italy, after reaching the IP, the radar simply

49. Faulkner's plane and one other had to jettison their bombs over the Adriatic. Confirming Mission Report, 454th Bomb Gp (H), Mission #124, September 23, 1944, Air Force Historical Research Agency, Reel B0601 – 454 Records, 629.

50. McComas was killed in an accident on Feb. 27, 1945. See Aviation Archaeological Investigation and Research, accessed on August 4, 2017, http://www.aviationarchaeology.com/src/dbasn.asp?offset=27675.

could not pinpoint its target below the thick overcast.[51] If we entered enemy territory, we would usually be given credit for a completed mission.

It was tough when the entire Group had to turn back. After getting up at four o'clock, sitting through the briefing, taking the short trip down to the field, dealing with all the gear and clothing, taxiing in line for takeoff, rendezvousing, and then spending hours flying to the target in formation, much of it in sub-zero temperatures, to have to turn back was incredibly deflating. I suppose that deciding to land so many planes with a super heavy load of bombs was a risk-reward situation. For several groups of thirty or forty planes each to jettison their bombs in the Adriatic would have been an expensive waste.

After landing from each mission, we would be taken back in trucks to the same building where we met for the briefing that morning. At this time, an officer would debrief each crew, reviewing the details of the day's flight. Here, all airmen returned their escape kits and were offered a shot of whiskey. I do not recall any of our men taking any, and I never understood the reason for it being available. The enlisted men were beer drinkers, and I always traded my beer coupons to them in exchange for more coupons for Almond Hershey bars. It is still my favorite candy bar. We were each given a certain number of ration coupons periodically for candy and beer and other food items available at our very small PX or commissary shed next to the post office. We were given enough for maybe one of these items every day or two.

### Mission 7 • October 4, 1944[52]
### Target: Marshalling Yards
### Munich, Germany

*Zowie! This was the roughest one yet—never saw so many "black clouds". I was number seven, tail-end-Charlie and after number two plane made an early return, we took number five position on the right wing of number four—which I like much better.*[53] *As we approached the target, flak bursting all around,*

51. Faulkner is referring to a mission on October 10, 1944, where his bomb group had to return. See Mahoney, *Fifteenth Air Force Against the Axis*, 251.

52. Over 110 B-17s and 219 B-24s, escorted by 112 P-51s and 138 P-38s, bombed Munich. They experienced severe flak. Ibid., 247–8.

53. Headquarters 454th Bombardment Group (H), Operations Order #259A – Plan Able for Force Able, October 4, 1944, Air Force Historical Research Agency, Reel B0601 – 454 Records, 728.

*Horvath, the nose gunner, saw a B-24 spin in. Leaving the target, McCorkle, the tail gunner, reported seeing another explode into a thousand pieces.*[54] *During the bomb run, the flak was light at first, but then they seemed to find our range and it was fairly close. I thought we were goners when they seemed to have our altitude after beginning the run. The harmless looking, silent puffs of black smoke got closer and closer and more dense all the time, until, over the target, we were completely surrounded by it. There was a thud under the fuselage and I thought we'd been hit. It was a miracle we got through the stuff with no injuries. When the flak stopped, I said over the inter-phone, "Well, I guess we made it." But I'd spoken too soon, for another barrage was hurled up at us, almost as bad as over the center of Munich. I'll never speak too soon again. On landing, we found only a small hole in the leading edge of the right wing next to the fuselage. Tomorrow, we fly again. This time at number six position. Good night.*

As my flight diary indicates, my position in the squadron boxes varied from mission to mission. The tail-end Charlie position at the very back of the squadron box was generally assigned to new crews. While I mentioned hating it in my diary entry for Mission 3, I came to not mind it that much; however, my favorite positions were the number 2, 5, and 8 slots because the pilot, seated on the left in the cockpit, has a clear view of the other plane out of his left window. The number 4 position, directly behind the lead ship (same as number 7, behind number 4), flies off of the tail of the plane above and it front. It is really easier; however, I still liked number 2, 5 and 8 positions best.

**Mission 8 • October 7, 1944**[55]
**Target: Winterhofen Oil Refineries**
**Vienna, Austria**[56]

*This is supposed to be the most flak-laden target in our range of operations. Vienna is protected by 317 anti-aircraft guns, but*

54. While all of the planes from Faulkner's squadron made it home safely, eleven B-24s from other squadrons did not make it back to their bases. Mahoney, *Fifteenth Air Force Against the Axis*, 248.

55. Faulkner's plane was part of a group of 231 B-24s that struck the oil depot. Ten of the planes were shot down. Mahoney, *Fifteenth Air Force Against the Axis*, 250.

56. Vienna was heavily industrialized and vital to the German war effort. "To: Co. R.D. Hughes," August 2, 1944," NA, RG 331 – Records of the Allied Operational and Occupation Headquarters, World War II, Box 113, Reel, 46D.

*only 131 would be in range of us.*[57] *We had Ancient and Honorable, an old B-24 D model, and it gave us plenty of trouble all the way. I guess Major Graham is peeved at us because we had such a delay before takeoff.*[58] *First, my bombardier had to have a harness fitted. He was late to the ship. Then I couldn't adjust the pilot's seat as the handle was broken and the crew-chief had to adjust it with pliers. Then the inter-phone wouldn't work and we horsed around trying to fix it. To top it all off, Nelson, the navigator, had to have the major take him back to supply to get a heated suit. So I guess we'll be flying tail-end-Charlie from now till the duration. We finally caught the formation before rendezvous, however.*

*All the way up, the old-style superchargers—which make formation flying a pain in the neck – were giving O'Brien and me hell.*[59] *We circled Vienna and before I knew it we were on the bomb run with those little black clouds bursting all around us. I put on my flak helmet. Over the target one of the ships in our group caught fire.*[60] *The whole ship became a ball of flames. One man bailed out. Another ship below us exploded.*[61] *After bombs-away, our squadron almost collided with the lead squadron, but our squadron leader put it in a 40-degree bank and dove it to 200 MPH. He headed for a clear space and hit it just right for there were perfect patterns of flak on both sides. The rally was really a rat race for ships were zooming in every direction. At the rally point there were only four ships together of the original formation. We lost the lead box. Four planes of other groups tacked on to us. I flew over to fill Number 3 position behind the leader. On the way home we received more flak—very light—from Kaprwinica at the west end of Lake Balaton. A little later the fuel pressure on Number 2 dropped to zero and it cut out. Number 1 propeller*

57. In reality, Faulkner and the other American bombers faced even more anti-aircraft guns than they realized. The Germans had placed 418 heavy and 383 light flak guns around Vienna by the fall 1944. See Westermann, *Flak*, 276.

58. Faulkner is probably referring to William F. Graham. "737th Bomb Squadron Crews – William F. Graham," Aircraft and Airmen from the 454th Bombardment Group in Italy during World War II, accessed on August 4, 2017, http://www.454thbombgroup.it/737th%20Squadron%20Crews.pdf.

59. For a good description of the supercharger and B-24 engines in general, see Douglas, *Consolidated B-24 Liberator Owners' Workshop Manual*, 109–10

60. The flak was "intense, accurate and heavy." Asch, Graff, and Ramey, *The Story of the Four Hundred and Fifty-Fifth Bombardment Group (H) WW II*, 127.

61. One plane from the 454th did not make it back. Confirming Mission Report, 454th Bomb Gp (H), Mission #129, October 7, 1944, Air Force Historical Research Agency, Reel B0601 – 454 Records, 743–4. Several planes from other bomb groups were lost as well. Mahoney, *Fifteenth Air Force Against the Axis*, 250.

*ran away, sounding like a siren at its loudest pitch. It kept us busy with the feathering buttons. We brought number 1 down and number 2 back in and it worked all right. Tomorrow, we're in Blue Force with maybe a milk run.*[62] *When we landed, we found a hole in the left leading edge and a foot-long gash in the left flap. O'Brien was amazed to find a silver-dollar size hole on the right side a little below his foot. He found the shrapnel, a nice souvenir from Adolf.*

Right after we landed in Italy, O'Brien's malady recurred, and as in Tonopah, he was apart from us for weeks. He was finally released from the Cerignola hospital and joined us for this mission over Vienna, his first. He then returned to the hospital and did not fly with us or even sleep in our tent for another two weeks. Meanwhile, I was hoping that during this time, when he was confined to the hospital and I was still being assigned other copilots, he might have forgotten about that regrettable incident in San Francisco which, to this day, I feel badly about. There seemed to be no animosity during our two-week flight to Italy from the United States, nor during the above mission when he rejoined us for the first time, but I was sure he was just resigned to his situation.

Additionally, I do not believe O'Brien ever cared for Runyan. I did not blame him for that, either. Runyan was a hard case and had a strong personality. Although Runyan was blunt and seemed uncaring with what anyone thought of him, he was almost always in a jovial mood and had a good sense of humor, and all-in-all, living with him and Arnie Nelson was a very pleasant experience during my six-month Italian sojourn.

### Mission 9 • October 10, 1944
### Target: Casarsa Railroad Bridge
### Tagliamento, Italy

*This was an unsuccessful mission because the entire formation had to bring back their bombs. There was a complete overcast of the target as well as all of northern Italy.*[63] *Very uneventful flight, but a good formation most of the time. We do get credit for the mission.*

62. Missions for October 8 and 9 were cancelled due to weather. Mahoney, *Fifteenth Air Force Against the Axis*, 250.

63. The target had solid cloud coverage to 15,000 feet. Confirming Mission Report, 454th Bomb Gp (H), Mission #129, October 10, 1944, Air Force Historical Research Agency, Reel B0601 – 454 Records, 748.

Damaged B-24 Leaves the Flak-Filled Skies Over Vienna, 1944 (National Archives)

When we first arrived at San Giovanni, we were told that, because some targets were a lot more hazardous than others (because of distance and heavier anti-aircraft gun emplacements), we would be given credit for *two* missions for those destinations. These included flights over Munich, Vienna, Regensburg, Linz, Budapest, Innsbruck, and other cities in Germany. For closer targets in Yugoslavia and northern Italy—where less flak or German fighter threat existed—we were to be credited for only one mission. With this simple formula, all airmen were required to have a total credit number of *fifty* before going home; however, before we left, the rules changed. The AAF dropped the two-mission credit altogether and announced that we would have to fly only thirty-five *actual* missions, regardless of the target, which usually worked out to be about the same number of missions flown under the old 50-mission system.[64]

When I returned home to Dallas in 1945, a brief article in *The Dallas Morning News* stated that I had flown forty-five missions,

64. On the switch in the number of required missions, see Mahoney, *Fifteenth Air Force Against the Axis*, 265.

which had to have been figured on the old formula since I had only completed twenty-eight *actual* missions, seven short of the thirty-five required. I do not know where their information came from and assumed then, and still do, that it was not from our squadron or group level, but some AAF central news source that had only fragments of the facts.[65] The article also said I had been recommended for the Distinguished Flying Cross, which I also figured had to be a mistake, and I completely dismissed that expectation and never gave it another thought.[66]

**Mission 10 • October 12, 1944[67]**
**Target: Warehouse Depot**
**Bologna, Italy[68]**

*Flew number eight position today and got #664 back. Couldn't ask for a better situation. The route of the sortie covered, or rather, paralleled the infantry fighting front lines.[69] We dropped forty 100-pound general purpose bombs. Were briefed for forty-five flak guns, but I saw very little flak. It was a milk run. We passed over some pretty country; the trees in the mountains were turning brownish-red. It seemed like the whole Air Force was concentrated over Bologna. I was more worried about running into other ships than the flak. On the coast, we saw what looked like four Navy ships with all guns*

65. "Fightin' Men: News of Texans in U.S. Service from Dallas County," *Dallas Morning News*, April 5, 1945.

66. The Distinguished Flying Cross is awarded by the president to any airman who "distinguishes himself by heroism or extraordinary achievement while participating in an aerial flight." It was first established in 1926. See 10 U.S. Code § 8749 - Distinguished Flying Cross: Award; Limitations, Cornell University Law School, Legal Information Institute, accessed on May 16, 2017, https://www.law.cornell.edu/uscode/text/10/8749. For the history of the award, see "Personal Decorations – Distinguished Flying Cross," The Institute of Heraldry, Office of the Administrative Assistant to the Secretary of the Army, accessed on, May 16, 2017, http://www.tioh.hqda.pentagon.mil/Catalog/Heraldry.aspx?HeraldryId=15249&CategoryId=3&grp=4&menu=Decorations%20and%20Medals&ps=24&p=0; and Barry L. Spink, "Distinguished Flying Cross and Air Medal Criteria in the Army Air Forces in World War II," June 25, 2015, Air Force Historical Research Agency, accessed on May 16, 2017, http://www.afhra.af.mil/Portals/16/documents/Timelines/World%20War%20II/WWIIDFCandAirMedalCriteriaCommand.pdf?ver=2016-08-30-150741-427.

67. As part of an infantry advance towards Bologna, Faulkner was part of a force of 228 B-24s that struck the warehouse depot. Mahoney, *Fifteenth Air Force Against the Axis*, 252.

68. Bologna was a large city in north central Italy and was a critical industrial and transportation center. It experienced extensive aerial attacks in the war and was close to the front lines from the fall of 1944 to its final capture by the allies in April 1945. See Holland, *Italy's Sorrow*, xxii, xxiv, 417–18, and 513–14.

69. The allied ground forces began a push for Bologna in the late summer and the Fifteenth Air Force began offering support by attacking targets around the city. See Craven and Cate, *The Army Air Forces in World War II*, Vol. III, 450–54; and Mahoney, *Fifteenth Air Force Against the Axis*, 252–3.

*blazing—think they were shelling a harbor. We were supposed to have helped the ground forces.*[70] *I'll be reading the Stars and Stripes to see if we did.*[71]

We seldom flew infantry support missions because B-24s, and for that matter, B-17s, were not designed for these types of attacks. From the cockpit, the pilot could not see the ground directly below and therefore could not be precise on bombing runs. We did practice medium altitude precision bombing using the Norden bombsight, but even then, perfect results were not guaranteed and some of our bombs were off the mark. This was not of serious concern in enemy territory, but when dropping bombs close to our own forces, we needed a level of precision that four-engine bombers could not normally provide.[72] Also, flying at lower altitudes to seek greater accuracy left our relatively slow-moving planes more vulnerable to flak.

This last mission to Bologna was my tenth mission, and surprisingly, after flying less than a month of missions, we had become one of the more experienced crews in the 454th. With other crews being lost in combat or rotating home, there were always new faces at the mission briefings. I was glad I had followed Warner Marsh's lead in joining the Air Force. I loved everything about it, about flying the B-24, about the men in my crew, about our semi-tough existence, about being in Italy where things were happening. All of my friends in high school were in some branch of the military. I did not know what was going on with them, but I knew I could not have been happier. I had learned, however, to take nothing for granted and that adverse events can alter all plans, especially here. In spite of our tenuous existence, I appreciated each day and looked forward

70. The attack on Bologna on October 12 did considerable damage. A later damage assessment reported, "Railroad and industrial installations in the city have been heavily damaged"; "An area of warehouses, garages, etc. is almost completely destroyed"; and "Three of four medium probably warehouses are gutted." "Interpretation Report No.3 P.T.S./D1.," October 22, 1944, NA, RG 331—Records of the Allied Operational and Occupation Headquarters, World War II, Box 38, Reel, 9B.

71. *Stars and Stripes* did not normally cover specific missions but would print articles on certain types of targets like marshalling yards.

72. For his mission on October 10, Faulkner and the other crews had strict orders to not release their bombs unless they could clearly identify their target. "If assigned targets cannot be positively identified and bombed visually, bombs will be returned to base." Headquarters 454th Bombardment Group (H), Operations Order #276 – Battle order Plan Able, October 12, 1944, Air Force Historical Research Agency, Reel B0601 – 454 Records, 753.

to the next, hoping to keep adding missions to our belt to reach the magic number of thirty-five. I knew of the sad consequences of a few crews, but somehow, did not relate it to us. We were now well into our task of a lifetime, but there were many more missions to fly. We had everything to gain, and everything to lose. We hoped for the best and prayed for our survival.

# Chapter 4

# A Grueling Stretch

After dropping our bombs over Bologna and returning to base, we found our names on the mission list for the next day. I was not all that superstitious, but I really did not look forward to flying over enemy territory on Friday the 13th. Mission-wise, we were moving right along. We had started in September and had flown ten missions in a little over three weeks and at this rate, if all went as it had, we would finish up by January! We had survived to this point with relatively few scares, and I was becoming a veteran in my unit, having flown with several newly arrived first pilots as my copilot on their first "orientation" missions.

By now, I felt confident in both my crew and myself and felt they had confidence in me. I did not worry too much about over-confidence, as it was daunting just trying to imagine the things that could go wrong on a mission. The B-24 was an enormous, complex airplane with so many parts, any one or several of which could go wrong, especially if damaged by flak. It was impossible to imagine every potential difficulty, but in my mind during those hours-long flights, I would try to rehearse my response to multiple combinations of breakdowns of different components. Also, there was the ongoing reality that my squadron had lost crews or at least suffered serious damage on almost every mission, which eliminated all temptations of becoming too self-satisfied.

Flying on Friday the 13th was a bit ominous. I am not superstitious now because I learned a few years after the war that Christians do not believe in such rot, but at that time, my mother's inimitable but innocent reactions to superstition still influenced me. One day, as a small boy in Helena, I watched as she yelled, "Oh, no!" slammed on the brakes, screeching us to a halt, and then made a quick U-turn to avoid crossing the path of a black cat. Not surprisingly under this influence, I did wonder on the night before that Friday the 13th mission, perhaps more than other nights, if I would be sleeping in that same bed the next evening. Otherwise, I do not recall dwelling on it.

**Mission 11 • "Black Friday" October 13, 1944[1]**
**Target: Factory**
**Mór, Hungary**

*This mission, I believe, I will remember above all the others. At briefing, we were told our target was to be the Szekesfehervar marshalling yards, north of Lake Balaton, in Hungary.[2] They told us there would be only three flak guns. It would be a milk run. Our squadron was in the low left, Charlie box, with only six planes per box. Captain Goosen was our box leader. When Lake Balaton was in sight, Nelson (our navigator) complained that the formation was way off course. When we neared the Initial Point I saw that our six ships were separated from the rest. I didn't know what was going on.[3] The lead ship opened his bomb doors way before he was supposed to. We flew for a few minutes and I had just put on my flak suit and was flying the ship when suddenly I felt a sharp pain in my thumb and my neck. I realized we must have been in flak. Then a few bursts appeared off to our left at*

1. Because of overcast, planes from Faulkner's 454th Bomb Group hit a variety of targets. Faulkner and five others hit the railroad marshalling yards. Mahoney, *Fifteenth Air Force Against the Axis*, 253.

2. Lake Balaton was a common assembly location for bombers of the Fifteenth Air Force. See Eby, *Hungary at War*, 179. Railroad marshalling yards were critical targets at the juncture of the war. General Eaker noted, "Prior to November, rail yards, bridges, tracks and rolling stock were the main targets." "The Effect of Allied Strategic Bombing on the Present Status of the War," n.d. LOC, Eaker Papers, Box I:29, Folder 6 – Press Conferences, April 1944-February 1945, Eaker Press Conference, February 2, 1945, 2.

3. Eighteen planes from Faulkner's squadron were supposed to attack Szekesfehervar, but because of the weather, six planes, including Faulkner's, took a wrong heading. Confirmed Mission Report, October 13, 1944, Mission #133, Air Force Historical Research Agency, Reel B0601 – 454 Records, 759.

*our altitude. They had our range perfectly. "Three guns"—what a laugh, I thought. I was afraid to look around, thinking my thumb would be something of a nub. Then number 3 ship's bomb bay caught fire just as bombs went away. It was Winfree's ship.*[4] *He was on his last mission. He peeled slowly off to the left, going down, flames pouring out of the open bay, more and more. I saw a couple of the men leave the ship.*[5] *I knew Winfree didn't have a chance. He was a blond, always cheerful fella. I had flown to Goia, Italy, as his copilot on my first local (non-combat) flight here and he's the one who gave me the tip for smooth landings. It was a dirty shame that he went down. His copilot was named Etaugh, a new first pilot just being broken in on his second mission.*[6] *The number 4 ship, on whose wing I was flying, began to drop back, I could see his number 3 engine was hit.*[7] *I stayed with him until clear of German fighter territory. Then I left and caught up with the rest. After we left the target area, I turned around and gave a quick glance at my thumb—still intact—felt my neck—no blood! What luck! A little later, Obie took the wheel and I relaxed. He pointed to a hole in the windshield on his side. Obie had seen what happened. The shrapnel had come through, and after knocking out the compass light rheostat, grazed my right thumb, the glass spraying my neck, then made a deep imprint in the steel casing of the steering-wheel column before dropping between my feet, about an inch and a quarter long. Willie Horvath, our nose-gunner, will get the Purple Heart. Glass splinters pierced his neck and had to be removed by the medics after landing. We were hit in other places, one piece lodged in to our Gibson Girl radio, saving our tail-gunner from a direct hit.*[8] *After landing, we found we had*

4. "737th Bomb Squadron Crews – Samuel C. Winfree," Aircraft and Airmen from the 454th Bombardment Group in Italy during World War II, accessed on July 14, 2017, http://www.454thbombgroup.it/737th%20Squadron%20Crews.pdf.

5. Bailing out of a B-24 was not an easy task. Those in front of the bomb bays (the four officers, nose gunner, top turret gunner-engineer) would bail out the front of the bomb bay. The four gunners in the rear would bail out the rear of the bomb bay. They could also use the waist gunner's window.

6. "2nd Lt. Howard A. "Utah" Etaugh," Find A Grave, accessed on July 14, 2017, http://www.findagrave.com/cgi-bin/fg.cgi?page=gr&GRid=3298732. See also "737th Bomb Squadron Crews – Howard A. Etaugh," Aircraft and Airmen from the 454th Bombardment Group in Italy during World War II, accessed on July 14, 2017, http://www.454thbombgroup.it/737th%20Squadron%20Crews.pdf.

7. All but Winfree's plane made it back to base, although two of the squadron's planes had been damaged by flak. Confirmed Mission Report, October 13, 1944, Mission #133, 759.

8. The Gibson Girl radio was a portable transmitter used in emergencies to reach help if a plane had to ditch at sea or crash land.

*bombed a secondary target, a factory in Mor.*[9] *From now on, I'm staying in bed on all Friday 13ths.*

[Written a few days later] *Winfree was medium height, blond hair, very pleasant, slight. After an indoctrination flight to Goia and then around the area with my crew, I came in and made a bumpy landing. I explained to him that my landings were usually pretty good but were not consistent. He took off again, came back to approach, and made a smooth, perfect landing. After explaining his secret to me, we took off and went around the traffic pattern once more. It was simple. After leveling off a foot or so above ground, he would wait until the precise time of stall, then jerk the wheel all the way back into his stomach for a soft, cushioned landing. I used this from that point on and rarely had a bad landing. I hated it that he and his crew went down.*

[Written a few weeks later] *We just learned that Winfree and all of his crew except one, had bailed out and were captured. For reasons unknown, the copilot, Etaugh, failed to make it out of the burning plane and lost his life. Etaugh, was a First Pilot. He flew his first mission with me as a copilot. He was on his second orientation mission with Winfree.*[10]

Over six decades after this mission, Mr. and Mrs. Paul DeCleva invited my wife, Ann, and me to a dinner party at their home with twenty-four other guests, most of whom we did not know, including two Catholic priests. Ann and I had recently joined the Catholic Church at Christ the King after being Episcopalians during our entire marriage. Sitting down and across the table from me in the dining room was one of those priests. We had not been introduced, but when I overheard him mention to another guest the word "Szekes-fehervar," my ears pricked up and moments later, I said, "Father, that name is familiar to me. Isn't it a town in Germany?"

He spoke with a foreign accent and replied that it was a small town in Hungary where he was born and raised. "Why do you ask?" Reluctantly, I said, "I hesitate to mention this, but I was a pilot in World War II and there was a target in that town that my squadron bombed. Were you living there during the war?" Since we hit most

9. Mór was a small town in north central Hungary about twenty miles north of Lake Balaton.

10. Only three men made it out of the plane, Winfree and two of his gunners. There were only nine men on the plane, and the other six perished. See Tom Parks, "A Box of Old Letters: WWII, Family Letters, & Strange Tangents," Stories – WWII, accessed on July 14, 2017, https://aboxofoldletters.com/tag/wwii/.

of our targets many times, it would be unlikely that he would be able to identify any particular attack in which I might be involved.

"Yes," he replied, "I will never forget it. It was on October 13, 1944. I was eight years old. Our little town was bombed twice, once at night, the other in the daylight."[11]

I knew that our group must have bombed his town on the daylight raid of October 13, 1944. He continued, "The front of my family's home was destroyed by fire during that attack and hundreds of people were killed." I offered my regrets and explained that we never intended that any civilians be victims, and that our target was probably the railroad yards. At this point, I was aware of the total silence in the room and that the host and the other ten guests had lowered their knives and forks to focus on the exchange between the priest and me. It was an awkward moment, and I questioned if I should have opened my mouth. Calmly, he told of the total carnage and destruction that took place 25,000 feet below our group after our bombs were dropped, when he, a small boy, and his family were forced to witness the fright of war, the deafening explosion of bombs, the destructive fire, and the deaths. His story was heart wrenching. It was a strange coincidence that I was sitting with a priest in Dallas and learning our lives had interacted in such a traumatic way on that fateful day.

The next day, I discovered that the priest was the head of the local Cistercian Preparatory School, and I wrote him the following:

*January 6, 2005*
*Rt. Rev. Abbot Denis Farkasfalvy*
*3550 Cistercian Road*
*Irving, TX 75039*
*Dear Abbot Denis:*

*What a pleasure it was to meet you last night at the DeCleva's dinner party. Afterwards, I could not wait to run to my study to look up the date of our mission over Szekesfehervar, Hungary. For some reason, the name of that town has remained in my mind since the war, and when I heard it mentioned across the table, I could not keep from injecting a personal experience into the*

11. The United States launched twenty-one raids against Hungarian targets between April and November. The Hungarians were shocked when the initial bombs fell because they had seen American planes cross Hungary for many months prior to the German occupation. See Eby, *Hungary at War: Civilians and Soldiers in World War II*, 157–8. Faulkner participated in six of the missions.

*conversation, taking the risk of a huge mistake. Yes, the Szekesfehervar railroad marshalling yards was our primary target for that day, October 13, 1944, the day that remains so vividly in your mind.*

*As a pilot of an American four-engine Liberator, B-24 Bomber, I flew 28 missions over Germany and German-occupied territory during the war. Usually, we would take off at dawn and, after rendezvousing over our base in Southern Italy, join other Squadrons and Groups and fly up the Adriatic. I can recall seeing as many as a thousand bombers in view at one time. Before reaching the Alps, each Group of 30-odd planes would turn toward their primary targets.*

*Every mission was a separate adventure, and after returning, exhausted from the eight-hour flight, and before bedding down for the night, I would jot down the day's events. Attached is a copy from my diary of what had happened to my crew and to me on Friday, October 13, 1944, the day that is so memorable to both of us and brought our lives so perilously close together. I also enclose a copy of a list of each of my missions; you will note the first two were over Budapest. As one of the dinner guests said last night (I paraphrase), "What are the odds of an American bomber pilot meeting someone sixty years after World War II who was at the target of his attack?"*

*Since the war, when meeting people who lived in Germany or German-occupied territory, I have avoided the subject, but last night, the coincidence was too great. When I heard the word, Szekesfehervar, even from a priest I had just met, I had to inquire. Concerned, of course, about your reaction, I was hopeful you would have no ill feelings. Muted only slightly by the six decades since, it was still shocking to me to realize that I played any part in a mission that caused you, as a small boy of eight, to witness your family's home being partially destroyed, and that bombs aimed and dropped by planes from my Squadron had killed many of your countrymen on that day. My diary description of that mission, my eleventh, tells it best. I also enclose the account of my first mission, which was over Budapest, as it is relevant to last night's conversation and will display the concerns and anxieties of the airmen flying 30,000 feet over your young head.*

*The British and American Air Forces played a significant part in ending the war. Most historians seem to agree that, while air power did not win the war, the war could not have been won nearly as soon without the destruction of Hitler's oil refineries and rail marshalling yards from the air, which inhibited his ability to move his Wehrmacht at will.*

*My wife and I are members of a Book Club, now reading John Steinbeck's East of Eden. He suggests that the youth of our country are taught from birth to love, respect, and protect one another. Also ingrained in him is the premise that killing another human is one of the worst sins, if not the worst sin of all. But then, as a soldier, we put a gun in his hand and expect him to shoot the enemy without hesitation. This, my generation did because of the clear division that seemed to exist between good and evil, and because of our assumption that God would forgive our actions, and also our belief that our cause was not only just, but absolutely necessary.*

*Please forgive me for preaching to the preacher. It stems from my concerns for what has bothered me for decades. I do thank God that you and, I hope, your family, were not physically harmed by our Friday-the-thirteenth bombs.*

*It was such a genuine pleasure to meet you and sit across the dining table from you at the DeCleva's beautiful home. I hope we will have occasion to meet again and perhaps spend time discussing more agreeable subjects than—war.*

*Sincerely,*

*Tom Faulkner*

The abbot replied with a courteous and considerate letter. He looked at my list of missions and wrote, "I also think that on Sept. 17 your mission at the "marshalling yards" of Budapest took place at night and included the bombing of the railroad of Szekesfehervar, as well. That was the night my (grandfather's) house was partially burned down. The date is locked forever in my memory." I carefully reread the diary account of the mission and made a startling discovery. It was clear that our six-plane Charley Box had become separated from the group and chose an alternate target. Our box had not bombed Szekesfehervar at all, but a *secondary* target, a factory in Mór, Hungary. Also, our attack was in daylight. Only the Royal Air Force flew night

View From Below of B-24 on Bombing Mission to Vienna, January 15, 1945 (National Archives)

missions.[12] We *never* did. Although relieved, I chose not to prolong the matter and did not reply to correct his impression. Yes, his town was the target of the rest our group, *but during daylight hours* of October 13. Based on his letter, neither the bombs from my plane, nor even the bombs from my Group, played any part in the nighttime fire at his family's house.

### Mission 12 • October 16, 1944[13]
### Target: Aeroworks
### Steyr, Austria

*This was the first mission I had flown without Runyan, our bombardier.*[14] *Nelson, the navigator, toggled off the bombs. My copilot was a new first pilot named Hefner, on his first mission.*

12. The Royal Air Force operated Group 205 at night from bases around Foggia from the beginning of 1944 to the end of the war in May 1945. Its squadrons flew a combination of Wellington and B-24 bombers. For their nighttime operations in Italy, see Alun Granfield, *Bombers over Sand and Snow: 205 Group RAF in World War II* (South Yorkshire, UK: Pen and Sword Aviation, 2011), 234–321.

13. Sixty-five B-24s from the 454th and 455th Bomb Groups attacked aircraft factories at Steyr. Mahoney, *Fifteenth Air Force Against the Axis*, 257.

14. Runyan was moved to the lead plane to replace the bombardier there who had to miss the mission.

Vapor Trails from B-24s on Bombing Mission to Vienna, January 15, 1945 (National Archives)

*On the way up we saw a few bursts over the coast. Never came close. The vapor trails of the ships above us were really beautiful. About halfway up, a supercharger amplifier went out but we fixed it so it maintained a constant forty inches.*[15] *There was an overcast beneath us all the way, so we must have dropped our bombs by radar in the lead ship.*[16] *The Germans also used radar to track us. The flak was fairly heavy—and accurate.*[17] *Our formation split up after bombs away and it seemed to be every man for himself. First chance I had to use evasive action – we were dodging in and out, up and down, trying to avoid the black puffs. They seemed to come in bursts of five in a straight line. 664 is up for*

15. When the throttle is moved up or back to maintain formation position, it effects the exhaust that powers the supercharger; so, the amplifier helped maintain a constant control. With an amplifier not working, the 40 inches was a constant setting that resulted in the least ill-effect during formation throttle adjustments.

16. Faulkner was correct about the use of radar. Headquarters 454th Bombardment Group (H), Operations Order #282-Plan Able, October 16, 1944, Mission #133, Air Force Historical Research Agency, Reel B0601 – 454 Records, 771. Ira Eaker and the Fifteenth Air Force increasingly emphasized the use of radar in the fall of 1944 to overcome many of the weather difficulties. Ira Eaker to Barney Giles, January 4, 1945, LOC, Eaker Papers, Box I:25, Folder – Giles, Barney, Vol. III, Dec. 1941-March 1945, 1.

17. The flak was "intense and accurate." Asch, Graff, and Ramey, *The Story of the Four Hundred and Fifty-Fifth Bombardment Group (H) WW II*, 128. The official mission report noted, "Intense, accurate, heavy flack was encountered at Steyr." Confirmed Mission Report, October 16, 1944, Mission #136, Air Force Historical Research Agency, Reel B0601 – 454 Records, 774.

*a two-day, 100-hour inspection, so tomorrow, we're scheduled for Gentleman Jim, an old khaki crate. We're naming 664 "Lotta Laughs". An Indian Sergeant is already busy painting a beautiful Lotta on each side, covered, partially, with a bath towel. She should look nice when he's through.*

As it turned out, #664 was assigned to us on ten of our first twelve missions. We all liked the idea of having our own plane, and the men wanted her to have a name. Most all planes eventually were given a name, always selected by the pilot or the crew. Bomber names were important. It gave the plane an identity all its own, separating it from all others. The most famous of all, as we knew even then, was *Memphis Belle*, a B-17 from the Eighth Air Force.[18]

We finally received permission to have a name painted on the nose under the cockpit on both sides. We all thought about what would be the best name as attachments grew to certain planes, as they became part of your life. We looked upon them like pets. Horvath, the nose gunner, knew of an Indian who had painted scantily clad girls on other planes for a fee and said he would talk to him. We all shared the expense, $10 per man. "Lots of laughs, guys, lots of laughs," was still a favorite phrase often repeated by everyone on our crew at times. On both sides the Indian artist painted that recurring expression, *Lotta Laffs*, along with an undressed girl holding a towel. What else could we have named our plane?

### Mission 13 • October 20, 1944[19]
### Target: Marshalling Yards
### Innsbruck, Austria[20]

18. For more information on the *Memphis Belle*, see Noah Adams, "At 75, A World War II Legend Gets A Full Makeover," West Virginia Public Radio, accessed on July 14, 2017, http://www.npr.org/2017/04/22/525106154/at-75-a-world-war-ii-legend-gets-a-full-makeover. The *Memphis Belle* was the focus of a documentary in 1944 and full-length movie in 1990. See "The Memphis Belle: A Story of a Flying Fortress," IMDb.com, accessed on July 14, 2017, http://www.imdb.com/title/tt0036152/; and "Memphis Belle," IMDb.com, accessed July 14, 2017, http://www.imdb.com/title/tt0100133/.

19. For a description of this mission, see Mahoney, *Fifteenth Air Force Against the Axis*, 259. Thirty-seven planes from Faulkner's Group took off for the mission, but seven planes had to return early for mechanical reasons. Confirmed Mission Report, October 20, 1944, Mission #137, Air Force Historical Research Agency, Reel B0601 – 454 Records, 778.

20. The Innsbruck Marshalling Yards were critical for the German forces in northern Italy. "Fifteenth Air Force – Innsbruck Marshalling Yard Attack," December 15, 1944, NA, RG 331 – Records of the Allied Operational and Occupation Headquarters, World War II, Box 114, Reel, 53D. General Eaker later described the importance of the Innsbruck rail yards and how the Fifteenth Air Force attacked them eleven times resulting in one of the "heaviest maulings of the whole route." "The Effect of Allied Strategic Bombing on the Present Status of the War."

Tom Beside *Lotta Laffs*

B-24 Leaves Munich Airspace after Dropping Its Bombs (National Archives)

*Today we were briefed to bomb the Munich Rhim Airdrome, the one we missed on my first Munich raid. We flew Gentleman Jim. We took off, got in formation, everything fine. On course, number 4 engine's RPM and MP started oscillating. The engine kept cutting out – then back in. It repeated this over and over. The cylinder head temperature was a very high 260 degrees. The formation hit a very strong headwind. The lead ships had to draw so much power that old Gentleman Jim, with her 55 missions, just couldn't take it. We flew a loose formation, fortunately, for as we hit the Alps we experienced the most severe turbulence I've ever seen. All formations were completely broken and I had quite a job trying to hold the ship steady: the wings were flopping as if they were going to come off. After fifteen minutes it quieted down. Then my number 1 engine started detonating.*[21] *My power settings were correct and the cowl flaps were open—there was nothing I could do but sweat it out. Nearing the target, number 2 started cutting out also. I knew if one engine went completely out that one or even two more could go. We struggled along – I thought of turning back, but had a hunch we could make it to the target. We were so near to it. Numbers 1, 2 and 4 got excessively hot and each would cut out frequently at different intervals. We really had a time controlling it. As we neared the target, I saw it was hopeless to stay with our box, what with all our trouble, and began dropping back and down, and finally got in the box behind us. They too, had too great a pace for us, so I was forced to drop even further behind, until we were flying beside the 459th Group, with the checkerboard tails.*[22] *The engines had cooled by this time and I had no difficulty in staying with them. They turned away from the Munich bomb run because cloud cover was too great – and went down to bomb their alternate at Innsbruck. One of our engines would occasionally cut out but come back in. We were all sweating it out something fierce. The only way I knew we were over the target was by the flak popping off to our right—moderate, but at our altitude. The engines had cooled down after we dropped the bombs and were able to pull back power. I stayed with the 459th all the way back to the Adriatic, then went*

21. "Detonating" is like when a car backfires, but it repeats at set intervals.

22. For a history of the 459th Group, see "459th Bombardment Group," 459th Association, accessed on July 14, 2017, http://www.459bg.org/index.cfm; and "459th Bomb Group," American Air War Museum in Britain, accessed on July 14, 2017, http://www.americanairmuseum.com/unit/4032.

*home alone, with Nelson navigating. All seemed well. We were low over the Adriatic, about 30 miles from the field when Jim Hamilton, the waist gunner, called over the inter-phone, "Lieutenant, feather number 3! It's falling apart, pieces flying everywhere!" We had to turn on the electric hydraulic pump in order to let the gear and flaps down for a three-engine landing. This was the first time I'd had any doubts about making it home. It's not a healthy feeling.*

Deciding what would cripple Hitler's war machine the most was paramount in the planning of missions, but weather conditions always were taken into account, along with intelligence reports and other factors.[23] The choice of targets involved coordination between General Eaker, commander of the Mediterranean Allied Air Forces (which included the Fifteenth Air Force), and General Spaatz, commander of the Eighth Air Force in England. General Twining, as commander of the Fifteenth Air Force, was in charge of carrying out the destruction of all selected targets.[24]

Most of our targets were either railroad marshalling yards or oil refineries. In planning and selecting targets, our commanders looked to avoid damage to churches and civilian property.[25] Of course, as my discussion with Abbot Denis revealed, it was impossible to avoid damage to civilian property located near target areas. Bombs that were dropped on our missions did not always hit the target. However, it was obvious even to us that the overall strategy worked.

When we arrived at San Giovanni Airfield on September 1, 1944, we found that German fighter aircraft were almost nonexistent. Our P-51s and P-38s had been equipped with long-range,

23. Italy's weather, as well as the weather patterns over target areas, made flying missions very difficult. In late November, General Ira Eaker lamented the disruptions caused by the weather, claiming "the weather has interfered frightfully with our air effort." Ira Eaker to Jacob L. Devers, November 17, 1944, LOC, Eaker Papers, Box I:12, Folder 2 – November 1944, Eaker to Devers, 1.

24. For a description of the priority targets in the fall 1944, see Craven and Cate, *The Army Air Forces in World War II*, Volume III, 646–7.

25. There is tremendous debate among historians about just how committed U.S. commanders were to precision bombing and avoiding civilian casualties. While not discounting the targeting of civilians, Conrad Crane concludes that, especially in Europe, the "persistence of precision-doctrine" and the desire to minimize civilian casualties when possible remained basic principles of the AAF's leadership. He does acknowledge that the "temptations to use terror bombing increased" in the later stages of the war and can be seen in the fire bombings of Japan. Crane, *American Airpower Strategy in World War II*, 10. For opposing viewpoints, see Sherry, *The Rise of American Airpower*; and Schaffer, *Wings of Judgement*.

disposable fuel tanks and could escort us all the way to the target.[26] Our fighters had mostly eliminated their fighters. In fact, the six gunners of our ten-man crew never had an opportunity to fire at an enemy plane. Germany was literally running out of gas, and also Messerschmitt 109s and Focke-Wulf 190 fighter planes. Our fighters shot down most of them, and our bombing missions against German airfields destroyed many others. Germany was also running out of fighter pilots due to their losses and also the difficulty in training new recruits because of material shortages.[27]

### Mission 14 • October 21, 1944[28]
### Target: Marshalling Yards
### Győr, Germany

*Today we flew the number 4 position. I like it better than the others. We were in Dog box and hit quite a bit of prop wash the entire trip.*[29] *On the way up, one of the superchargers acted up and we got behind a little. We had trouble catching up because number 4 engine was smoking a good bit. We went right through a thin overcast and for a few minutes all I could do was follow the vapor trails of the planes ahead. It was a beautiful day and from the rear of the Group, the hundred or so white vapor trails against the bright blue sky was a sight to see. We passed right over Lake Balaton—very pretty.*[30] *I had a new first pilot flying as my copilot, Conrad Leslie. He had little recent time in a B-24 in the past two months mostly because of the long boat crossing,*

26. The P-38 "Lightning" and P-51 "Mustang" were the main Allied fighter escorts by this point in the war. For a description of the P-51, see Michael O'Leary, *North American Aviation P-51 Mustang* (Osprey Publishing, 1998). See also McFarland and Newton, *To Command the Sky*, 247–8.

27. By the fall of 1944, the Luftwaffe was suffering severely. The strategic bombing campaign had destroyed German access to key resources, especially oil, and the growing number of allied fighter planes had overwhelmed the Luftwaffe. Whereas earlier in the war, German fighter pilots made seventy-five flights in their assigned aircraft before being assigned to combat, by the fall of 1944, they only flew ten. Adam Makos concludes that the summer and fall of 1944 "witnessed the slaughter of the [German] Air Force." Adam Makos, *A Higher Call: An Incredible True Story of Combat and Chivalry in the War-torn Skies of World War II* (New York: Berkley Caliber, 2012), 261. See also Tilman, *Forgotten Fifteenth*, 185 and 195–97; and Craven and Cate, *The Army Air Forces in World War II*, Vol. 3, 304.

28. The target for this mission was the Gyor, Hungary Marshalling Yard. Fifty-four P-51s escorted forty-nine B-24s. Mahoney, *Fifteenth Air Force Against the Axis*, 260.

29. Four squadrons of seven planes each from Faulkner's Group flew on the mission. Dog box was the last of the four formations and in the lower middle of the formation. Headquarters 454th Bombardment Group (H), Operations Order #286, October 21, 1944, Air Force Historical Research Agency, Reel B0601 – 454 Records, 784.

30. Balaton is a major tourist attraction today because of its natural beauty. "Lake Balaton," Hungarian Tourism Agency, accessed on July 24, 2017, http://balaton.gotohungary.com/.

*in which two ships of his convoy were sunk by German U-boats.*[31] *We dropped our bombs - think we did some damage – and made a nice fast rally out of moderate flak, all low, only twenty guns. Colonel Aynesworth, the Group Commander, led the formation and used way too much power after the rally. We had to use climbing settings to stay with his descent. He was doing about 190 mph. Coming back, our box closed up and flew a good tight formation. Tomorrow, we stand down. Think I'll see if I can test hop Lotta Laughs, check controls and the new cylinder on number 3 engine.*[32]

In 2014, I self-published a scaled down version of this memoir, with the title, *Combat Missions from Italy*, and that version somehow reached a few former airmen of my 737th Bomb Squadron or their families. Almost all of the airmen of our squadron have passed on, but I have had the pleasure of being in communication with their spouses or children and grandchildren.

One of the airmen who contacted me was Conrad Leslie. He was a first pilot who had just arrived with his crew and was my copilot on his orientation mission, which was my fourteenth mission. Leslie, from Xenia, Ohio, was twenty-one years old at the time, a couple of years older than myself. He ultimately completed thirty-five missions and returned home just as the war in Europe was ending. Leslie and his crew, and I with mine, would fly together in the same squadron formation box on seven missions. If anything, he ran into more scrapes than I did, and he received the Distinguish Flying Cross for his valor.[33]

Leslie's most harrowing mission occurred on February 28, 1945, when the 737th squadron was charged with knocking out a railroad bridge along Brenner Pass in the Italian Alps. The squadron's lead ship was flown by recently promoted Captain Ted Schindler.[34]

31. For background on Conrad Leslie, including a description of his thirty-two-day trip crossing the Atlantic Ocean in a Liberty ship with a maximum speed of seven knots, see Conrad Leslie, "Welcome to the Diary of Conrad Leslie's 35 Bombing Missions over Germany as a 21 Year Old B-24 First Pilot," unpublished memoir, in author's possession. See also "737th Bomb Squadron Crews – R Conrad Leslie," Aircraft and Airmen from the 454th Bombardment Group in Italy during World War II, accessed on July 17, 2017, http://www.454thbombgroup.it/737th%20Squadron%20Crews.pdf.

32. Faulkner occasionally made test flights to see if repairs fixed known problems and to determine whether the plane was ready for long fights.

33. For a description of Leslie's postwar career, see Leslie, "Welcome to the Diary of Conrad Leslie's 35 Bombing Missions Over Germany." See also "Crop Forecaster Is Market Maverick," *New York Times*, September 19, 1983, D2.

34. For information on Ted Schindler, see "737th Bomb Squadron Crews – Ted K. Schindler," Aircraft and Airmen from the 454th Bombardment Group in Italy during

Schindler, a tall, dark and lanky, nice looking young man and his older brother, Hally, were inseparable. Hally was also a pilot with his crew in the 737th Squadron. Both had gone through their military careers together from cadet training. They were so close that they even interchanged members of their crews.

Leslie's navigator, Hal Stricker, was pulled from his crew to be Ted Schindler's navigator, just for this mission. This would be Stricker's first experience as a lead navigator. From Leslie's number four position, he would be looking up at Schindler's tail gunner, Sergeant Ray Zisk. Zisk was sitting in his cramped tail turret, which is centered between the plane's large twin rudders.

The targeted bridge in Brenner Pass was located in a valley in the Italian Alps, and the Germans had placed their anti-aircraft guns near the top of the mountain peaks around the bridge, bringing them 8,000 feet closer to the formation, giving the German gunners an enormous advantage.

The 737th squadron's seven-plane box consisted of two planes flying on Schindler's wings with Leslie directly behind and below Schindler, and two planes flying on Leslie's wings with the tail-end B-24 just behind and below Leslie. Heavy flak pounded them as they flew over the target. After "Bombs away," while turning from the target, Leslie was looking up at Schindler's tail turret when an explosion occurred just behind the tail gunner's position. The direct hit severed the tail turret, with Zisk inside, from Schindler's plane. Zisk fell free and his body almost collided with Leslie's plane. The entire double-fin tail section then separated from Schindler's mortally wounded plane. While Leslie was able to avoid Zisk's body, the loose tail section slammed into his own right rudder. Leslie's copilot was calling frantically over the radio to Schindler and Hal Stricker (Leslie's regular navigator) to bail out. Despite his damaged rudder, Leslie was able to keep his own plane in the air as Schindler's tail-less plane drifted down, spinning away, out of control. No one saw any open parachutes.

Colonel Aynesworth sent the distraught Hally Schindler and his crew home immediately. By a strange and inexplicable coincidence, the day after tail gunner Ray Zisk's tragic death, his brother, Phil Zisk, also a sergeant in the Air Force, reported for duty at the 737th squadron. He was looking forward to surprising his brother,

---

World War II, accessed on July 14, 2017, http://www.454thbombgroup.it/737th%20Squadron%20Crews.pdf.

whom he had not seen for months. He was, of course, shocked to hear the circumstances of his brother's death the day before.[35]

Conrad Leslie has had an interesting life ever since. He served 45 years as a member of the Chicago Board of Trade and interacted with many financial luminaries. After reading *Conrad Leslie's Guide for Successful Speculation, Stocks, Commodities and Gold*, fabled financier, Bernard Baruch, commented to him, "You and I think alike."[36]

**Mission 15 • October 23, 1944[37]**
**Target: Marshalling Yards**
**Trieste, I.taly**

*Today was, without a doubt, the most trying mission we have had. I think I'd rather go over Vienna five times than go through another ordeal like today's mission. We were supposed to bomb Regensburg, way north of Munich, but due to 10/10 cloud cover, we were forced to bomb Trieste, a secondary target.*[38] *We were assigned San Antonio Rose, a good old ship, but very cold. We were briefed for a bombing altitude of 23,000 feet but the group leader (cuss his hide) climbed to 27,000 feet. We were at that altitude for at least three hours and the temperature was 38 degrees below. Worst of all, my heated suit wouldn't work and my hands and feet, I thought, were surely frozen solid. I was really in agony, sitting on one hand and flying with the other. We had good escort, P-51's buzzing around us all the time. Regensburg was overcast so we headed for Innsbruck after an ample amount of flak had been thrown at us, all too low. Innsbruck was also covered, so we headed back southeast for Trieste. Flak on the way—through the overcast. By the time we dropped our bombs over Trieste, our formation was half its original size since a lot of the ships simply couldn't keep the pace. We rallied from Trieste, letting down rapidly to get through a hole in the overcast. The whole cockpit*

35. For a careful study of what happened to Schindler's plane, see Erik Goldstein, "Ray's Story: The Lost Air Gunner of the 454th Bomb Group," accessed on July 17, 2017, http://www.454thbombgroup.it/Ray's%20Story%20EMAIL%20614.pdf, 94–104.

36. Conrad Leslie, *Conrad Leslie's Guide for Successful Speculating: Stocks, Commodities, Gold* (Chicago, IL: Dartnell, 1970).

37. For brief details of this mission, see Mahoney, *Fifteenth Air Force Against the Axis*, 261.

38. Trieste was not even listed as an alternative target on the operational orders. The first alternate target was the Rosenheim Marshalling Yards and the second was Innsbruck. Both were overcast. Headquarters 454th Bombardment Group (H), Operations Order #289A, October 23, 1944, Air Force Historical Research Agency, Reel B0601 – 454 Records, 789.

Bombs Falling on Trieste, 1944 (National Archives)

*iced up with frost; the controls were very stiff. My hands and feet began to thaw out. They began to hurt, but by the time we reached the bottom of the overcast, it was O.K. There were only 8 of the original 24 ships with us. Some, low on gas, had headed for emergency bases on the north Italian coast.*[39] *We flew through*

39. As Allied forces advanced in Italy, Yugoslav partisans gained control of parts of Yugoslavia, and Russian forces drove the Germans out of the Balkans, Fifteenth Air Force airmen had more options if their planes were damaged and could not make it back to

B-24 Leaves Smoking Target in Italy, 1945 (National Archives)

*many rain showers, sweating out our own gas supply over the Adriatic. Reaching home, we landed on a wet, slippery runway. On the approach, I could see Star Dust, one of our ships, nosed over short of the runway, a wreck now. At the other end there was a second ship, tail high in the air, demolished. After we taxied in and parked, a plane flew in with two flat tires and he also nosed over. I began thinking that this was a costly day for the 15th Air Force.*[40] *That morning Squadron leader, Captain Goosen, blew a*

their main bases around Foggia. The allies developed emergency fields where the crippled planes could land. The most widely used airstrip was on the Isle of Vis in the Adriatic. See Mahoney, *Fifteenth Air Force Against the Axis*, 424; Ambrose, *The Wild Blue*, 194–95; and "Adriatic Island Base Succors Allied Airmen," *Torretta Flyer* 11 (Winter 1984): 27. Five planes on this mission had to land at emergency airfields. Confirming Mission Report, 454th Bomb Gp (H), Mission #140, October 23, 1944, Air Force Historical Research Agency, Reel B0601 – 454 Records, 791.

40. Leslie flew his first mission as a first pilot on October 23, and his plane was one of the ones that got separated from the main formation due to the weather and also flak knocking out one of his engines. He writes, "Rainstorms over home field at time of return. Ordered the crew to brace for an emergency landing. Attempted landing in rain and wind, the crosswind was very strong. ... During landing, one wheel went off into the mud and pulled ship into a drainage ditch, breaking the nose wheel." Leslie, "Welcome to the Diary of Conrad Leslie's 35 Bombing Missions Over Germany." Twenty-three planes, including Faulkner's, participated in this mission. Four planes returned to base without reaching the target, including Leslie's crew. According to a post-mission report, "A solid undercast of several layers of clouds from 1500 ft. to 18,800 ft. persisted throughout the entire mission." Confirming Mission Report, 454th Bomb Gp (H), Mission #140, October 23, 1944, Air Force Historical Research Agency, Reel B0601 – 454 Records, 792.

*tire on take-off, breaking his landing gear off, another wrecked Liberator. Quite an exciting day, but I hope I never have another one quite like it. I now have 100 hours of combat time. Lotta Laffs will be ready tomorrow. Hurrah!*

**Mission 16 • November 1, 1944[41]**
**Target: Supply Depot**
**Graz, Austria[42]**

*Today was one of those exciting, eventful missions. We were briefed for a Vienna ordnance depot. With Obie still ailing, I again had Major Harmon for my copilot.[43] We were to fly Number 5 position, one of my favorites. The major hasn't had much time in B-24's and made one or two boners. On take-off, he pulled back power too soon and (with our heavy bomb load) we hugged the ground for ten or fifteen miles. On course, we ran into quite a bit of weather over the Adriatic and went headlong into a layer of thin stratus clouds. At times, the lead box would be out of sight, but I stayed close and never lost sight of my lead man. We were in it for a couple of hours. Number 3 supercharger went out on the way up. I had little Will Gorman, our engineer, set the amplifier at 40 inches and it didn't give us too much trouble. It worked, but the power of that engine could not be adjusted, making formation flying more difficult. The adjustment caused us to fall back and, in catching up, we had excessive cylinder head temperatures. Before we knew it, bomb bay doors were open—still in the soup. We would be bombing by the lead ship's radar.[44] Flak was bursting all around. After a couple of minutes, I was surprised when bombs were away—then it hit. I heard a sharp crack and felt a sudden pain around my eyes and forehead and nose. I looked up and saw a three-inch hole in my windshield. I looked down to see broken glass in my lap. The flak was still close. I thought my face*

41. This mission started out as an all-out assault on Vienna, but because of bad weather, most of the planes attacked alternative targets. Faulkner was part of a flight of twenty-eight B-17s and 139 B-24s that hit marshalling yards at Graz. Mahoney, *Fifteenth Air Force Against the Axis*, 267–8.

42. Graz was especially known for a supply depot that processed artillery. "Target Information Sheet – Graz," March 18, 1945, NA, RG 331 – Records of the Allied Operational and Occupation Headquarters, World War II, Box 113, Reel, 46D.

43. Major William A. Harmon had recently transferred from the Group Headquarters to the 737th Bomb Squadron. 454th Bombardment Group (H), AAF, History for the Month of October, n.d., Air Force Historical Research Agency, Reel B0601 – 454 Records, 705.

44. The orders indicated that using the PFF radar for bombing was expected. Headquarters 454th Bombardment Group (H), Operations Order #295-Plan Able, November 1, 1944, Air Force Historical Research Agency, Reel B0601 – 454 Records, 916.

B-24 Dropping Bombs in Support of Ground Troops in Italy, 1945 (National Archives)

*might be a bloody mess, but kept in formation and kept my head. Another sharp crack in the cockpit. We rallied and then Major Harmon pointed to the instrument panel. All four cylinder head temperature gauges and all four-oil temperature gauges, also 3 and 4 engine fuel pressure and oil pressure gauges and number 3 RPM gauge all registered zero. I asked for a crew check. All okay. Later, I looked at my reflection in the gauges and could see the two scratches above my left eye. The piece of flak had broken the lens of my goggles and stopped inside my coffin seat.*[45] *I put the flak in my pocket. After we landed, Runyan showed me a hole large enough to put his foot through in the top of the nose. That burst almost hit Nelson. At interrogation, we were told we bombed Graz, an alternate target.*[46] *Lotta Laffs is out tomorrow*

45. The G and J silver models of the B-24 had pilot and copilot seats that allowed them to sit back during the bomb run with steel protected sides and shaped to allow them to be protected on three sides. The seat was around 1/8 inch steel. It was called the coffin seat.

46. Graz was the second alternate target. Headquarters 454th Bombardment Group (H), Operations Order #295-Plan Able, November 1, 1944, Air Force Historical Research Agency, Reel B0601 – 454 Records, 916.

*for repairs. We won't fly. I don't mind. We're almost half way through our missions – hurrah! I'm beginning to wonder whether I have a charmed life, or rather if I'm a flak magnet.*

People often ask the question, "Were you afraid going over the target?" The standard answer is, "Anyone who says he's not afraid while being shot at is either lying or is a fool." It would become very tense when the black puffs were close, especially when shrapnel burst into the cockpit as it did a few times. I still have some of the grooved steel shrapnel pieces. One imbedded itself in my control column just above my thigh. Another broke my goggles, grazing my brow and leaving two scratches, but not enough to seek medical attention. Nose gunner Willie Horvath is the only member of my crew to have received the Purple Heart—because of plexiglass fragments puncturing his neck.[47] Flak was dangerous, of course, but only a few times did I ever hear any explosion, and their puffs looked harmless enough while flying through it.

However, I know for sure that, if a German fighter came roaring at me, guns blazing away, I would have been scared as hell, especially if I could see his face. Having one fighter after another making passes at my ship was the worst thing imaginable, and this is exactly what happened to those who flew missions before we arrived in September 1944 and before the P-51s and P-38s destroyed the Luftwaffe fighter groups. The slow and tense six to eight minute Russian roulette ride through a bursting field of impersonal flak firing randomly at us from five miles below was bad enough, but a highly personal and up close *mano a mano* test of whether the German pilot could destroy us before we destroyed him would test the bravest of all.

I am not minimizing the fright that flak could engender. Fellow pilot Conrad Leslie tells of a pilot on one of his early missions turning the wheel over to him as they approached the bursting flak and burying his face in his hands. I could not believe any of our pilots would be so obviously afraid until I realized he just did not want his face disfigured. On another occasion, I heard of a waist gunner that sat on his parachute during each bomb run, choosing to protect other important parts of his body. But, I sensed no

47. 454th Bombardment Group (H), AAF, History for the Month of November, n.d., Air Force Historical Research Agency, Reel B0601 – 454 Records, 861.

panic or fear from any of my crewmen. We all behaved like brave soldiers, but I was concerned about some of the crew, particularly those four situated behind the bomb bay, cut off from the flight deck altogether, and what they were feeling, depending largely on a nineteen-year-old pilot to get them though every mission. I talked to the sons of our tail-gunner, Tony Barone, not long ago. They all said he never wanted to talk about the war, but he could not have been too shaken up. I had talked to Tony not long before he died and he expressed to me utter disappointment that we completed only twenty-eight missions instead of thirty-five.

**Mission 17 • November 4, 1944[48]**
**Target: Marshalling Yard[49]**
**Linz, Austria[50]**

*Today we bombed Linz by radar because of the overcast.*[51] *It's rumored that we did a good job. Their flak was erratic and some of the bursts were red instead of black. I was uneasy after turning at the I. P. toward the target. Another box was crowding us on the left and I had to watch three or four ships at once. We were number 7 in the formation, directly behind and under number 4. When bombs went away, number 4 turned, nosed down and chopped power. His wing man overshot him. I slid directly under, all power cut and still almost collided with his tail. O'Brien lowered 20 degrees flaps to slow us. It was close. Coming back, the snow-capped Alps were—as usual—beautiful. I had Gorman transfer all fuel from the Tokyo tanks.*[52] *On the base leg of the traffic pattern, number 1 engine cut out, so I made a three-engine landing, my third one. On landing, we discovered*

48. Forty-five P-51s escorted 130 B-24s that struck an oil plant in Linz. Mahoney, *Fifteenth Air Force Against the Axis*, 270.

49. Headquarters 454th Bombardment Group (H), Operations Order #299 – Battle Order, November 4, 1944, Air Force Historical Research Agency, Reel B0601 – 454 Records, 926.

50. Linz was a vital communication and transportation hub in Austria. Allied Headquarters considered it "the most strategically located communication target in Southern Europe." It concluded, "The combination of the port on the Danube, the large rail yards, important industries, as well as its position on main road and rail routes, all make Linz of great importance to the Germans." "Inland Towns – Austria – Linz," n.d., NA, RG 331 – Records of the Allied Operational and Occupation Headquarters, World War II, Box 114, Reel, 56D.

51. For a description of the pathfinder method, see Asch, Graff, and Ramey, *The Story of the Four Hundred and Fifty-Fifth Bombardment Group (H) WW II*, 129. The mission report indicated 10/10 overcast or complete cloud cover. Confirming Mission Report, 454th Bomb Gp (H), Mission #143, November 4, 1944, Air Force Historical Research Agency, Reel B0601 – 454 Records, 929.

52. Tokyo tanks were extra fuel cells in the wings that supplied the engine tanks as needed.

*number 1 tank to be bone dry, yet there was plenty of gas in the other tanks. Guess that will teach us to pay more attention.*

D-Day, the Allied invasion at Normandy across the English Channel, had taken place on June 6, 1944, three months before we began our tour.[53] Hitler's Germany, coping with Russia's advancing armies from the east, was still strong, and Hitler threw his infantry and Panzer Divisions with their thousands of tanks at the American and English troops on the western front. It was slow going for the Allies, but we were winning the war, and we knew it. It was just a question of time. The allied advances from both the east and the west took their toll on the German forces, including the Luftwaffe, contributing to our seldom seeing German fighter planes.[54]

**Mission 18 • November 5, 1944[55]**
**Target: Oil Refinery**
**Vienna, Austria**

*Today was another uneventful mission. There was a complete overcast and again we bombed by PPF (radar). No flak till bombs away, then lots of it from 70 guns in our range—all scattered, not too accurate. Number 1 engine was hit but still worked. All PPF runs are long. It's a hell of a feeling; sitting there, waiting, waiting, waiting. The seconds seem like hours. It's actually almost a relief to see the black bursts. Part of the tension is relieved. Just talked with Williams' navigator. He just got back from pre-briefing. He says tomorrow's mission is as rough as they come.*

Prior to joining the military, I could not imagine not knowing where my high school friends were; however, once I began training and especially after I left the United States that changed dramatically.

53. There are several very good books on the D-Day Invasion. See Stephen E. Ambrose, *D-Day, June 6, 1944: The Climatic Battle of World War II* (New York: Simon & Schuster, 1994); Adrian R. Lewis, *Omaha Beach: A Flawed Victory* (Chapel Hill: University of North Carolina Press, 2001); and Cornelius Ryan, *The Longest Day: The Classic Epic of D-Day, June 6, 1944* (New York: Simon & Schuster, 1959).

54. There was widespread optimism in the late summer and early fall that the war would be over soon. Much of this optimism was misplaced. In early October, General Ira Eaker called it "the silly optimism about an early finish to the war." Ira C. Eaker to Peter Beasley, October 4, 1944, LOC, Eaker Papers, Box I:12, Folder 1 – October 1944, 1. A day later Eaker wrote the Assistant Secretary of War for Air, Robert Lovett, "I feel we have been done much harm by the wave of optimism which swept the United States, Great Britain, and even the combatant Armies and Air Forces as the result of the quick capture and liberation of France. All of our boys here are receiving letters saying that they are expected home by Christmas. It is going to be a rude shock both to them and to their families when in fact they do not get home this year at all." Ira C. Eaker to Robert A. Lovett, October 5, 1944, LOC, Eaker Papers, Box I:26, Folder 2 – Lovett, Robert A., January 1944-February 1945, 1.

55. Faulkner's plane joined 360 B-24s and 143 B-17s on the mission to Vienna. They were escorted by 139 P-38s and 198 P-51s. Mahoney, *Fifteenth Air Force Against the Axis*, 270.

With the exception of Warner Marsh, with whom I corresponded every few months, I really did not know where anyone else was—even my own brother, Jim. All I knew about Jim was that he was on some kind of boat somewhere in the Pacific. We just did not keep up with our friends—probably because we were so involved with our own very fluid situations and writing to our parents and maybe a girlfriend was all most of us could handle; so, we seldom had knowledge of friends who might even be stationed nearby.

One day, as I lay on my cot, reading, I was surprised to hear a familiar voice, "Hello, Tommy." No one had called me that since high school, so I knew instantly someone special was speaking. I turned and looked up, delighted and surprised to see my old friend, Kenneth Higgins, standing in the entrance of our tent. We had gone all the way through school together since Armstrong Grade School in Highland Park. I was unaware that he was in the Army Air Forces. Kenneth had somehow learned I was nearby. He was in a squadron of the 455th Bomb Group located across the runways. Though using the same field, the two groups operated independent of each other. The two parallel runways might as well have been the Mississippi River. We never saw anyone of the 455th Bomb Group, except in the air.

Kenneth and I spent the afternoon talking about old times and old friends. We also compared notes on the missions we had flown. Kenneth was the radio operator of a crew whose pilot was George McGovern, the same George McGovern who later became a senator from South Dakota and eventually the Democratic Party's nominee for president of the United States in 1972. McGovern lost that election in a landslide to incumbent Richard Nixon.

Weeks after Kenneth's visit in my tent, McGovern, as pilot, and with Kenneth on board, made an emergency crash landing on the Isle of Vis in the Adriatic after being hit by flak over a German target. A transport plane picked up McGovern and the rest of the crew the next day and flew them back to San Giovanni. McGovern would receive the Distinguished Flying Cross for making a difficult landing with a badly damaged aircraft and saving his crew.[56]

56. McGovern and Higgins flew on a mission on December 20, 1944, and their plane was severely damaged. For a description of McGovern's crash landing, see Ambrose, *The Wild Blue*, 194–96.

### Mission 19 • November 6, 1944[57]
### Target: South Ordnance Depot
### Vienna, Austria

*Today was a rather run-of-the-mill mission, except for a hell of a lot of flak. Expected over Vienna. One navigator said we were in flak for eight minutes. It seemed like an eternity.*[58] *I saw an engine on a ship in another group seem to blow up – I'm sure it went down. Although we were in range of 130 guns, the flak wasn't accurate, thank the Lord.*[59] *Willie Horvath, the nose gunner, said he'd never seen so much. He has a much better view than the pilots. My copilot was a new first pilot named Tolson.*[60] *He was in Liberal, Kansas, when I was—really a swell kid.*

For the above three missions, we were assigned *Gentleman Jim*, an older, olive colored D model. The D models were okay, but the newer, silver J models were better, and certainly more reliable. Several times, a malfunction would occur serious enough to warrant returning to the base before reaching the target. The D models were also more prone to engines overheating. During my stay in Italy, I made seven three-engine landings after taking off for a mission. While three landings were from flak damage, the four others were engine failure due to overheating. This was a continual problem with Pratt and Whitney B-24 engines. "Early returns" were not good. Alone, we had to drop our bombs in the Adriatic more than once after being unable to continue with the formation, usually because of engine problems.

On one mission, a rare milk run over Yugoslavia, we returned because the plane kept stalling out. The higher we flew, and the thinner the air, the more we would just drop from the formation—without warning and without any reason we could discover. I had everyone look over the outside of the ship. We had no idea what was happening. The instruments were all reading at normal levels,

57. 266 B-24s, escorted by ninety-two P-51s and ninety-four P-38s, attacked the Southern Ordnance Depot in Vienna. Mahoney, *Fifteenth Air Force Against the Axis*, 271–2.

58. Faulkner flew in the number 4 position in Box F, the last group of planes in his squadron. Headquarters 454th Bombardment Group (H), Operations Order #303 – Battle Order, November 6, 1944, Air Force Historical Research Agency, Reel B0601 – 454 Records, 939.

59. "Flak at the target was intense but inaccurate." Asch, Graff, and Ramey, *The Story of the Four Hundred and Fifty-Fifth Bombardment Group (H) WW II*, 129.

60. "737th Bomb Squadron Crews – Patrick H. Tolson," Aircraft and Airmen from the 454th Bombardment Group in Italy during World War II, accessed on July 14, 2017, http://www.454thbombgroup.it/737th%20Squadron%20Crews.pdf.

but we continued to stall out. I would nose down after each stall to keep from spinning in, and we watched in frustration as the formation finally disappeared, far up and away. I hated turning back especially since there was no danger of fighters or even any flak, and we would lose credit for this easy mission. Reluctantly, however, I finally turned back to the base in disgust. We talked to the crew chief after landing, and he found that the elevator trim tab had stuck in the extreme position. The trim tabs help stabilize the plane in flight. They stabilized the rudders, ailerons, and elevators, keeping the plane on course and level, and the wings from tending to dip. The takeoff checklist requires all trim tabs to be in a neutral position. In this case, there was a malfunction. I would never have guessed one trim tab could cause that much trouble. However, it did at altitude. I was just glad it did not have a similar effect during the takeoff.[61]

**Mission 20 • November 7, 1944[62]**
**Target: Troop concentration**
**Novi Pazar, Yugoslavia**

*Aha! Today, at last, what I'd been hoping for the last eight missions – a real, genuine MILK RUN! No flak! No flak! No flak![63] It was really an enjoyable mission. I was the number 4 with a newly arrived first pilot named Woods.[64] After take-off, we had a nice rendezvous, and on course, it was in no time that we were in Yugoslavia over the initial point. There were lots of stratus clouds and again I was flying instruments and formation, and never lost sight of my lead. I got vertigo once. Not bad – thought I was level and the flight indicator showed a 30 degree bank. Bombs away! We hit the town where the troops were directly in the middle. Charlie Box and Dog Box didn't get a chance to drop,*

61. This mission was probably on Christmas Day. Faulkner was scheduled to fly, and he was in one of three planes that had to return to base because of mechanical issues. One of the planes, which was probably Faulkner's, returned "because elevator trim tabs broke loose and stuck." Confirming Mission Report, 454th Bomb Gp (H), Mission #172, December 25, 1944, Air Force Historical Research Agency, Reel B0601 – 454 Records, 1119.

62. Faulkner flew with 110 B-24s to attack troop concentrations in Yugoslavia. Mahoney, *Fifteenth Air Force Against the Axis*, 273.

63. The official report for the mission described the flak as "Scant (4–8 bursts)." Confirming Mission Report, 454th Bomb Gp (H), Mission #147, November 7, 1944, Air Force Historical Research Agency, Reel B0601 – 454 Records, 945.

64. "737th Bomb Squadron Crews – Kenneth J. Woods," Aircraft and Airmen from the 454th Bombardment Group in Italy during World War II, accessed on July 14, 2017, http://www.454thbombgroup.it/737th%20Squadron%20Crews.pdf.

*so we all made another run. It seemed strange that there were no little black clouds puffing about us, or rather, it seemed wonderful. On the second time over, I got a good glimpse of the target – the first target I'd ever gotten to see from the air. Tomorrow we're being stood down. Captain Pitts says we've worked plenty hard for the past week and deserve a rest. I guess I'm glad, but I'd just as soon keep plugging the missions in. It gives me quite a thrill to see our sorties pile up so quick. Made a bad landing - 30-mile per hour crosswind.*

The two parallel gravel runways at San Geovanni airbase were fine—as long as the wind was running in the same, or opposite, direction of the runways. They were constructed to face the most prevalent wind of the area. Most airports of any size, anywhere, usually have a second, crossing runway in order to avoid having airplanes land or takeoff in a direct, heavy crosswind. A plane approaching a runway must line up exactly with that runway on the approach, which requires the pilot to crab into the crosswind as he glides in. At the last second, just before the wheels touch, he has to pull the plane's nose in line with the runway. It is almost impossible to have a smooth landing. Just getting a B-24 down safely on a narrow gravel runway in a very high, direct crosswind was always something of a relief.

**Mission 21 • November 16, 1944**[65]
**Target: Marshalling Yard**
**Munich, Germany**[66]

*Today was eventful! And how! Yesterday we were told to pack and get ready to go to Capri, the Air Force rest camp, for a week. While we were packing, our leave was cancelled. We had to fly. I had a hell of a premonition that the worst would happen if we flew; all night I thought about it. At briefing they pulled the curtain and the target was Munich, which ain't good! Our flight path would take us in range of up to 280 guns. All during briefing, and before takeoff, I had an uneasy feeling. At the ship, I discovered there was a camera in the rear section, behind the bomb bays,*

65. All of the bomb wings of the Fifteenth Air Force participated in the attack on Munich, including 101 B-17s, 348 B-24s, 53 P-38s, and 203 P-51s. Mahoney, *Fifteenth Air Force Against the Axis*, 276–7.

66. The mission on November 16 was the first of four consecutive days of more than 1,000 planes from the Fifteenth Air Force attacking German targets. Eaker to Arnold, November 21, 1944, LOC, Eaker Papers, Box I:24, Folder 7 – Arnold, Henry Harley Gen., Vol III, Sept. 1944-March 1945 (2 of 2).

*but it had not been set up or mounted. I had it taken off. The crew was superstitious about cameras on board. Mac, the tail gunner, said he would set it up, but I was already running up the engines. We were flying "The Joker", in number 4 position. The flight up seemed long and I was apprehensive all the way.*

*We had a green navigator named Robinson.*[67] *Finally, we reached the I. P.—the first flak hit in brackets to the right. Then it got heavier—and heavier.*[68] *Over the loud roar of the engines I could hear the flak hitting our ship. Flak hit Runyan in the head, leaving a dent in his steel helmet. My heated gloves went out and my hands were freezing—the temperature on the gauge registered minus 45 degrees Fahrenheit. Bombs away, right rally. A fast one. Flak close. After the run, clear at last, the waist gunner, Gorman, called and said Number 3 engine was pouring oil by the bucket full. My hands were killing me now, but they warmed up as we descended. We watched number 3. It seemed O.K. Coming back over the Italian coast, O'Brien saw four P-51's chasing an ME-109. Other German fighters were reported by other crews after we landed. There was a strong crosswind and after we parked, Major Pitts drove up to say I'd made the best landing of the group. Quite a compliment—even mentioned it at the squadron pilot's meeting held earlier tonight. But up at operations, after flight interrogation, Pitts told me I had to see Colonel Mears about having the camera taken off the ship.*[69] *I was shaking in my boots, but the interview wasn't so bad. Captain Jacobs fixed it so that I could still go to Capri tomorrow. Colonel Mears had told me I would have to stay and receive some sort of disciplinary action. So tomorrow, Capri! P. S. Lotta Laffs is finally ready to go again. Hooray!*

Just thinking about a week away from the grueling routine of San Giovanni was invigorating. Outside of my short visit to Cerignola, I had seen only the men in my squadron for almost three months. The thought of a hot shower and good food was almost

67. "737th Bomb Squadron Crews – Carlyle F. Robinson," Aircraft and Airmen from the 454th Bombardment Group in Italy during World War II, accessed on July 14, 2017, http://www.454thbombgroup.it/737th%20Squadron%20Crews.pdf.

68. "Intense, accurate, heavy flak was encountered at the target." See Confirming Mission Report, 454th Bomb Gp (H), Mission #151, November 16, 1944, Air Force Historical Research Agency, Reel B0601 – 454 Records, 961.

69. James F. Mears, 454th Bombardment Group, accessed on July 14, 2017, http://www.454bg.org/mears-james-m9732-454bg.cfm. See also Obituary of Col. James. F. Mears, *Savannah Morning News*, January 18, 1995, 2D. Mears was upset because the camera would have helped headquarters determine target damage.

overwhelming. We did not frequent the small squadron mess hall with any regularity at San Giovanni. The breakfast fare consisted of powdered eggs and powered milk (neither of which I would eat or drink), coffee (which I never drank), marmalade, and Italian bread. Lunch and dinner always offered some variety of spam—cold spam, pan broiled spam, or grilled spam.[70] The mess hall also seemed to serve Jell-O often. It was pretty good, just a little grainy. My enlisted men told me the Jell-O was suspect. In Italy, we never saw any women; so, I assumed that is why there was no frustration, not the usual talk or interest to speak of in—well, "sex." My enlisted men swore that the Air Corps was involved in a conspiracy to feed us some kind of chemical, probably in the Jell-O that cut back on the usual male sex drive. At nineteen years old, it made sense to me. We thought our K-rations were safe.

We had high expectations when we left San Giovanni for Capri.[71] From the time we left San Francisco to the time we returned to Miami seven months later, I did not encounter a single girl, except one and what a girl she was. Her name was Marie. While on Capri, the officers stayed at the Quisisana Hotel, the most luxurious on the island.[72] There were earmarks of the Nazis having stayed there only months before. I still have a small Nazi flag from Capri. There was a small gift shop next door to the hotel. I wandered in and found a young, beautiful Italian girl standing behind the counter. She spoke halting English and, after visiting with her a couple of times, I asked if she would go out with me to dinner. She left for a minute, slipping behind an opening covered by a curtain, then returned to decline my offer, but said

70. For a description of Spam and its importance to the allies in World War II, see Dwight Jon Zimmerman, "A War Won With Spam (and a Few Other Things)," May 19, 2011, accessed on July 13, 2017, http://www.defensemedianetwork.com/stories/war-won-spam-things/.

71. For a description of Capri, see Asch, Graff, and Ramey, *The Story of the Four Hundred and Fifty-Fifth Bombardment Group (H) WW II*, 119; and Chalker, *The Flight of the Liberators*, 58–63. The 454th leaders recognized the benefits from leave: "Rest camps on the Isle of Capri, at Village Mancuso, Rome, and in Cairo were used to excellent advantage, most of the men preferring a week's rest at Capri. While it is true that many combat crew members could have completed their tour of duty without such a rest, it is a fact that the prospect of going to a rest camp gave them something to look forward to; and all in all, the rest camp leaves were of great value to the combat personnel, for in all cases the men appeared to be physically and mentally improved after taking the rest." "Medical History of the 454th Bombardment Group: Initial Report 1 June 1943–30 September 1945," Air Force Historical Research Agency, Reel B0601 – 454 Records, 7.

72. For the history of the Quisisana Hotel, see "History," accessed on July 17, 2017, http://www.quisisana.com/en/history. See also Jack R. Myers, *Shot at and Missed: Reflections of a World War II Bombardier* (Norman: University of Oklahoma Press, 2004), 134.

that she lived behind the shop and invited me to visit her there after closing that evening.

All day, I looked forward to seeing her, the first girl I had laid my eyes on in over three months. That evening, with great anticipation, I stepped inside the shop, and she motioned for me to come with her behind the curtains. Waiting for us inside were her parents, her grandparents, and an aunt in a small, square cubicle behind the curtain that was their living room. They were all sitting in chairs around the room, facing us as she and I sat together on the sofa. None of her family spoke English. She explained to me that she could not leave, but that we could talk there as long as we wished. There was no offer of any refreshments. While I would not have been surprised with *one* chaperone, we had *five!* I looked around at the elderly relatives, all with their hands folded in their laps, looking at us. Even though none of them could understand what Marie and I were saying, I was completely uncomfortable with her family sitting in silence, all watching Marie and me struggling to carry on a conversation. No one was enjoying this. After ten awkward minutes, I gave up. The shortest date I had ever had was over. My great romance with the beautiful Marie of Capri was just not to be.

# Chapter 5

## Slow March towards Thirty-five Missions

I hated going more than a few days, or as long as a week, without flying. I just did not want to lose my touch at the wheel. Like a young teacher returning to the classroom after summer vacation, so it was with me. The B-24 was a demanding beast, and I would never take her for granted. The week's leave at Capri, combined with bad weather before and after, left us with not flying a single mission for almost a month. During our first two months, we flew twenty-one missions, rarely having more than a few days off between flights. Returning to San Giovanni from Capri, we found the pace of our operations much different. Because of poor weather mainly, but also, because of the arrival of many new crews, I flew missions less regularly, only two missions each in December and January, and then three in February.[1] This was a frustrating time, mostly cold and rainy, sloshing through mud to get anywhere. We flew a couple of practice missions, but outside of that, things were dull. The three months after Capri proved a challenge in many unanticipated ways.

1. By December, the Fifteenth Air Force had two crews for every bomber. Mahoney, *Fifteenth Air Force Against the Axis*, 294.

### Mission 22 • December 11, 1944[2]
### Target: Southeast Goods Depot[3]
### Vienna, Austria

*At last! After twenty-five days without flying—a completed mission. The weather has kept us down a lot.*[4] *The last few days we have taken off, but failed to reach the target because of heavy weather. On one of those aborts, number 1 engine lost power on the takeoff run, but I pulled back all engines before the wheels left the ground.* [5] *And yesterday, I became separated from the formation in clouds just as they were turning for home, lost them and returned to the base alone. Many others had the same experience. We came in over the Adriatic under a 500 foot ceiling, landed on a muddy runway in a heavy rain.*[6] *Today, I had a new first pilot fly as my copilot, Lieutenant Frick – a good boy – keeps us supplied with cigarettes.*[7] *We flew number 3 position in Able box.*[8] *We were briefed for bad weather and 190 heavy guns. Uneventful trip up. Target finally in sight, good bomb run. Lots of flak but none hit Lotta Laffs. One ship in Baker box blew up over the target. The crew counted six chutes coming out.*[9] *It was really cold, 45 degrees below. At one time my throttles almost froze solid. Tomorrow, we are deputy lead in a 3 ship box.*[10] *Our group will be sending up only 12 to 15 ships, less than half normal. I hear it's a sort of experiment. It'll be either*

2. Forty-nine B-24s with an escort of forty P-51s attacked the Southeast Freight Depot in Vienna. Ibid., 295.

3. Freight depots were often adjacent to railroad marshalling yards and were part of the focus of Fifteenth Air Force in trying to disrupt the German transportation system. Robert Ehlers argues, "The chaos brought on by the bombing is difficult to overstate. Every main and alternate route closed, most permanently, to anything but small trains rushed through after the repair crews made the lines operational until the next raids." Ehlers, *The Mediterranean Air War*, 380–1.

4. The 454th was able to fly missions on sixteen days in December. The weather prevented missions on the other days. 454th Bombardment Group – Heavy – For the Month of December, n.d., Air Force Historical Research Agency, Reel B0601 – 454 Records, 1066.

5. The 454th began missions on December 7 and 9 but could not complete them. The mission Faulkner had to abort was probably one of these. See Mahoney, *Fifteenth Air Force Against the Axis*, 292–4, and 454th Bombardment Group – Heavy – For the Month of December, n.d., Air Force Historical Research Agency, Reel B0601 – 454 Records, 1066.

6. Mahoney, *Fifteenth Air Force Against the Axis*, 294.

7. "737th Bomb Squadron Crews – Russell J. Frick," Aircraft and Airmen from the 454th Bombardment Group in Italy during World War II, accessed on August 11, 2017, http://www.454thbombgroup.it/737th%20Squadron%20Crews.pdf.

8. Headquarters 454th Bombardment Group (H), Operations Order #347 – Battle Order, December 11, 1944, Air Force Historical Research Agency, Reel B0601 – 454 Records, 1084.

9. Various crews reported seeing between one and seven parachutes. See Confirming Mission Report, 454th Bomb Gp (H), Mission #165, December 11, 1944, Air Force Historical Research Agency, Reel B0601 – 454 Records, 1086.

10. Deputy lead meant that Faulkner's plane would lead the bombing mission if the mission commander's plane could not complete the bomb run.

*a milk run – or a rough one. I do notice that only the most experienced crews are going. Probably a roughie-toughie.*[11] *G'night.*

I would have loved to have known what and where the target was for that reduced number of planes, mentioned above, but I never found out. The mission was ultimately cancelled.

The "twenty-five days" referred to above was a time of complete boredom, outside of our trip to Capri.[12] On arrival on September 1, 1944, we found our small tent to be hot, dusty, and wind-blown. Now, in December, it was cold and windy, and the constant rain created a sloppy sea of deep, sticky mud between the tents. The tents were set up a good distance from one another, probably spread out initially to avoid concentrating crews who would have been vulnerable to German strafing. Rather than struggling in the mud, we found it simpler just to stay in the tent and read, talk, sleep, and eat.

Keeping the floor of our tent clean was a real problem. Some tents had wood planks for floors, but our tent was staked out over a concrete slab that had been poured by local Italians. They had used such a poor quality of concrete and sand that the floor was always covered with a layer of light gray powder that flaked and crumbled on contact. Sweeping the floor only exacerbated the problem, and stepping into pants and flight suits was tricky. Any part of the pant legs touching the floor would be instantly covered with the chalky powder.

After we had moved into our tent, the first rain revealed a series of slow leaks along the seam directly above my bunk. When rain was imminent, I would hook up a row of tin dishes and cans on a string under the leaks—just above my head to catch the drips. More than once, forgetting what was above my head, I would rise up in the dark, upsetting the tenuous balance of cans and tins, dousing myself—and my bunk.

We were surprised to find that winter in southern Italy was extremely cold, and the crew would laugh about what was advertised as "sunny southern Italy." Keeping warm was a real effort. When all went well, our primitive heating system proved reasonably efficient, and on a cold, windy day or night, it was even cozy. Runyan, Arnie and I would often sit on the edge of our cots and

11. Faulkner's mission the next day ended up being cancelled.

12. Because there were limited recreational facilities available, boredom was a constant problem for the men. See 454th Bombardment Group – Heavy – For the Month of December, n.d., Air Force Historical Research Agency, Reel B0601 – 454 Records, 1005–6.

reach out with cold hands for the comforting heat, or watch as our cheese sandwiches, with their delicious aroma, toasted away on top of the round, hot stove that actually glowed when we overdid the gasoline.

Our stove was the top half of a 60-gallon steel drum. The half-drum sat on the cement floor in the center of our small area. A full barrel of high-octane aviation fuel rested just outside my bunk, and gasoline would flow through a copper tube running under my bunk and across the floor to the drum, where it would drip to the cement floor. A metal smokestack on top of the drum reached up through the top of the tent. A small opening had been cut at the base of the steel drum-half at floor-level so we could reach in and light the gasoline. We adjusted the gas drip with a small clamp, squeezing the two-inch section of rubber tube near the stove, controlling the flow of gas and the size of the flame. At first, it was a little scary sleeping two feet from a full drum of high octane aviation fuel, with it flowing under my bunk, but we all got used to it because it seemed to work and the freezing alternative was not enticing at all.

None of us complained too much about this or the other inconveniences or obstacles related to living in tents. Frequent issues of the *Stars and Stripes,* depicting the trials of cartoon infantry dogfaces Willie and Joe were constant reminders of the infantry struggling through the mud and freezing cold of the rugged Apennines, under heavy fire, while slowly pushing the Germans north up the Italian boot. Nor did we bemoan our plight as opposed to the England based airmen of the Eighth Air Force, who we knew were living in the comfort of warm barracks, decent food, and located near beautiful towns and villages of a modern and civilized Britain, presumably populated with attractive and available British girls. What a difference!

On severe nights, with the gas flowing as much as we dared, the barrel stove would actually become red-hot and glow, and sparks would fly out the top of the stack. During our stay, a couple of nearby tents caught fire and burned to the ground along with everything inside—another reason why each tent was placed a good distance from the other.

Almost every night, to avoid the spam dinners in the small stone mess hall, we would scramble through our mountainous stack of K-ration boxes searching for the small, round, khaki-colored tins of

American cheese. Early on, we had discovered that the Officers' Club (as well as the enlisted men's club) would provide heated cheese sandwiches made with American cheese and delicious Italian bread.[13] They were stacked on plates on the bar counter and absolutely the best sandwiches we ever tasted, and we were able to duplicate them right in our own tent. I have been searching for something similar ever since. We would slice the K-ration cheese over Italian bread and place it on bent coat hangers, a makeshift grill resting on top of the half-barrel stove. When the steel drum became hot enough to toast the sandwiches, what a delicacy it was!

The K-rations contained many food items we quickly tossed, like spam and scrambled eggs in tins, but we appreciated the chocolate bars in tinfoil and the two cigarettes. I finally began smoking because of the free K-ration cigarettes. I did not break the cigarette habit until twenty years later, but I am, to this day, an unrelenting chocoholic.

All of these years, I have wondered why the AAF placed 1,000 boxes of K-rations inside our new plane before our San Francisco takeoff without any instructions or reasons given. I worried a little at not advising some superior about our taking them off the plane in Bari and dividing them up between the ten of us. It may be that what we did was not so unexpected. I now believe they were put there for our use. Many B-24s flew over South American jungles on the southern route to Italy, and we flew over barren deserts of northern Africa. If we had gone down for some reason, those K-rations could have been lifesaving.

After all this conjecture, I have to get back to the more obvious conclusion of all. Those K-rations were there for a very specific reason—to be our meals on eight-hour combat missions. The Air Force may have considered this so obvious that no explanation was necessary. But really, now. That cannot be the answer, can it? A hundred boxes for each? With our tour finished after thirty-five missions?

13. The men valued the Officers' Club as well as the clubs for enlisted men, but they only solved some of the problems with boredom. Bad weather often forced men to stay in their tents and limited access to other activities. Morale improved in February in large part because of improvements in the weather. A monthly summary of the bomb group noted, "The lack of rain made it easier for the men to get around the area, and galoshes gave way to low shoes." Headquarters 454th Bombardment Group – Heavy – For the Month of February, n.d., Air Force Historical Research Agency, Reel B0601 – 454 Records, 1212.

### Mission 23 • December 20, 1944[14]
### Target: Marshalling Yard
### Linz, Austria

*After dozens of briefings and being stood down while waiting inside Lotta Laffs, or even after takeoff, we finally got one in.*[15] *The other day I had an early-return. They don't like that. I got half way to Odertal and number 1 cut out, so we came back on 3 engines. Had trouble diving through the overcast. Picked up a little ice on the wings.*[16] *On today's mission to Linz, I had Mullins for a copilot.*[17] *O'Brien finally got his own crew, so I've been assigned the job of checking out new pilots and copilots on their first mission. We've had a lot of trouble with just weather. Low hanging clouds, ground fog. Right after takeoff I made a left turn, hit a cloudbank, climbed on instruments and after breaking out, saw another B-24 barreling straight for us. He swerved and I did likewise, just in time. After finally getting on course, we hit the bottom of another overcast above the Adriatic. The group leader must have been awfully eager (I can't see why, for our primary target was Brux—325 flak guns—our most dangerous and furthest target yet, only 100 miles south of Berlin). He ordered the entire group of almost 30 planes to climb through it in formation. We were flying number 2 position and I quickly lost sight of the box leader. All 30 planes had the same problem. I shoved the coals to the engines and broke out at 15,000 feet. There were only a few single ships flying around. I couldn't spot the formation for it had completely broken. After vainly attempting to find it, we spotted a formation way off to the left. I caught up with it. It was the 459th Group; I got in number 7 position of Able box, assuming we were still on the way to Brux. After a while, the lead ship opened his bomb bay doors and started throwing out chaff—to distort the antiaircraft guns' radar, unable to see us through the overcast. So we were hitting some other target,*

14. Because of bad weather, a force of thirty-one B-17s and thirty-five B-24s hit their alternative target at Linz, Austria. Mahoney, *Fifteenth Air Force Against the Axis*, 302.

15. Bad weather limited the number of missions the Fifteenth Air Force flew between December 11 and 20. See ibid., 296–302.

16. Faulkner and two other planes had to abort the mission because of engine failure. See Confirming Mission Report, 454th Bomb Gp (H), Mission #169, December 17, 1944, Air Force Historical Research Agency, Reel B0601 – 454 Records, 1103.

17. "737th Bomb Squadron Crews – Lynn D. Mullins," Aircraft and Airmen from the 454th Bombardment Group in Italy during World War II, accessed on August 11, 2017, http://www.454thbombgroup.it/737th%20Squadron%20Crews.pdf.

*probably Linz, Austria.*[18] *On the long bomb-run, number 6 pulled out for home. I caught up with 1, 2 and 3, and dropped my bombs when they did.*[19] *Some large bursts exploded off our right wing. We rallied and headed for home with them. I peeled off over the coast and let down to come in over the overcast. I felt safe over the Adriatic and let down through the overcast, breaking out at 500 feet, visibility. We finally found the field. I lost sight of it in the landing pattern, made one pass, missed, went around, tried again and still couldn't see a thing. Approaching again, Nelson almost directed me to land on our own row of tents. I swerved over and hit the runway to bounce in. Bad landing but I felt like kissing the ground when I got out.*

Notwithstanding his history of illness, and only being available for about half of our training in Tonopah, O'Brien had made it known when we arrived in Italy that he eventually wanted to be a first pilot and have his own crew. After having flown only a handful of missions with us and after three months, he was gone—along with his barracks bag and personal effects—without any goodbyes or so-longs to any of us that I know of. I do not recall ever seeing him after that. He finally got his way. At some point after the first of the year, he was given a makeshift crew of airmen assembled from a pool of men that, because of injuries or illness, had dropped out from their original units. After he left us, he may have lived with officers of his own crew, assuming he had overcome his illness. I did not know. The last time he flew with me, I found him to be tentative at the controls and his inexperience showed. I did not feel he was ready to be on his own. It was not his fault. He just had not had enough flight time.

Despite his sudden and unannounced exit, I cannot help but admire O'Brien. Our unfortunate personal confrontation in San Francisco, instead of dampening his spirit, may well have goaded him on, the straw that thrust him into refusing to accept the subservient role of spending the war sitting in the right-hand seat of a B-24 next to a teenage superior, whom I am sure he felt had

18. Linz was actually the third alternate target behind Brux, Pilsen, and Regensburg. Headquarters 454th Bombardment Group (H), Operations Order #366 – Battle Order, December 20, 1944, Air Force Historical Research Agency, Reel B0601 – 454 Records, 1084.

19. Faulkner and one other plane from his bomb group dropped their bombs on Linz. Confirming Mission Report, 454th Bomb Gp (H), Mission #171, December 20, 1944, Air Force Historical Research Agency, Reel B0601 – 454 Records, 1114.

betrayed him. Most men would likely have resigned to this fate for the duration. Not O'Brien. In spite of his debilitating illness, which put him physically down for long stretches, he pressed on, determined to become an airplane commander with his own crew. I do not know how many missions he flew, but the records show at least a dozen and maybe twice that many before the Germans surrendered. In effect, he received a battlefield promotion, all the result of his own dogged determination. He may well have still hated me all that time, prompting him to ask our squadron leaders to change his status. To do that would require his satisfying them of his competency. O'Brien was about the same age as our Squadron leaders and they well may have identified with his situation. Their faith in him was justified. He flew most of his missions after our crew had left, and he even earned a Distinguished Flying Cross. No other copilot that I know of set out to win a field promotion to first pilot during our time at San Giovanni. I wonder how many accomplished what O'Brien did during the war.

Since O'Brien had not been available and I was without a copilot for almost all our missions, I was logically the one selected to break in the new pilots. My copilots would continue to be newly arrived first pilots flying their first missions. I also was the pilot assigned to most of the test-hops of new or just-repaired B-24s. Usually, it would be to check out an engine, but sometimes we would have to go to 30,000 feet to make certain the radar was working. This would call for at least two radar-trained navigators to join us. I would be assigned a copilot. My crew was not normally involved in any of these test-hops, but sometimes, a few would go along for the ride.

On one test-hop, I remember sighting another B-24 and tagging onto his wing. Feeling confident, I inched closer and closer, so close that I slightly overlapped his silver wing and could have gently tapped his with my own. One of its crewmen stood at the waist window, and I could see the flat expression on his face. We were close. On a few occasions I would come almost that close on missions, but on a test-hop we were not surrounded by dozens of other planes. *Lotta Laffs*, with her stiff controls, would respond to the slightest pressure on the wheel. No movement of the steering wheel was visible here, just imperceptible pressure, but I felt by this time that the B-24 and I were practically one.

The crewman standing at the other plane's open window looked at us with concern, but I also had eye contact with his copilot and recognized that he knew all was okay. The pilot could have pulled away at any time. We flew for a while, holding the same steady position, the crews of the two planes only a few feet from each other, when the other plane very slowly banked in a turn to his left and I followed, maintaining the same tight, wing-over-wing position until he leveled off, then turned away for home. While this kind of wing overlapping in formation-flying is routine stuff for *fighter* pilots, it is not for four-engine bombers. The above exercise may sound foolish, but it was one of the high points I remember about flying in Italy.

Despite the hope provided by the holidays, December proved to be a difficult month personally for me. The war had been going well, but the Germans launched a major counterattack in Italy in the middle of the month that coincided with the Battle of the Bulge.[20] Through *Stars & Stripes*, we knew in general what was going on. While it did not threaten us directly, it was an indication that the war was not as close to being over as many had hoped. We would often think of friends who were serving in other parts of the war. Other than knowing my brother, Jim, was serving in the Pacific, I did not know exactly where he was or what dangers he faced. My high school friends were all occupied in different areas and facing enemies bent on killing them just like those German flak gunners trying to shoot down my crew and me. It was in this atmosphere that I received some horrific news about Warner Marsh through a letter from home.

Warner was in the cadet class right behind mine. I was in 44-A because I graduated in January 1944, while he was part of class 44-B, and a February graduate. He spent his first six months at airfields all located within a fifty-mile radius of Dallas, primary in Corsicana, and basic training at a field in Fort Worth.[21] I believe that his father, as a former World War I fighter pilot, had friends in the military and may have used his influence to have Warner

20. For an overview of the Battle of the Bulge, see Weinberg, *A World at Arms*, 766–71. There are numerous full-length accounts of the battle. For one of the best examples, see Peter Caddick-Adams, *Snow and Steel: The Battle of the Bulge, 1944–45* (New York: Oxford University Press, 2014).

21. The Army Air Force opened Corsicana Airfield in 1940 and it operated as a training field until 1944. See "Airport History," City of Corsicana, accessed on August 14, 2017, http://www.cityofcorsicana.com/index.aspx?NID=590.

stationed nearby. Warner would write to me about how he loved flying and was not ashamed to express his feelings about it—how exciting it was for him far above the earth among the cool, soft clouds, and what a thrill it all was to him. I cannot recall his exact words, but I had believed then in reading his descriptions that he was trying to tell me that, all alone in the air, flying was a spiritual experience for him. I loved flying, too. Although my cadet days of flying alone were over, I knew how he felt. Warner would be a great pilot. After receiving his wings, he was sent to fighter pilot transition school to fly the oversized, bulky fighter plane called the P-47 Thunderbolt. Months later, soon after D-day and the invasion of France, Warner was sent to England to join a Thunderbolt fighter squadron.

It was sometime in December when the letter from my mother came. I could not believe it. It did not seem possible. Warner Marsh was dead. The one I had thought of as my best friend since our junior high days… gone. Warner was killed while on a combat mission in his P-47 over northeast France.[22] I did not react at all walking back with Runyan from the little structure that was our post office; I read the tragic news from my mother, and then mentioned it to Runyan in an almost casual manner. I did not understand my reaction, except by then I had seen other men and friends killed. Accidents were expected and not to be brooded about. Later, Warner's death would bother me a lot, and I have had dreams many times over the years about seeing him. He was such a likeable, kind, and thoughtful person.

After the war, I dreaded calling on his parents. Everyone knew how much they adored and worshiped him. Mr. Marsh was six-foot-four and robust, with wavy, dark gray hair, a rakish mustache, and a deep, resonant voice. He was a man's man and could not have been much over fifty. But, Mr. Marsh was out of town and I never saw him. Mrs. Marsh, Anchen was her name, was heartbroken and tearful when I called on her. They had another son, Rogge, who was too young for the war, and who died in his early eighties. They loved

22. For descriptions of what happened to Marsh, see "2nd Lt. Warner H. Marsh and His P-47 Soon to be Uncovered?," *Argunners Magazine*, April 15, 2015, accessed on August 14, 2017, https://argunners.com/2nd-lt-warner-h-marsh-and-his-p-47-soon-to-be-uncovered/; and "67 Years Ago: The 362nd FG Moves Airfields," Flat Spins and Milk Runs, accessed on August 14, 2017, https://obscureco.wordpress.com/2011/11/06/67-years-ago-the-362nd-fg-moves-airfields/.

and cherished Rogge, whom they called "Butch," but it seemed to me that Warner was their heart.

Before Rogge's death, I received a letter from him telling me about his visit to a monument on the French/German border where the names of American airmen missing in action in that area were displayed. *Warner Harrison Marsh* was among those names carved in stone. I am proud to say he was my friend, the finest boy I ever knew. The world lost a truly great young man when Warner's P-47 Thunderbolt went down on the French-German border in 1944. Warner was—I hate this well-worn phrase, but there is none more apt—a very class guy. The classiest, by far, that I have ever known. He indicated that after the war, he might choose to become a doctor. I thought then, and still do, that for all the good a great physician can do, Warner would have done more good for more people by going into politics. He was not at all a glad-hander or loud or brash or the least bit a show-off, and I was not alone in recognizing, even then as one still in his teens, his magnetism, charisma, and just downright natural goodness. I have run into people who met him just once and all remember and admire him. Do not ask me to explain. I cannot.

After graduation, one of the Highland Park teachers told me—and this was *before* he joined the Air Force—that Warner was the most outstanding student ever to attend that school. It may sound foolish to speculate that anyone, particularly one so young, would be a good candidate for president of the United States, but he had every quality that would be a natural for that position. Even then, I thought he could and actually would have made it to the highest level. I would certainly have hounded him, and I am sure others would have, too. Is that any more farfetched than to have speculated then that another Highland Park standout student would be so singularly and nationally recognized—as was Doak Walker—winning the Heisman Trophy in 1948? What are the odds of *that*?

Another of Warner's good friends was our classmate, Bill Erck. Bill was in my cadet class of 44-A, but at different bases, and became a highly decorated fighter pilot. He flew over 100 missions out of Italy. Bill stayed in the Air Force reserves after the war and ultimately retired as a very young full colonel. He was able to find out that Warner died while flying in formation with a squadron mate on a mission near the northeast corner of France. While escorting a flight of A-20 twin-engine bombers, one of the two P-47s flying in close formation accidently flew into the tail of the other. The planes went down killing both pilots. No one knows exactly how the two Thunderbolt P-47's came together, but split-second acts of war are often unexpected and unforgiving. Such occurrences cast aside human traits of intellect or physical prowess and reduce combatants to a sometimes futile, but hopeful reliance on ability, training, experience, and luck. But war produces incidents so unpredictable that no amount of those qualities guarantee survival.

The other pilots in their squadron were devastated upon hearing that their two comrades had gone down in a common accident. This occurred on November 5, 1944, at the same moment I was flying *Gentleman Jim* on a mission over Vienna to drop our bombs on an oil refinery. The last letter I received from Warner had come from Paris. It sounded to me like he was having the time of his life and relishing reliving his father's World War I experience.

**Mission 24 • January 4, 1945[23]**
**Target: Marshalling Yard**
**Verona, Italy**

*What a madhouse! It was the first Pathfinder (or Mickey) radar ship I'd flown on a mission. I had three navigators plus my regular crew. Flew number 2 position in Charlie box. Had to climb above the 7,000 foot overcast in order to rendezvous over the field. Hit prop-wash on takeoff and really sweated until we had some altitude. The target was clear as a bell. We didn't need all that extra baggage after all. The navigator in the nose, Hoffman, almost got hit by flak.*[24] *We did evasive action all the way to the coast, dodging dozens of small flak areas.*[25] *A couple of miles at sea, we thought all was well; then Venice started throwing up a thick barrage that made me wish I hadn't taken off my flak suit and helmet so soon. 'Night.*

23. Forty-one B-24s and ninety-one B-17s bombed the marshalling yards in Verona; 103 P-38s provided escort cover. Mahoney, *Fifteenth Air Force Against the Axis*, 313.

24. "737th Bomb Squadron Crews – Jacob H. M. Hoffman," Aircraft and Airmen from the 454th Bombardment Group in Italy during World War II, accessed on August 11, 2017, http://www.454thbombgroup.it/737th%20Squadron%20Crews.pdf.

25. "Flak at the targets was moderate and accurate." Asch, Graff, and Ramey, *The Story of the Four Hundred and Fifty-Fifth Bombardment Group (H) WW II*, 133. See also Confirming Mission Report, 454th Bomb Gp (H), Mission #176, January 4, 1945, Air Force Historical Research Agency, Reel B0601 – 454 Records, 1181.

Flak Over Vienna, 1945 (National Archives)

The awful January weather not only hampered our missions from San Giovanni but also effected one of my friends a few hundred miles to the north. While I did not know it at the time, my newly acquired cousin-by-marriage, Bob Tetley, was fighting just to the south of the Battle of the Bulge. Bob's mother, having married my uncle, had made us step cousins and more importantly life-long friends. Soon after the wedding, Bob enlisted in the infantry. In late December 1944, he was advancing through northern France as part of the renowned 42nd Rainbow Division, under the command of General Harry Collins. Bob was involved in German Operation North Wind, one of Germany's most vicious counterattacks of the war.[26] Under heavy fire, mired in deep snow for days, Bob's unit was short of ammunition and food, and wearing inadequate clothing for the freezing weather. By the time Bob's company finally penetrated the Siegfried Line, they were exhausted and their ranks decimated. Only six of the original forty men in Bob's platoon emerged unscathed. All others were wounded, captured, or killed.

26. For a short history of Operation North Wind, see Steven J. Zaloga, *Operation Nordwind 1945: Hitler's Last Offensive in the West* (Osprey Publishing, 2010).

Bob Tetley

Bob was found near the Rhône River, lying alone in the snow, unable to move. If fellow soldiers had not discovered him and quickly secured medical aid, he would have frozen to death. Another hour, the doctor said, and he would have lost both legs. As it was, infection spread over his entire body. He spent three months recovering in a Marseilles Hospital and was sent back to the United States for further treatment. Rainbow Division commander, General Harry Collins, was from Helena and a good friend of my parents. I still have the personal letter he wrote to them from his snow-bound tent three weeks after the Battle of the Bulge.[27]

27. As an interesting side note, General Harry Collins took the time from his duties to write an interesting personal letter to Faulkner's parents from his tent on the battlefront shortly after the Battle of the Bulge. Faulkner's parents were not aware that Bob Tetley was in General Collins's Division.

Years later, Bob became highly successful in the cosmetics business, joining Estee Lauder Company when Mrs. Lauder was still in charge. Bob eventually became the number two vice-president under President and CEO Leonard Lauder.

**Mission 25 • January 15, 1945[28]**
**Target: Vienna East Station**
**Vienna, Austria**

*We flew another Mickey ship (radar - pathfinder). It's a comforting feeling to have three navigators (Benson for Mickey, Hutcheson for D.R., and Hoffman for Nose).[29] Nelson, our regular navigator, would not fly with us this mission. Tolson was my copilot.[30] He had been grounded for two months for pilot fatigue as a result of a Yugoslavia bail-out and a couple of minor accidents. He took the mission swell as far as I could see. One of the Schindler brothers, the box lead, was hard as hell to follow.[31] Vienna was overcast and on the bomb run I could see quite a lot of puffs below us, though nothing like the previous raids. Bombs away! Then quite a lot of evasive action to avoid the flak.[32] Twenty minutes after target, number 3 engine oil pressure dropped to 40 lbs. I hit the feathering button and she ran away to 3300 rpm! A high-pitched scream that scared hell out of all of us, but she finally stopped after cutting all switches. On three engines, we couldn't keep up with the formation, but could keep them in sight. Alone, we sweated out enemy fighters, but couldn't contact our fighters for protection. Rest of trip, O.K.*

January proved a very challenging month because of the weather, and that is saying a lot considering the issues with weather we had experienced previously. I learned later that the winter of the Battle of the Bulge was one of the worst in European history—and so it was with us. My squadron only flew six missions the entire month,

28. Faulkner's plane joined 235 B-24s and 153 B-17s on the mission to Vienna. They were escorted by eighty-two P-38s and 188 P-51s. Mahoney, *Fifteenth Air Force Against the Axis*, 315–16.

29. Besides Hoffman, who had flown on Faulkner's January 4 mission, the other navigators were Clifford L. Benson and Robert W. Hutcheson, see "737th Bomb Squadron," Aircraft and Airmen from the 454th Bombardment Group in Italy during World War II, accessed on August 11, 2017, http://www.454thbombgroup.it/737th%20Squadron%20Crews.pdf.

30. "737th Bomb Squadron Crews – Patrick H. Tolson," Aircraft and Airmen from the 454th Bombardment Group in Italy during World War II, accessed on August 11, 2017, http://www.454thbombgroup.it/737th%20Squadron%20Crews.pdf.

31. The Schindler brothers are discussed in Chapter 3. Faulkner flew in Charlie Box, position 2. Headquarters 454th Bombardment Group (H), Operations Order #15 – Battle Order, January 15, 1945, Air Force Historical Research Agency, Reel B0601 – 454 Records, 1188.

32. "Flak at target was intense and accurate," Asch, Graff, and Ramey, *The Story of the Four Hundred and Fifty-Fifth Bombardment Group (H) WW II*, 134.

and I participated in just two of them.[33] The Pathfinder radar my plane carried on the two missions I flew that month did make it easier to reach targets even if there was overcast, but it was far from foolproof. It did not in inclement weather help with take-offs or landings and was useless when trying to fly in formation in heavy cloud cover. It did help with navigating to the target and to a degree with hitting it. The radar was able to detect cities, but could not pinpoint specific targets within a city; therefore, when we used it, our bombing lacked the precision that we normally tried to achieve on our missions.[34]

**Mission 26 • February 1, 1945[35]**
**Target: Graz Marshalling Yard**
**Graz, Austria**

*We had to bring back our bombs today even though we flew over our first, then the second alternates.[36] Lots of weather. I got vertigo once very bad. I love formation flying, but not in an overcast. Because of the effort, we get credit for the mission.*

Sometimes we would sit inside the plane for up to two or three hours, waiting until the tower would signal with flares that the mission was a stand-down, or scrubbed. The reaction would vary usually depending upon the announced target. It would be a disappointment if the target was perceived as a milk-run; but cancellation of a flight over Munich or Vienna would be greeted with less regret. Vienna and Munich were heavily defended by flak guns. Because of their size and importance, our bomb runs over these cities lasted the longest. I never timed it, but I believe those two, and a few other targets, took about eight minutes, although it seemed even longer. On more than one occasion, the entire group took off, rendezvoused above the field, and headed out over the Adriatic for Germany, only to be turned back because of weather.

33. "The month of January, operationally, was the least active which the Group has had in its twelve months of combat. Although twenty-six missions were briefed, only six were actually flown. Weather was the fly in the ointment." Headquarters 454th Bombardment Group – Heavy – For the Month of January, n.d., Air Force Historical Research Agency, Reel B0601 – 454 Records, 1148.

34. For an overview of the effectiveness of Pathfinder-assisted bombings, see Mahoney, *Fifteenth Air Force Against the Axis*, 414–16. Stephen Ambrose argues that "dropping bombs by radar instead of visually meant few of them hit what they wanted them to hit and the damage was minimal." Ambrose, *The Wild Blue*, 165.

35. Mahoney, *Fifteenth Air Force Against the Axis*, 323.

36. The PFF radar on both the Lead and Deputy Lead planes failed and the alternative target was cloud-covered. Confirming Mission Report, 454th Bomb Gp (H), Mission #183, February 1, 1945, Air Force Historical Research Agency, Reel B0601 – 454 Records, 1249.

I loved flying in formation, but the biggest problem and the one creating the tensest moments of all, at least for me, was flying in formation through an overcast. With visibility barely beyond the wingtips, the other planes would suddenly disappear when climbing through a thick, heavy cloud cover. I would simply hold the exact heading, continue ascending, and hope to avoid colliding with another plane. It was not fun. The term "flying blind" took on new significance when there were thirty or forty planes in very close proximity, and none of the pilots were able to see the other planes.

There was also always the fear of icing. Freezing rain or moisture inside winter clouds can cause a rapid build-up of ice on the leading edge of wings and the tail. The sheer weight of the ice and distortion of the wings could be disastrous for the entire group. Some pilots, like Conrad Leslie, experienced severe carburetor icing, but I did not have this problem on the missions I flew.

On days that I did not fly in the scheduled missions, I often flew practice flights or tested newly arrived planes. I took one of these test flights on February 3, 1945. Just a few days prior, a brand-new B-24 equipped with a new radar arrived and was designated for the exclusive use of Colonel Aynesworth, our Group Commander. I was assigned the task of taking it up with Lieutenant Harman, a PPF radar specialist, who had been my radar navigator on a couple of other missions when I had been assigned a mickey (PPF) ship. Harman was to check out the highly technical, special equipment on the new plane at high altitude. By this time our crew had flown over twenty-five missions, but because of bad weather and a few mechanical mishaps, we had flown only a handful of missions since mid-November. To relieve the monotony of being cooped up all day in their tent, three enlisted men from my crew and a couple of their friends decided to go along for the ride. We ducked into the bomb bay and climbed inside. Having just come from the factory, it smelled like a new automobile. From 33,000 feet, we completed the radar check. I remember looking out over miles of beautiful rolling Italian countryside. A Mustang P-51 suddenly made a mock pass at us and so I put the new plane in a steep bank and feigned chasing him. We had a brief "dog-fight" in and out of the scattered white clouds, and I finally nosed down and headed for the field.

I wanted to make an especially good landing in case the colonel or any of his staff were watching. By now, my landings were almost

B-24 Flown by Tom that Crashed on Landing Due to Mechanical Issues

always reasonably smooth, but this time, the plane pulled to the right as it settled to the runway. I applied full left rudder, but the plane still pulled right. Our gravel runways were narrow and had deep drainage ditches on both sides. I pushed the throttle for power on number four engine and then number three to what seemed like full throttle to offset the strange, dogged pull to the right—without response. Suddenly we were angling through the drainage ditch, snapping off the nose-wheel. The nose dropped and we were skidding rapidly through the mud. It all happened in a matter of seconds. Tail up, the shiny, silver plane plowed along the muddy field, finally stopping, with our entire cockpit section collapsed, rolled over and twisted back parallel to the wing. The propellers were bent back and the engines had dug into the mud, leaving the rear half of the plane and its twin tails sticking up at a 45-degree angle. The entire nose section, including the cockpit, had rolled over on its left side to the ground, like a wounded elephant, the glass cockpit canopy, shattered.

Although the B-24 cockpit sits high above ground, while strapped in my seat, my left shoulder had scraped the ground and my flight suit was caked with mud. Even worse, my legs were pinned in the jumbled mass of rudders and controls. Fire crews quickly jumped

Close-up of B-24 Cockpit Section from Which Tom Had to be Cut Out

up on the wings, showering the engines with white foam, while an emergency crew worked to remove my steering wheel, which was pinning my leg against the cockpit wall. When they finally pulled me out to the ground, my left thigh was in pain and already swelling. After they hauled me away, the medics had to rip up the leg of my heated suit to pull it off. The enlisted men in the rear were shaken, but no one else was hurt. The injury was eerily identical to the high school football injury of my left thigh that sidelined me for two weeks towards the end of the season my senior year. One of my crew-members brought me the steering wheel. It is the only memento I salvaged from the war, and I gave it to my grandson, Matthew Faulkner, on his 16th birthday.

I had no idea what had happened and felt terrible about destroying the colonel's new airplane. I was relieved, however, to learn that ground crewmen of the 455th Bomb Group across the field had seen and heard the hissing tire deflate as they watched the landing. The air intake stem on the right tire had snapped off on impact due to faulty tire alignment with the tire's steel rim.[37]

37. For a listing of Faulkner's accident, see February 1945 USAAF Overseas Accident Reports, Aviation Archaeological Investigation and Research, accessed on August 14, 2017, http://www.aviationarchaeology.com/src/AARmonthly/Feb1945O.htm.

A B-24 Goes Down in Flames During Mission Over Germany, 1944 (Tom was in Hospital with Photographer of This Well-Publicized Picture) (National Archives)

I spent two weeks recovering in the Cerignola hospital surrounded by other injured airmen. On one side of my bed was a radio-operator from another squadron in our bomb group. He was the only survivor of a crash in the Adriatic. His pilot had been buzzing an Italian fisherman's sailboat, trying to blow it over with the prop-wash of his four engines. The B-24 wingtip dipped into the sea as he banked, ripping the plane apart. All on board were killed except this radio-operator who was thrown out and saved by the fisherman. The pilot of his ship, I would later learn, was Lt. McComas, who had flown as my copilot on my sixth mission, which was his first orientation mission.

On the other side of my hospital bed was a prize-winning Air Force photographer who had flown on several missions. He had been awarded a citation for a now-famous picture he had taken. I have seen it several times over the years since the war. The photograph shows a B-24 receiving a direct hit over its target, its right wing peeled back in flames against the fuselage as fire engulfs the ship.

On my return to the base from the hospital, two officers from the colonel's staff visited me in my tent to finalize their accident report.

Mortally Damaged B-24 After Attack on Vienna, 1944 (National Archives)

Flak Damage to Wing of B-24, 1945 (National Archives)

The B-24 reacts just like an automobile with a blowout at high speed. In flight, if we knew a tire was damaged, we could tie the cords of a parachute to the machine gun mounts on the opposite side and toss it out as the wheels touched down to balance the drag and prevent a crash. My friend, Kenneth Higgins, and his crew had done this in mid-December after flak damaged their plane on a mission and both sets of brakes were inoperative. The crew tied the parachutes to the inside of the plane and then threw them out from both waist gun windows as they landed. The billowing parachutes helped slow their plane, although they still ran off the end of the runway and crashed in a ditch.[38]

**Mission 27 • February 24, 1945[39]**
**Target: Marshalling Yard**
**Mestre, Italy**

*Mission was uneventful and ineffective as we had to bring back our bombs due to complete cloud cover. We were flying number 2 position and had to take over the lead as the squadron leader was forced to drop out and return after an hour or so.[40] This was my first mission since my crash landing in which my left leg was injured. I was in the hospital for two weeks.*

While I was in the hospital, the Fifteenth Air Force was very active. The 454th flew twenty-one missions in the month, including missions every day from February 13 to 25.[41] If I had not been in the hospital, I know I would have been assigned to several of them, and my mission total would have probably grown to over thirty. This would have left me much closer to the magic number of thirty-five that would have signaled the completion of my tour. However, that was not the case, and I knew, based on the number of missions I had flown since November, it might now take several more months for us to reach the end of our tour and return home.

38. See Ambrose, *The Wild Blue*, 243–4.

39. See Mahoney, *Fifteenth Air Force Against the Axis*, 341.

40. The mission commander's plane was the only one that had to return to base early. The overcast was complete over both the primary and alternate targets. Confirming Mission Report, 454th Bomb Gp (H), Mission #200, February 24, 1945, Air Force Historical Research Agency, Reel B0601 – 454 Records, 1306.

41. See Headquarters 454th Bombardment Group – Heavy – For the Month of February, n.d., Air Force Historical Research Agency, Reel B0601 – 454 Records, 1212. General Ira Eaker was so excited about the consecutive days of missions that he sent a telegraph to General Hap Arnold highlighting the Fifteenth Air Force's efforts. On February 23, he wrote, "Fifteenth Air Force is operational today for an eleventh successive large scale effort." He added that his air force put 1,150 bombers in the air for the previous day's missions. AOWAR for Arnold for Giles from Eaker, February 23, 1945, LOC, Eaker Papers, Box I:25, Folder – Giles, Barney, Vol. III, Dec. 1941-March 1945, 1.

# Chapter 6

# Mission to Augsburg and Internment

**Mission 28 • February 27, 1945[1]**
**Target: Rail Yard**
**Augsburg, Germany**

Throughout my time at San Giovanni, I kept a mission diary. On those nights after each mission, I would take a few minutes to write down my thoughts on that day's flight. The only exception was this twenty-eighth mission. When going to bed on nights *before* missions, I would often wonder if I would be sleeping in that same bed the *next* night and be there to record the mission. As it turned out, after the twenty-eighth mission, I would not.

On the morning of that cold February day, we got off to a bad start and, as time passed, things got progressively worse. Just before taxiing out for takeoff, our navigator, Arnie Nelson, was pulled from our ship to fly in the lead plane with the squadron commander.[2] Howard Runyan, our bombardier, now also had to perform as our

1. There were 160 B-17s and 272 B-24s involved in the attack on Augsburg. They were escorted by seventy-seven P-38s and seventy-eight P-51s. Mahoney, *Fifteenth Air Force Against the Axis*, 343–4.

2. Faulkner does not know why his navigator was switched. He assumes the squadron commander's navigator must have been ill. Since Arnie was one of the most experienced navigators in the squadron, it made sense for the squadron commander to want to use him.

navigator, should the need arise. It did. And after it was all over, we would realize that the absence of our navigator was critical, and that Runyan's navigation skills had completely deserted him.[3]

The day was bright and clear as we circled above San Giovanni Airfield and rendezvoused with our squadron at 3,000 feet as usual. *Lotta Laffs* was not available, so we were assigned a silver J-model with no name, but numbered 458. When our seven-plane squadron was all in place over the field, we headed for Cerignola, climbing to 5,000 feet. Lieutenant Colonel William Large was the deputy commander of our 454th Bomb Group, and he flew in the lead ship of Able box, the lead squadron of our four-squadron group.[4] Colonel Large was in charge of the investigation following my crash landing of Colonel Aynesworth's new B-24 and completely absolved me of any pilot error.

Able box was circling and waiting for us. Our squadron, Baker box, would fly on their right and slightly above them. Several minutes later, Charley box came in and flanked them on their left and slightly below them. Dog box followed, forming up directly behind and below Able box, bringing all four squadrons of the 454th Bomb Group in place before heading for the Adriatic to take our place entrain with the other groups.

Since we were Baker squadron and I was flying the number five position, our plane's identity and call sign was Baker Five. We rarely had occasion to communicate on the radio between planes, but today would become far from an ordinary day.

The four squadrons of our diamond shaped 454th Bomb Group was now headed northwest over the Adriatic.[5] I asked the crew to test all guns, a routine exercise. The rattle of the fifty caliber guns could be heard over the loud drone of the four engines, especially from the twin fifties of Will Gorman's top turret, located right above and behind us. There had rarely been any problem before, but this day, Willie Horvath reported that his nose turret was inoperable. This was followed by Jim Hamilton's stating that his .50 caliber waist guns were jammed. So two of our six machine-gun stations

3. Runyan never talked to Faulkner about what happened. It was just one of those strange situations in World War II where Runyan was thrust into a very difficult position for which he was not adequately prepared.

4. For William Large's account of his time in the 454th, see *454th Memories* (Dallas, TX: Taylor Publishing Company, 1991), 17–18.

5. Twenty-eight planes from the 454th bomb squadron left San Giovanni on Mission 202. See Mission Report, 454th Bomb Gp (H), Mission 202, February 27, 1945, Air Force Historical Research Agency, Reel B0601 – 454 Records, 1282.

B-24 Over Alps, 1945 (National Archives)

were not working. Horvath and Hamilton would now be just going along for the ride. We did not consider this a huge problem either since no German fighters had attacked us on previous missions, and our own P-38s and P-51s would meet us over Germany and fly an "S" pattern above us as we climbed to the target.[6]

The next problem was more serious. As we moved up the Adriatic approaching the Alps, the turbo-supercharger on the number two engine suddenly went dead. Superchargers are not essential except at high altitude where they transform an engine struggling and gulping for oxygen into one that operates normally by ramming the engine's exhaust down through the canted flanges of a round, foot-wide, flat disc mounted on the bottom of the engine. The disc rotates at enormous speed, compressing the thin oxygen levels at high altitude into a chamber, so that normal combustion

6. To compensate for the differences in cruising speed between fighter planes and bombers, the P-38s and P-51s "constantly weaved around the bombers to reduce their speed so they could stay with them." Mahoney, *Fifteenth Air Force Against the Axis*, 418. Former fighter pilot Norman Fortier described how his squadron would follow a weaving flight path where they flew a "follow-the-leader pattern that kept the bombers in view and closed off potential avenues of attack." Norman "Bud" Fortier, *An Ace of the Eighth: An American Fighter Pilot's Air War in Europe* (Presidio Press, 2007), 86.

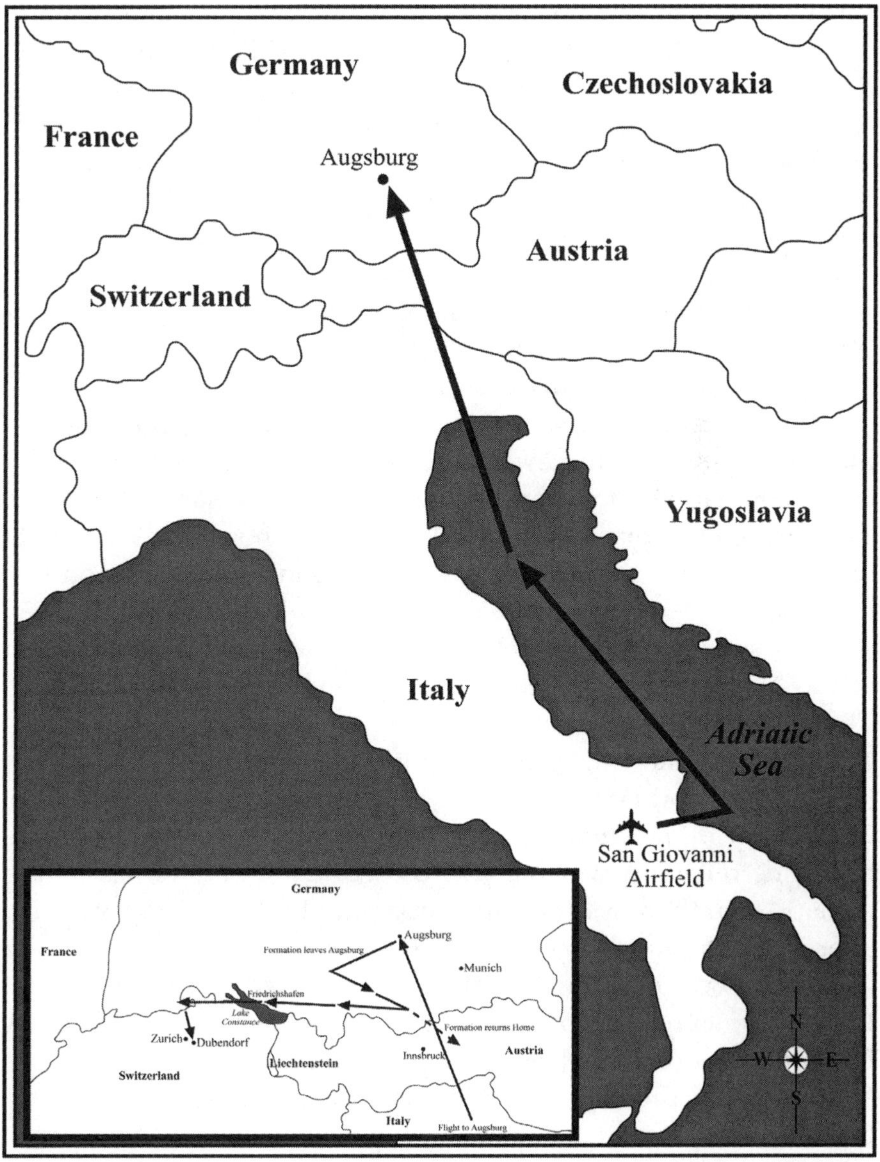


Tom's last mission

occurs in the engine cylinders. Without the supercharger, an engine at high altitude is dead weight, a liability, and virtually useless. Although there is enough combustion to turn the propellers, the engine is unable to produce any thrust; therefore, still far from the target, we would be climbing to our bombing altitude of over 23,000 feet on just three engines, with no navigator, and with two of our six gun-stations out.[7] We had flown many times on just three engines, but always with the squadron nosed down for a gradual descent on the way home. But now, still a good distance from the target and still having to climb, we were taxing the three good engines and subjecting them to overheating because of the extra power required to keep up with the formation. However, since we had flown with only three engines before, I had no real concern—not yet.

Also, this was our copilot's first mission. He was a young Pennsylvanian named William Knauer who had only recently arrived at San Giovanni with his crew. This was his first "orientation" mission.[8] Again, this was no real problem. Having been assigned the task of breaking in new pilots, I had not flown with an experienced combat pilot for months. I never had the luxury of a regular, experienced copilot, as had all other crews, whose opinions would have been useful and his presence comforting—especially on this mission.

Only scattered clouds below impeded our view. Looking down at the Alps was always exciting. This time they looked different. There was always snow at the tops, but on this day, the glistening bright snow looked like soft, luscious whipped cream rounding the jagged edges and flowing to the deepest valleys. We were nearing 20,000 feet by now and had just left the blue Adriatic. The sun's brilliance reflected over the entire earth and once we passed the Adriatic Sea, there was nothing but a pure bright, white landscape ahead, blanketing everything below. As we moved beyond the Alps and toward the target, wisps of clouds covered the ground. It was 50 degrees below zero inside our plane and well below freezing at ground level.

The target, the Augsburg railroad center, would not be fun for two reasons. First, it had a high number of flak guns because of the German infantry retrenching on the ground.[9] As they retreated

7. Mission Report, 454th Bomb Gp (H), Mission 202, February 27, 1945, Air Force Historical Research Agency, Reel B0601 – 454 Records, 1282.

8. Knauer was a second lieutenant from Reading, PA. He was twenty-two-years old at the time of the mission. Escape Statement, March 12, 1945, Air Force Historical Research Agency, Reel B0601 – 454 Records, 1655.

9. By the end of the war, Germany devoted well over 1.1 million men and women to anti-aircraft defenses. If these forces could have been used against advancing allied armies, the attacks would have been even more costly. This was an important side effect of the strategic bombing campaign. Tillman, *Forgotten Fifteenth*, 192.

B-24 Falling from Formation After Being Hit by Flak Over Munich, 1944 (National Archives)

from France, they brought their 88mm and 128mm guns with them, and concentrated these additional guns around Augsburg.[10] And second, Augsburg was beyond Munich, and our missions to Munich stretched the limits of our B-24's fuel capacity. Now, with our plane using fuel in greater amounts to compensate for the supercharger loss, there was more than the usual concern.

Over the target, the flak on the bomb run was the worst we had ever experienced. Large, black clouds burst all around us, closer than ever before. The Germans had pinpointed our altitude at 23,500 feet. The plane even shook, and we could hear the explosions over the engines' roar. I remember thinking it sounded as if someone was on top, pounding the ship over and over with a baseball bat.

As we reached the target, our bombardier, Runyan announced, "Bombs away," over the intercom. Our plane lurched as it always did at the sudden release of our three-ton load. We were carrying six 1,000-pound high explosive bombs, and we could see the rest of our squadron releasing their bombs at the same time.[11]

Suddenly, during our banking and turn from the target, our number three engine lost all power after being hit by flak.[12] Copilot Knauer, whom I had just met that morning, quickly reached up above the windshield and pushed the red feathering-button, but instead of the number three propeller blades stopping and knifing steady into the wind to eliminate drag as they were designed to do, the propeller just wind-milled.[13] As we turned from the target,

10. The 88mm was the most common anti-aircraft gun in the German arsenal. However, since its maximum ceiling was around 20,000 feet, the Germans added both 105 and 128mm guns. B-24s typically dropped their ordnance between 22,000 and 26,000 feet. See McFarland and Newton, *To Command the Sky*, 52. For a great overview of German anti-aircraft guns, see Terry Gander and Peter Chamberlain, *Weapons of the Third Reich: An Encyclopedic Survey of All Small Arms, Artillery and Special Weapons of the German Land Forces 1939–1945* (Garden City, NY: Doubleday and Company, 1979), 147–58. The two types of guns Faulkner references were probably the 8.8 cm Flugabwehrkanone 41 and the 12.8 cm Flugabwehrkanone Zwilling 40. See ibid., 155–7. The 12.8 cm Flugabwehrkanone Zwilling was the most effective anti-aircraft gun, but the Germans were never able to manufacture it in large numbers. In early 1945, it made up only five percent of the total flak guns in Germany. See Westermann, *Flak*, 293.

11. For the bomb load of Faulkner's squadron, see Mission Report, 454th Bomb Gp (H), Mission 202, February 27, 1945, Air Force Historical Research Agency, Reel B0601 – 454 Records, 1282.

12. Flak damage for bombers was quite common. The Fifteenth Air Force lost 1,046 heavy bombers to flak, including Faulkner's plane, during its roughly eighteen-month existence. Another almost 12,000 were damaged by flak. Westermann, *Flak*, 286–7.

13. Pilots would feather propellers "so that they turn edgeways on to the airflow when an engine needs to be shut down." This would reduce the overall drag of the non-working propellers. See Douglas, *Consolidated B-24 Liberator Owners' Workshop Manual*, 97.

we dropped like a rock and slid below and behind our formation. I had never had any experience even close to this. I applied more power to number one and number four, now our only two good engines. To keep from stalling, I had to push the nose down at what felt like a steep, 45-degree angle.[14] The bomb bay doors were still open, and they refused to close, and we could hear the freezing wind rushing inside.

Our engineer, Will Gorman, came quickly down from his top turret gun position. We all knew that number-three engine contained the fluid tank that supplied the hydraulic system. The hydraulic pump and fluid tank were located inside the number three engine housing and depended on that engine to perform all its functions. It operated the propeller feathering mechanisms of all four engines, the bomb bay doors, and the landing gear. With number three dead, Will had to close the bomb bay doors manually. There was no remedy for the wind-milling propeller. Still falling fast, the formation was far above us, pulling steadily away. The wind-milling number three propeller began to run away, and it screamed like a banshee just outside the copilot's window.

We were falling at over 500 feet per minute. The two good engines, with their throttles pushed far above cruising power, were in danger of overheating and could not last long at that setting. At our rate of descent, we could not make it back to the Alps, much less over them. The Alps' highest peaks were over 11,000 feet.[15] If we could make it over the Alps, we had a chance to reach Ancona, the location of an emergency airfield on the Adriatic, beyond Venice and half way down the Italian coast.[16] Finally, it became obvious that we had no chance of reaching friendly territory in Italy. We watched the formation steadily leaving us, high above and now far in the distance. Although I did not know exactly where we were, I knew we were still far from the Alps. The crew was well aware of our plight as they could see our

14. The stalling speed of a B-24 is ninety-five mph. If a plane stalls, the pilot loses all ability to control it, and the plane will go into a free fall or spin.

15. For an overview of the Alps, see National Geographic Society, *The Alps* (National Geographic Society, 1973).

16. Ancona was a city on the east coast of Italy about 140 miles south of Venice and 240 miles north of San Giovanni. Allied forces liberated Ancona in July 1944 and used several airfields in the area until the end of the war. See Ehlers, *The Mediterranean Air War*, 345; and Maurer Maurer, *Combat Squadrons of the Air Force, World War II* (Washington, D.C.: Government Printing Office, 1982), 28.

precipitous and rapid descent. I made the decision, banked the plane, turned to a southwesterly heading, and then announced to the crew that we were going to Switzerland.

We had flown twenty-eight missions and spending the last weeks of the war sitting on the sidelines in some Swiss prison camp was the very last thing any of us would want. But I did not see any other option. We could end up as German prisoners of war if we reached the Alps at an altitude so low as to deprive us of passage. Or worse, if we attempted to go through the Alps while still pushing already sorely taxed engines—we would likely not have survived at all. Without minimizing the impossible challenges faced by other airmen flying their crippled ships over the vast reaches of the hostile African desert or the deep oceans of the world, they would at least have some hope of survival. But parachuting into the deep, snow-covered and uninhabited frozen Alps could result only in a certain freezing death, as many of our Fifteenth Air Force airmen had experienced. I recognized the absolute duty of returning with my plane and my crew from every mission, but the hope of reaching the Alps and attempting to fly over or through them ceased to be a reasonable possibility.

Ultimately after our turning from the formation, the runaway number-three propeller jolted to an abrupt stop, and the annoying

Postcard of the Palace Hotel in Adelboden, Switzerland Where Tom Was Interned

siren scream also ceased. Un-feathered, its wide blades were frozen flat against the wind, adding even more drag than before. We were dropping to heavier air and more normal oxygen levels, but not quite at the same precipitous rate because the lower we dropped, the more effective number two engine became as it no longer had to rely on its dead supercharger. We had a new option. I realized we could make it to France. It was not far, and the Allies had recaptured all of it at that time.[17]

Almost immediately after the turn from the formation, I headed 270 degrees, due west, and announced to the crew over the intercom, *"We're going to France. We can look for an airfield there or bail out if we have to."* And I added, over the open mike, addressing the bombardier, *"Runyan, keep us fifty miles north of Switzerland in case of more engine trouble."*

My assumption that we were at least fifty miles north of Switzerland was woefully wrong. We were not. I had assumed that Runyan, stationed in the glassed-in nose and now acting as our navigator—and trained for just this situation—knew where we were and would be following my instructions. He never indicated he was unable to pinpoint our position. This was critical. Had Runyan admitted there was any question about our location, the copilot and I would have gotten involved and at least been aware of the additional problem. Had my normal navigator Arnold Nelson not been taken from us just before takeoff to fly in the lead ship, none of this would have been an issue. Nelson always knew our exact position in flight at all times.

I should never have expected Runyan to possess Nelson's capabilities. I should have known he was in over his head, that his silence throughout the entire ordeal was an indication we were not on the same page, especially in this highly stressful situation which he faced. Runyan had no clue at all as to where in the world—nor tragically, where in Germany—we were.

As we left the target, nose down, falling, I do recall Runyan's voice sounding high and excited. But later, I would learn that during the flight from the target to the point where we turned for Switzerland, we had actually flown almost to Innsbruck, Austria which is *east* of Switzerland. We were not 50 miles north,

17. By January 1945, allied forces had recaptured almost all of France, including Alsace-Lorraine. See Weinberg, *A World At Arms*, 810.

as I incorrectly assumed. Our due west course would skip us in and out of Switzerland's jagged northern boundary with Germany.

Our P-51s and P-38s had so dominated German fighters over the recent months that they were now rarely able to mount an attack against our formations. Still, I was concerned that, isolated and alone, we were easy prey, and they could come up and pick off a crippled American bomber, especially one with two of its six machine-gun stations unable to fire back.[18] At our briefing that morning, we were advised of the possibility of the Germans sending up their new ME 262 jet fighter.[19]

It was clear now why we had fallen so rapidly. With no supercharger on number-two engine, that engine was useless at 23,500 feet. Further, when flak knocked out the number three engine, we were flying with just two good engines in the thin air of 23,500 feet. Even after we left the formation, now far away, we were still falling. In addition, on landing, we found a three-foot gash in the leading edge of the right wing, which, with the frozen propeller of number three engine, had created significant drag. Number two engine, which would gradually come back to life as we dropped to lower altitudes, was smoking, later discovered impaired, and low on oil.

Alone and having dropped to 8,000 feet, I pulled back slightly on the throttles, still dropping, but at a lower rate of descent. The dead supercharger on number two no longer was a limiting factor, and, though number three's frozen propeller still created drag, at this lower altitude, we now had three good engines, raising the question: Could we have made it back over the Alps? That question haunted me for almost seventy years after the war.

I was now holding level at 6,000 feet—heading west for France, still thinking we were well north of Switzerland. Suddenly a large burst of flak exploded off our nose, directly in front! I banked the plane over on its side and looked down to see we were over the center of a large German city. How could Runyan have let this happen? B-24 pilots cannot see the ground ahead, only a fringe of distant horizon, but the bombardier's glass-bottom nose allows him to see everything. What was he doing? I took evasive action as the

18. See Makos, *A Higher Call*, 299–310.

19. Headquarters, 455th Bombardment Group, Field Order No. 206, February 27, 1945, in author's possession.

Germans fired at least a hundred rounds at us and continued due west for France. I later learned that we had flown directly over Friedrichshafen, a large German city across a large lake from Switzerland.[20] We continued west for a good while without incident, certain we were over Germany and that France was not all that far ahead, unaware we were still skirting the northern irregular edges of the German/Swiss border.[21]

About fifteen minutes later, my radio operator Jim Hamilton, now manning the impaired left waist guns, said over the intercom, "Fighters coming up from seven o'clock." I remember it well, and said, "Okay, everybody, get ready." I held the western course, certain we were not too far from France and safety, still thinking we were far north of Switzerland. All of us assumed we had a fight on our hands. Minutes later, waiting for the fighters to start attacking, someone said, "Lieutenant, they're not German. They're *Swiss* fighters."

The Swiss lead ship came up on my left wing. Coming in close, he looked at me and pointed down with his thumb. I kept flying. He dropped away and the fighters took turns making passes at us without firing, letting us know they would shoot us down. The leader returned to my wing and pointed down again. I stalled as long as I felt I could and finally asked Gorman, the engineer, to roll down the landing gear manually, a signal of surrender, but I kept flying west, hoping we could reach the French border. The Swiss pilot motioned for me to follow him once again, and I finally gave up.

He led us south to Zurich's Dübendorf Airfield. He buzzed the runway on which we were to land. On the approach, there seemed to be a high building at the end of the short runway. I came in way too high, saw the end of the runway looming ahead, pulled back on the steering wheel to stall out at twenty feet above ground and made the worst landing of my life. Crashing down to the concrete runway, I was certain the wheel struts would come through the wings. We followed a jeep-like vehicle to the parking area.[22]

20. Faulkner's crew had flown close to Lake Constance.

21. Faulkner had flown approximately 120 miles by the time he reached Friedrichshafen and had roughly another 100 miles to reach the French border.

22. Upon landing, Faulkner and crew joined the over 1,700 American airmen who reached Switzerland and became internees. Stephen Tanner, *Refuge from the Reich: American Airmen and Switzerland During World War II* (Rockville Centre, NY: Sarpedon, 2000), 2.

There were dozens, maybe more than a hundred B-24s and B-17s lined up two deep, wing-tip to wing-tip, all repaired and in apparent good condition.[23] On that one day, eight four-engine bombers (six B-24s and two B-17s), along with their eighty crewmen, crossed over the Swiss border and became interns.[24] I am sure all of them were hit and brought down by the accurate anti-aircraft guns of Augsburg. I saw three B-24s land after me at Dübendorf.[25] One appeared to have no damage. All four engines were running smoothly as it taxied in to park. I talked to the pilot, Donald Fortheringham. He was short, red-headed. This was his first mission with his crew. His engineer advised him that the fuel gauge indicated they had lost almost all their fuel. I never heard of a fuel gauge malfunctioning; so, he did have a problem. Still, a thousand gallons of aviation fuel does not just suddenly disappear unnoticed. But ignoring the gauge might have resulted in his crew's having to bail out in uninhabited, snow-covered mountains.[26]

We four American B-24 pilots were informally interviewed together by two Swiss uniformed interrogators in a small hotel room at the airport.[27] They were friendly, offered us a hot beverage,

23. According to the Hague Convention of 1907, "A neutral Power which receives on its territory troops belonging to the belligerent armies shall intern them, as far as possible, at a distance from the theatre of war." Convention (V) respecting the Rights and Duties of Neutral Powers and Persons in Case of War on Land, The Hague, 18 October 1907, International Committee of the Red Cross, accessed on May 18, 2017, https://ihl-databases.icrc.org/applic/ihl/ihl.nsf/Article.xsp?action=openDocument&documentId=3C5ACCA7CF58497CC12563CD00516A15. For an overview of Switzerland's internship policies during World War II, see Controversial Refugee Policy, Swiss Federal Archive, accessed on May 18, 2017, https://www.bar.admin.ch/bar/en/home/research/searching/topics/die-schweiz-im-zweiten-weltkrieg/umstrittene-fluechtlingspolitik-im-zweiten-weltkrieg.html.

24. For a list of the American planes that landed in Switzerland or were shot down by the Swiss Air Force, see "Aircraft Listing by Order of Arrival in Switzerland," Swiss Internees Association, accessed on May 16, 2017, http://swissinternees.tripod.com/aircraft.html. Six of the planes that Faulkner notes landed in Switzerland, while two others were shot down by the Swiss Air Force.

25. Dubendorf was a large airfield near Zurich. See Dubendorf Airfield, American Air Museum in Great Britain, Imperial War Museums, accessed on January 20, 2017, http://www.americanairmuseum.com/place/168639.

26. 1st Lt. Donald Fotheringham was flying a brand new B-24 when it was hit, and he was forced to land at Dubendorf. The Swiss found only twenty-four gallons of gas in the fuel tank. Hans-Heiri Stapfer and Gino Kunzle, *Strangers in a Strange Land; Vol. II: Escape to Neutrality* (Carrollton, TX: Squadron/Signal Publications, 1992), 69. See also Roy Thomas, *Haven, Heaven, and Hell - Part 1: The United States Army Air Force Aircraft and Airmen Interned in Switzerland During WWII* (Monroe, WI: Puka Press, 1991), 78.

27. It is unclear who the other two pilots were besides Faulkner and Fotheringham. Four other B-24s landed on February 27. Their pilots were 1st Lt. Ray Grooms, 1st Lt. Joseph Clayton, 2nd Lt. Jess Foster, and 1st Lt. Douglas Lambert. See Thomas, *Haven, Heaven, and Hell*, 77–9.

Tom's Crew in Naples after Internment in Switzerland, 1945—Bottom (left to right)—Archie Rosencutter, Jim Hamilton, Willie Horvath, Tony Barone, and Talmidge "Jonesie" Jones; Top (left to right)—William Knauer, Howard Runyan, Tom, Will Gorman

and expressed interest in our latest radar equipment. The war would be over soon, and they indicated serious concern that the Russians, whose troops were approaching German borders, would keep on marching and take over Switzerland.[28]

The next day, with white snow covering everything, the Swiss took us by train to Frutegan, and from there by bus up a winding road to a beautiful luxury hotel and ski resort in the mountains. I would spend my twentieth birthday, March 3, 1945, here, at The Palace Hotel, in Adelboden, Switzerland.[29]

28. In 1945, the European war was coming to a close with Allied forces converging on Germany from the east and west. Further, the Allied strategic bombing campaign continued relentlessly from the skies. See Glantz and House, *When Titans Clashed*, 302–324; and Weinberg, *A World at Arms*, 780–818.

29. Adelboden was a small village of several hundred people during World War II. Because of its relative isolation, it was an ideal location for internees. The Nevada Palace Hotel catered to skiers and tourists. For a description of the village and hotel, see Mrazek, *To Kingdom Come*, 270–1.

At least fifty or sixty other American airmen were kept there. From a spacious glassed-in dining room in back, we could look out and see some of them skiing down the slopes toward us. At the next table, one airman was on crutches, wearing a leg cast, his leg broken while skiing. On a trip to Switzerland many years later, Ann and I would learn that the Palace Hotel had burned down a few years after the war.

I talked at length to a B-17 pilot from the Eighth Air Force in England. He said we would never have made it to France and were lucky to have been forced to land in Switzerland. He explained, "The German artillery on the battle front along the French border would have shot you down easily at 6,000 feet."[30]

We were watched by the Swiss, but barely aware of it. I felt more like a guest than a prisoner and had not expected our confinement to be so easy and comfortable. We knew the war would be ending soon (it was over seven weeks later). Bordering Germany, the Swiss seemed to have favored the Germans during most of the war with supplies and information, but they now appeared to want good relations with America.[31]

After dinner on the first night, Runyan, Knauer, and I walked out of the hotel and down to the shops in Adelboden. It was a small, beautiful little village. There was no wind, and it did not even seem all that cold. I remember light snowflakes slowly floating straight down on us like feathers. Our feet crunched through the fresh snow as we strolled along the narrow streets with quaint, dimly-lit shops. There were horse-drawn sleighs, but no automobiles. Children walked along with their parents, their cheeks colored like red disks. A church with its bell tower reaching to the sky was bathed in soft light. This was a strange experience for airmen accustomed to living in the mud and being confined to a tent, and who considered their high-point as living on portions of K-rations.

Five days later, the Swiss took our crew, along with about thirty other American airmen, by bus to Bern and marched us in formation across the downtown area to a train station. We rode the train

30. As the Germans retreated from France and other occupied territories, they did strengthen the air defenses of their homeland dramatically by concentrating their antiaircraft guns. See Westermann, *Flak*, 234, 247, and 273.

31. Switzerland's situation in World War II was precarious to say the least. Through most of the war, it was surrounded by Axis or Axis-occupied countries, and shared a roughly one hundred mile border with Germany. For a short description of Switzerland's situation, see Tanner, *Refuge from the Reich*, 103–18.

to Geneva and were then taken across the nearby French border to waiting Allied forces.[32] We boarded several canvas-top trucks that were open in the rear and rode on a winding, two-lane road some 200 miles to Lyon, France. I sat on a bench, and while bitterly cold, I saw beautiful winter scenes of snow and ice-covered trees that I will never forget.[33]

From the Lyon airport, we boarded a twin-engine C-47 transport and were flown to Naples, where we deplaned and were met by three-star General Ira Eaker. As we lined up in formation, he stopped to shake hands with each airman and talked to some of us about our experience.[34] I had no idea at that time that General Eaker had played such an important part in the air war over Germany, had worked closely with Winston Churchill while briefly in charge of the Eighth Air Force in England and was now head of the entire Mediterranean area, including the Fifteenth Air Force and all RAF operations. He was also the leader of the first shuttle-run mission of a hundred four-engine bombers over Germany to and from Russia, and was possibly next in line under four-star General Hap Arnold, head of the Air Force.

That evening, we were flown back to San Giovanni Airfield to pick up our personal items and spend one last night in our tent. There, we were taken to the villa of our 454th Group Commander, Colonel Aynesworth, where all nine of us were his dinner guests. We sat around the table with him and enjoyed a sumptuous meal with Italian wine.

By the time we returned to our tent, it was late, and the rest of the squadron was asleep. The next morning the crews we had

32. While Faulkner did not know it, his release occurred because of a previous agreement between American, Swiss, and German diplomats. Brigadier General Bernard Legge, the American military attaché in Bern, negotiated with Swiss and German representatives between mid-December 1944 and mid-February 1945 to obtain a swap of U.S. airmen in Switzerland with German forces interned there. The first batch of around 475 American airmen were released on February 17 and another one hundred were released over the next month. Faulkner was part of that release. Ibid., 203–5.

33. While Faulkner remembers the idyllic winter scene of the French countryside, another airman, Clinton Norby, remembered the destruction. Norby remembered, "On the road we traveled [to Lyon], there was very little damage to the countryside; most of the damage was centered on small villages. When we reached Lyon, we saw more damage." Ibid., 238.

34. Eaker took a special interest in meeting with former prisoners of war, escapees, and other returnees. He wrote in October 1944, that he "suffered a deep disappointment" when he did not get to meet with some airman returning from captivity and ordered his assistant to "take the necessary steps in the future" to make sure he had the opportunity to visit other returnees. Meeting Returnees and Ex-Prisoners of War, October 12, 1944, LOC, Eaker Papers, Box I:24, Folder 1 – Army Air Forces, Mediterranean Theater of Operations – February 1944-June 1945 (1 of 2), 1.

lived with for six months had left early for that day's target briefing and then down to the flight line for takeoff. It was disturbing to not have the opportunity to say proper goodbyes to our friends from other crews; however, we were able to talk to the navigator from Willie Williams's crew.[35] His navigator, Max Cutler, told us that while we were gone, Ted Schindler and his crew had gone down on a mission to destroy a bridge over Brenner Pass in Northern Italy.[36] There were no survivors. It had happened the day after our mission over Augsburg.

Cutler also said he had heard that on our Augsburg mission we had dropped from the formation and headed to Switzerland *"with all four fans flying."* This was not good to hear. The inference was obvious and haunted me for many decades. If the men in my squadron believed all four propellers on my plane were working, then they must have questioned why I could not finish the mission by returning to San Giovanni. Although Colonel Aynesworth seemed completely satisfied with our response to what had happened to us, I had an unsettling feeling as we left our base for the last time.

From Naples, the ten of us, including my Augsburg copilot, Bill Knauer, who had flown only that one mission, flew back to the United States in an almost empty C-54 cargo plane, not under a cloud, but feeling somewhat like a dazed boxer, reeling in the corner between rounds. I slept on the floor of the open cargo bay most of the way over the Atlantic. To begin our combat tour, our crew had flown a new B-24 from the United States to Italy and now we were being flown back home. We were lucky because most all other B-24 crews were transported to and from Europe on slow-moving boats. Our four-engine C-54 transport landed at Miami Airport. The first thing we did was sit down in a lunch area and order a cheeseburger and a chocolate milk shake. It was unbelievable how good it tasted: that such simple things could feel so important.

We stayed in a small hotel on the beach for a week. We swam every day, staying close to the hotel. It was a sort of rest camp for Air Force crews returning from combat. On a deep-sea fishing trip,

35. Willie was the nickname of Sumner M. Williams, Jr. His navigator was Maxwell Cutler. See 737th Bomb Squadron Crews, 454th Bombardment Group, accessed on January 21, 2017, http://www.454thbombgroup.it/737th%20Squadron%20Crews.pdf.

36. For a description of what happened to the Schindler and his crew, see Chapter 3.

I hooked a huge Swordfish and watched it dance on the water until it got away. After a week of rest and fun, we were all sent to our homes from Miami and went our separate ways. In 1965, our waist gunner Talmage (Jonsie) Jones, of Houston, stopped by my office and my radio operator, Jim Hamilton, traveling from California with his wife, stayed with us a few days in 2007. But, I never again saw the other members of my crew.

When I arrived at San Giovanni for the first time six months earlier, I learned that pilots in the Air Force who completed their thirty-five combat missions were rewarded with two prizes, both of which I would covet more with each passing mission. There was, of course, no guarantee of either, but upon completion of thirty-five missions, all aircraft commanders before had been awarded the Distinguish Flying Cross and also received a promotion to the rank of captain. Earlier, I had thought that at the rapid rate we were completing our missions, there was the distinct possibility that I could have achieved both and still at the age of nineteen. The opportunity and challenge were both exciting. As it turned out, I left Italy with neither.[37]

Looking back, I have my doubts as to whether we would have completed our thirty-five missions even if we had *not* been shot down. The war was over on May 8, 1945, two months after we went down. It was still winter with bad weather. Further, several new crews had recently joined our squadron, and they would have shared in mission assignments. Since I had only flown five missions in January and February combined, I do not know if I would have been scheduled to fly seven more missions before April 25, the day the Fifteenth Air Force flew its last mission over Europe.

* * *

Willie Williams's navigator's comment about *"all four fans flying,"* continued to bother me after I returned home. Unfortunately, I experienced another unsettling incident in Dallas a year after the war that made me question my actions on that fateful February day in 1945. One of the 737th squadron leaders during my time in Italy was Captain Billy Jacobs. I remembered that Jacobs was

37. After returning to the United States, the Army Air Forces recognized Faulkner as a "Repatriated Internee" who could not be assigned outside the continental United States without special authorization from the War Department. See "Reclassification of Faulkner, Thomas Pettit," April 28, 1945, in author's possession.

from somewhere in Texas, and while in the golf shop at the Walnut Hill golf course in 1946, I was certain I saw Jacobs walking with another golfer. I called out to him, "Captain Jacobs," loud enough for him to hear, but he never turned around to look and just walked out with the other golfer. I was fairly certain it was Jacobs and wondered if he purposely avoided speaking to me. These two events, the navigator's "four fans flying" comment and Captain Jacobs's apparent snub bothered me for almost seventy years. If it *was* Jacobs, neither he nor Williams's navigator really knew what my crew and I experienced on that last mission. And this was the only solace I could muster. Still, I relived that mission over and over, year after year after year.

Over the next seventy years, I was plagued with a chronic health condition, not realizing that it stemmed from my doubts about my mission on February 27, 1945. In New Orleans in 1950, at the age of 25 and five years after being discharged from the Air Force, I was placed in charge of a small Marine Insurance branch of the Aetna Casualty Insurance Group. There, I began having sore throats, and they became more troublesome each year. This continued after Ann and I, with our two small children, moved back to Dallas, where I opened an insurance agency in 1955. After several throat operations during the ensuing years, and with doctors unable to find a cause or cure, I agreed to see a psychiatrist. After three sessions, I gave it up, but later learned they had diagnosed me with OCD, or Obsessive Compulsive Disorder. I never quite understood what that meant until reading a *Time Magazine* article years later. It concluded that OCD results when an issue is so great that *it becomes your life*. Knowing this helped, but the sore throats continued. Now, because of an unexpected lightning bolt from out of the blue in March of 2013, this lifetime problem is completely and miraculously over.[38]

Preoccupation with that mission caused me many sleepless nights as I would rehash every detail over and over. Countless numbers of Air Force veterans who had flown bombing missions during the war were forced to deal with far greater combat issues than this one, but after 68 years I was resigned that I would go to my grave without any

38. For an interesting article showing the possible link between OCD and Post Traumatic Stress Disorder, see Matthew Tull, "Trauma, PTSD, and OCD," January 31, 2017, Very Well, accessed on May 16, 2017, https://www.verywell.com/ptsd-and-other-anxiety-disorders-relationship-2797549.

B-24 Damaged by Flak During Munich Bombing Mission, 1944 (National Archives)

resolution. I was never proud of the fact that I landed in Switzerland because of the stigma felt by most airmen who landed in a neutral country. Regardless of how bad any of us felt about it, it was a free pass out of the war and there was no escaping that. [39] After the war, my high school friend, Steve Schneider, would continually razz me that while he was risking his life protecting America's soft underbelly flying dangerous patrol missions out of Corpus Christi looking

39. Many pilots felt this same guilt. See Mrazek, *To Kingdom Come*, 270.

for German submarines in the Gulf, I had spent the war living it up in a Swiss ski resort.

What did others in my squadron think? This was my decades-long concern. I was just not able to ignore the issue and just say, *who cares?* I cared—a lot. Also, there was a possible second issue, a little whisper, lurking in the back of my mind. A question I had to resolve. Was there ever any thought, before or during the mission over Augsburg, that I was influenced, even subconsciously, by the slightest urge to drop out of the war? In other words, was I a coward? I did not like thinking such thoughts. Abhorrent, but it had to be put on the table and dealt with. This kind of introspection is not easy. I knew I had never liked even verbal confrontations and recalled thinking I had never, ever been in any kind of one-on-one physical joust with anyone, not even in grade school. Had I spent my life avoiding conflict? Was this a clue to my nature or character? Did I lack the degree of courage that is expected of all men? All my life, I had taken for granted that I was as brave as the next guy, but never having been confronted with a serious challenge, now I had to wonder.

The answer to the question about my courage quotient came about twenty-five years after the war at a party of about thirty people at a private home for an engaged couple. The entire family of the bride-to-be had been close friends of my family since way before the war. The groom was from Chicago, and his father was the owner of a huge electrical manufacturing company with over 5,000 employees. His mother was a still-beautiful former movie actress named Martha O'Driscoll.[40] She had played mostly bit parts in over fifty movies.

There were not enough chairs at the party to accommodate all the guests, so after mixing and mingling for a while, Ann and I sat on the floor of the entrance hall by the front door with our backs to the wall, facing the stairway on which others were sitting, balancing our plates in our laps. Suddenly, we heard raised and angry voices coming from beyond the staircase, and the groom's father emerged into the entrance hall, yelling something back over his shoulder. He stopped right in front of Ann and me, and, ignoring us, growled to one of his other sons, "Take this," peeling off several bills from

40. For a description of Martha O'Driscoll and her career, see Martha O'Driscoll Biography, IMDb.com, accessed on August 16, 2017, http://www.imdb.com/name/nm0640930/bio.

a roll, "and find a liquor store and bring back some scotch, some vodka, and gin. We need to get this party going."

From the hall next to the staircase came the little bride-to-be, fury in her eyes. She stopped before her future father-in-law, grabbed his coat lapels and said, "You go back and apologize to my mother." For what, I never knew. It was obvious that neither of them cared who heard. All conversation in the adjoining rooms stopped. "I don't know what the hell you're talking about," the groom's father said. One of the guests—I had never seen him before—emerged from the living room, his fists clenched as he walked toward the older man. I jumped up and stood in his path and raised my hands.

"Outa my way," he said, looking over my shoulder. He was not quite as tall as I, but he was stocky and probably outweighed me. I said, "Now you don't want to cause any—" *Wham!* Like in a movie, in a split second, the fist grew larger and larger, until it crashed into my left eye, launching my glasses into the air. *The time had come!* Had the twenty-eighth mission revealed an unknown lack of courage? That lingering question actually did flash through my mind. There was no way I could let this opportunity pass. I swung back hard, catching him on the jaw. We stood, swinging, mostly trading blows to the body, moving, circling. In the middle of the living room, we were still swinging away when the host, obviously oblivious to everything before, rushed in, yelling, "See here, if you two want to do this, you'll have to go outside."

As I ignored him and continued trying to avoid getting killed, my seventeen-year-old son, Tommy, came into view. Instead of grabbing the other guy and stopping the fight, as I expected, he grabbed me around the waist from behind. Go figure. He held me tight, becoming my partner as we danced together around the room, my opponent and I still swinging at each other. Only now, I was burdened with the extra weight and not having a full range of motion for my arms and fists.

Suddenly, my opponent's wife, a head shorter than all of us, came storming in the room. She yelled his name and then, *"Stop it! Stop it!"* She jumped between us and slapped her husband hard on the face. "You idiot," she said, jerking her head toward me, *"He's on your side."* I knew her. Everyone knew her. She had been *Sweetheart of the University of Texas* during her senior year, chosen by a student body of some 40,000 students. She pulled him away. They ran out, slamming the front door behind them.

While Ann, Tommy, and my daughter, Linda, were hovering over me to see if I was bleeding or maimed, we heard screeching tires and a loud metal on metal crash out in the street. We all rushed outside to see that my opponent had sideswiped a few of the other guests' cars parked on the street.

At the large wedding reception a week later, Ann and I were waiting in the buffet line when my adversary and his wife came up behind us. I turned around, hoping he was not seeking revenge, as someone nearby tried to introduce us.

"Oh, I know Tom very well," my new friend said. "He's my sparring partner."

Brawling was not new to him. He was a truly rugged man. He had worked in all phases of the Texas oil industry. He had known the young bride as a child. When he perceived that someone had made her cry, that is all it took. Strangely, neither of us came out of the contest with any scars. I may not be a good fighter, but, ashamed as I was at making a complete ass of myself, at least I learned I was not afraid to fight. From that point on, I ceased worrying about being deficient in personal courage, satisfied there was no hidden fear or cowardice lurking in my brain. However, this did not solve the basic problem, which was—did I make the right *decision?* And what did the others in the 737th squadron think?

The sore throats continued, as did the sleepless rehashing.

My memory had always carried the assumption that I had left the formation only a short time after being hit, and that we were still way north of Switzerland. I had no memory of how far we had dropped, only that it was so precipitous that to continue on would have been foolhardy.

Right after my 88th birthday in March of 2013, new discoveries made about that mission turned my previous assumptions upside down. As if revealed by a sleeping genie finally released from its bottle, I was suddenly made aware of ancient facts I had no knowledge of before.

They were found by a person whom I had never met, Dan Matthews.[41] Dan lives in Minnesota and was introduced to me through

41. Dan Matthews is a retired airline executive who investigated Faulkner's last mission. He graciously shared with me many of the documents I am using in this chapter.

Dan Matthews

email by Charley Cleaver, the son of one of my best friends, Jim Cleaver. Charley, who lives in the Dallas area, and Dan have known each other for years as executives in the airline industry and they still communicate often. Charley knew of Dan Matthews's search for details surrounding the wartime experience of both his father and his uncle. Dan's uncle was a B-24 gunner in the Fifteenth Air Force and flew out of a base only a few miles from San Giovanni. He had been killed when his plane was shot down over Linz, Austria, on his ninth mission. I had flown two missions over Linz, a tough target, but on different days. Dan was determined to find out all he could about the circumstances surrounding his uncle's death, and through Air Force archives, had actually discovered when, where, and how his uncle had died.

After learning of my twenty-eighth mission concerns from Charley, Dan, on his own initiative, began a similar search on my behalf. He communicated with the same Air Force offices he had worked with before, and he also contacted a Swiss World War II amateur historian who helped in providing Swiss airport records and translations of those records from German to English.

Dan already owned a book by an American author called *B-24 Liberator Units of the 15th Air Force* and a Swiss book entitled *Strangers in a Strange Land*. The first information he sent to me was taken from these books. Both books offer comments about my twenty-eighth mission.[42] Both also give brief accounts of the crippled American planes that landed in Switzerland during the war, and one of them includes an artist's rendition of *our* plane.[43] They quote my emergency call to our group leader. I had no recollection of attempting any radio call. One book has a photograph of our plane turning off the runway at Dübendorf Airfield taken the moment after I landed.[44] The short narrative in each book reads roughly the same:

> 1LT Thomas P. Faulkner's B-24G-16-NT (42-78458) was hit over the target at 1359 [actually 1330]. Faulkner attempted to call the lead ship but received no answer. His call was acknowledged by 1LT Loren S. Loomis who took the message, "I'm losing 500 feet per minute and flying to a neutral country." The Liberator dropped out of formation and was escorted by a number of P-38s towards the Swiss border. The flak had knocked out the number two and three engines, the latter being completely locked. Shortly after crossing the border, Swiss Morane fighters intercepted and guided the stricken bomber to Dübendorf, where it landed normally.[45]

During the next few days of March of 2013, Dan sent me dozens of emails, all dealing with his findings about my last mission. It was exciting as the daily messages and copies of Air Force archives continued to pour in. He sent all the data given at the briefing, formation positions of each plane, pinpointed clock times, maps of our flight path, and mission results—everything from takeoff to landing—they all kept coming. He sent copies of signed statements of other pilots from my group describing what they had seen of our ship. He sent the 454th Group Mission reports showing the exact time we dropped our bombs, thus establishing the minute we were hit. He even sent the map showing coordinates of Wallgau, the small German village over which we were reported turning away and the exact minute we were seen leaving the formation. I was reminded of Watergate, beginning

42. See Robert F. Dorr, *B-24 Liberator Units of the Fifteenth Air Force* (Botley, Oxford, UK: Osprey Publishing, 2000), 94–95; and Stapfer and Kunzle, *Strangers in a Strange Land*, 69.

43. Dorr, *B-24 Liberator Units of the Fifteenth Air Force*, 30.

44. Stapfer and Kunzle, *Strangers in a Strange Land*, 67.

45. Ibid., 69.

with the small news items at the bottom of the front page blossoming rapidly over the following days and weeks into the complete news headlines across the top. What a difference it would have made if only I had known all this before the war ended.

Dan even sent copies of the Dübendorf Airfield Mechanics Report of the damage found in the inspection of our plane. This report, along with the Air Force records, removed my concern of not having tried to reach the Alps and fly over them. When Dan first called and told me of his early discoveries, I was uneasy, fearing he would find criticism of my leaving the formation. Over the next few days, however, he found this was not the case, and everything he discovered indicated my concerns over the years were baseless. Thanks to Dan Matthews, my seven-decades-old dilemma was finally over.

Yet, while relieved and delighted with these unexpected new revelations, I had lived for seven decades certain I had left the formation after just 15 minutes of leaving the target and still well north of Switzerland. Even when writing my self-published book a year later about this mission, I was still unable to wrap my mind around the mass of data Dan had sent. I wrote in that book "turning toward Switzerland fifteen minutes after leaving the target" and that I was at a height of 16,500 feet, assumptions all contrary to the data Dan had sent, and way off base. But all of this new information was more than enough to dispel my feelings of guilt.

The written statements of other crews tell of my calling the squadron leader several times but receiving no response. I have no recollection at all of this. Lt. Victor Calvo, a copilot on another plane in our Baker box, took my message, "I am losing five hundred feet per minute and am going to a neutral country." 2nd Lt. Loren Loomis reported my plane leaving the formation northwest of Innsbruck, Austria, adding, "all four engines were running," but "losing altitude fast." [46] Another pilot, 2nd Lt. Wallace Andrews also reported my plane losing altitude fast at 1359 hours, and that I had turned to a 270 degrees (due west) heading at coordinates 47/35N at 11/12E.[47] 2nd Lt. Robert Rankin also heard my radio message and reported that my No. 2 engine was smoking, and my plane was dropping "rapidly." One of them provided a hand drawn map

46. Headquarters, 737th Bombardment Squadron, Statement (Loren Loomis), February 28, 1945, in author's possession.

47. Headquarters, 737th Bombardment Squadron, Statement (Wallace Andrews), February 28, 1945, in author's possession.

showing the exact spot above the village of Wallgau, Germany, where I turned from the formation.[48]

There could be no mistake or miscalculation about my statement of losing 500 feet per minute. Engineer Gorman was standing behind me every second, listening anxiously and watching. My copilot Knauer, although this was his first mission and a total stranger to all of us until that morning, was there as well.

So now, after carefully sifting through all of Dan Matthews's data, and based upon his verification and also the acknowledgement of these conclusions by editor David Snead, I can say with certainty that we were hit over Augsburg at 23,500 feet at 1330 hours. We flew with our group in view for almost a half hour (twenty-nine minutes, not fifteen), dropping to an altitude of 9,500 feet, and were still falling. We were not even half way to the Alps when I judged we could not make it over them. We turned away from the formation for Switzerland. Immediately after turning I realized we could make it to allied controlled France, which would have allowed us eventually to get back to San Giovanni. After flying due west and being fired upon over Friedrichshafen, we continued on for another fifteen minutes, still assuming we were north of Switzerland. We were less than fifteen minutes away from the French border, and safety, when the Swiss fighters forced us down. We landed at Dübendorf Airfield, near Zurich, at 1436 hours, an hour and six minutes after being hit over Augsburg [49]

Yet, *even now*, I have just realized I still had not completely used everything Dan had made available. Drawing a line across the map from the exact point of my leaving the formation, over Wallgau, (47/35N at 11/12E) to the center of Friedrichshafen is not a perfect 270 degrees, but is closer to 278 degrees. Why? I know

48. Headquarters, 737th Bombardment Squadron, Statement (Robert Rankin), February 28, 1945, in author's possession.

49. Tom's twenty-eighth mission was the 202nd mission flown by the 454th Bomb Group. His plane, one of twenty-eight from his group's four squadrons that took off from San Giovanni at 8:50 a.m., was the only one from the group that did not return. His squadron was part of a much larger force that consisted of 160 B-17s, 272 B-24s, seventy-seven P-38s, and seventy-eight P-51s whose orders were to attack the Augsburg Marshalling Yards. The P-38s that escorted the bombers were from the 14th Fighter Group, 306th Fighter Wing, 15th Air Force (37th, 48th, and 49th Fighter Squadrons, and flew from Triolo Airfield in Italy. Post-mission photos show our attack was a success. See Mission Report, 454th Bomb Gp (H), Mission 202, February 27, 1945, Air Force Historical Research Agency, Reel B0601 – 454 Records, 1682–83; Headquarters, 455th Bombardment Group, Field Order No. 206, February 27, 1945, in author's possession; John W. Lambert, *The 14th Fighter Group in World War II* (Atglen, PA: Schiffer Military History, 2008); and Headquarters, Mediterranean Allied Strategic Air Force, Intops Summary No. 586, February 27, 1945, in author's possession.

my compass heading was due west, or 270 degrees, still thinking I was way north of Switzerland. Finally, it is just now dawning on me. Just before signing off for North Texas Press to send this to the printers, and having worked with David Snead for over two years in organizing and expanding on this Italian experience, I am just now figuring it out. That north-leaning line has to be the result of—*wind drift*. Some sharp pilot *I* am! Concluding this after five years of being given all the data! And to carry this one more step, if we extend that map line beyond Friedrichshafen towards France, then the clear likelihood of the Swiss fighters being so impatient for me to give up and turn back with them, was because I was very likely—*over Germany*.

What a relief it is to relax, knowing these additional facts about what occurred and why. For me, Dan blew away Willie William's navigator and his "all four fans flying" comment. He dispatched Captain Jacobs as if he was never in the golf shop (which may have been the case). And, based on the Dübendorf Mechanics Report, with the "blocked" number three engine, smoking number two needing oil, and the supercharger not working, I believe any B-24 pilot would agree that we would never have made it through the Alps, much less over them. Although we did not have our regular navigator, we *did* have a navigator after all. God was surely overseeing our safe landing that day.

Dan's discoveries did not end there. He later found that I actually *was* awarded the Distinguished Flying Cross. He chose to have my son tell me at a private family gathering, holding out a silver framed color photograph of the medal. At first, I did not believe it. When he showed me a copy of the official citation, it was hard not to tear up. The citation, issued by the Headquarters of the Fifteenth Air Force, was dated April 20, 1945 and I was one of twenty-four recipients of the DFC. I received it because of the twenty-eighth mission.[50] So, it was sixty-eight years before I learned about the DFC. Notice of the award eventually reached my official military records, but not until after I was discharged at Shepherd Air Force base in Wichita Falls in November of 1945. I had no idea it existed. It remained in limbo until resurrected by Dan Matthews in 2013.

50. Citation for Thomas P. Faulkner, April 20, 1945, in author's possession. For the list of all the recipients, see Headquarters, Fifteenth Air Force, General Order No. 2368, in author's possession.

Ann and Tom Faulkner at Distinguished Flying Cross Reception, 2013

Dan's efforts led to coverage in the *Dallas Morning News* and also an appearance on the local ABC television station about my twenty-eighth mission and being awarded the DFC.[51] At a special ceremony at the Fort Worth Naval Air Station on September 19, 2013, General John F. Nichols, Texas Adjutant General and Commander, Texas Military Forces presented me with the DFC in a special ceremony at the Fort Worth Naval Air Station. In my words of acceptance to the 75 airmen present, I explained, "I may not be the bravest pilot to ever receive the DFC, but I'll bet anyone here I'm the oldest."[52]

51. Steve Blow, "War Wound Finally Heals for WWII Pilot from Dallas," September 18, 2013, Dallas News, accessed on May 16, 2017, https://www.dallasnews.com/news/news/2013/09/18/blow-war-wound-finally-heals-for-wwii-pilot-from-dallas.

52. Elizabeth Gilbert and Phil Fountain, "WWII Pilot Presented Distinguished Flying Cross, after 68 Years," October 17, 2013, Air National Guard, 136th Airlift Wing, accessed on May 16, 2017, http://www.136aw.ang.af.mil/News/Features/Display/Article/866721/wwii-pilot-presented-distinguished-flying-cross-after-68-years/.

Charley Cleaver, Tom, Dan Matthews, and General John Nichols after Ceremony Where Tom Was Awarded the Distinguished Flying Cross, 2013

Although I have a raspy voice, with only half my vocal cords intact, I have not been sick or had a sore throat since Dan Matthews's revelations, over five years ago.

Life is full of "ifs." If the DFC award had reached me before my discharge, if I had known there had been no condemnation for my landing in Switzerland, but instead, a waiting medal, I would never have engaged in any nocturnal post-war questioning of decisions made on that Augsburg mission. It is so incongruous to me that the DFC, which I admit to coveting while in Italy, was actually in place almost from the time we left Naples when I had just turned twenty. And if our navigator had not been pulled from our plane; if the supercharger had not gone bad; if we had been able to feather number three engine—if any one of those had not happened, we would have made it back.

I endured decades of unnecessary anxiety resulting in throat problems, even throat operations, all the while convincing myself I had failed as a combat pilot. I re-flew those frantic last minutes of the mission thousands of times over thousands of nights in a futile attempt to find relief. I sifted through every possible option, every solution, searching in vain for the answer that would have avoided our being corralled by the Swiss fighters, and instead, allowed us safe passage over the Alps or sanctuary in a friendly France allowing us to complete our thirty-five missions.

Now I realize. *Without all the facts, there can be no resolution to the lingering problems of a past event.*

# Conclusion

While my crew and I went separate ways after returning to the United States, I still cherish the time I had with them in our Tonapah training and on our tour in Italy. We had flown twenty-eight missions and played our part in defeating Adolf Hitler, probably the most dangerous man who ever lived. I still wish we could have finished our thirty-five missions, but that was not God's plan for us. Looking back, aside from the 28th mission, and my losing a decent relationship with my copilot, there were no real negatives. The stigma, real or imagined, of not trying to return to our base that day is now gone. I wish I had kept in touch with Arnie Nelson, Runyan, and the six enlisted men I thought so well of. Still, I consider my two-year Air Force experience—especially the six months flying missions out of Italy—as the greatest of my life.

After a two-week leave in Dallas at Maple Terrace with my parents, the Air Force sent me to the ATC, Air Transport Command, in Memphis, which occupied one half of the Memphis commercial airport. I enjoyed the seven months in the 4th Ferrying Group even through stretches of inactivity and boredom. There were times when life was great, but there was little flying and much time to burn. However, the Air Force was good about seeing to it that pilots were scheduled to fly enough each month to at least qualify for flight pay.

In Memphis, in addition to flying the C-47 cargo plane, I also checked out in my very favorite twin-engine plane of the war, the North American B-25, named after Billy Mitchell. It had twin rudders like the B-24, and its engines made the greatest engine sound of all. They would cough, spit, and chug along the taxi ramps, an exciting sound, like no other plane. The B-25 Mitchells were the ones that took off from the short deck of a Navy carrier, the *Hornet*, to bomb Tokyo soon after Pearl Harbor.[1] You had to feel like a hot pilot behind the wheel of a B-25 and even more so with the A-26 Invader. It was sleek, powerful, maneuverable and almost as fast as a fighter ship. It went into action toward the last part of the war.

I felt really lucky to have had the one flight in the A-26 that I did. I was assigned to pick up a new one in Augusta, Georgia, and fly it to Fresno, California. I had never been inside an A-26, but the Air Force expected B-25 pilots to fly them with no problem. Of course, I was new to the B-25, designed for a pilot and copilot, and I discovered the A-26 also called for a copilot, but I would be alone on this A-26 delivery flight. This would be a totally new experience. I had never before flown a combat aircraft without a copilot.

In Augusta, I carefully followed the checklist duties for both pilot and copilot, or at least thought I did, and taxied to the end of the runway. I cleared with the tower and pushed the throttles forward and it jumped like a racehorse, gaining speed, and then I was startled by a strange, loud and overwhelming noise—apart from the engines' roar—sounding ominous and unfamiliar, and I knew something was drastically wrong. Too far down the runway to pull back, I had to ignore it and hope for the best. Still climbing away from the field, I looked behind. *There* was the problem! I had failed to close the bomb bay doors! How stupid! Furious wind blew around the cockpit as I reached for the bomb bay door control.

Landing in Phoenix to refuel, I stopped, parked, and unbuckled, then stood up behind the pilot seat and reached up to release the canopy. I pulled myself out to the top of the fuselage. The plane's aluminum skin was so hot my fingers were burned. Standing on top of the aircraft, I felt the sun beating down with a heat I had never

1. Faulkner is referencing the Doolittle Raid, which occurred April 18, 1942.

felt before. Inside the pilot's lounge, I was told the temperature outside was over 120 degrees.

The only other time I was in Arizona was to deliver an old B-24 to a field in Tucson—again, all alone, no copilot, just me. Now this *was* a challenge. With a two-engine plane, I could understand how one pilot could manage, but this I could not believe. Always before, I had the help of a copilot, navigator, engineer, and radio operator. Had a mistake been made? Then I realized maybe this was not such an unreasonable expectation. After all, the checklist was not mandatory as to who performed what. I could sit in the copilot's seat during the engine startup, then move over to the pilot's seat and from there, manage both pilot and copilot duties and all four engines. I had her all to myself. The prospect was exciting, and it was one of the strangest experiences of the war for me. I closed the bomb bay doors, called the tower, took off alone, raised the wheels, followed the prescribed course and delivered the loud, rattling old B-24, making one final landing, all alone. What a joy it was being behind a Liberator pilot's wheel that one last time! It had been eight months since I had flown one—eight months since that twenty-eighth mission. I turned off the runway and was met by a waiting jeep. I taxied behind it past several long rows of parked B-24s, hundreds of them, maybe a thousand, parked side by side.

This was the B-24 graveyard.[2] The war in Japan was over. I parked and cut its four engines and ducked down through the bomb bay to the ground. It was September now and in weeks I would be discharged and going home. No more flying. The jeep and its driver were waiting to take me to the operations room. This was a tough moment. I stood there, remembering the thrill of that first flight in Liberal. I have thought of that moment many times since—taking off with that deafening roar from the dreary, snow-covered Kansas airfield with the other student pilots, to enter the dark overcast, finally emerging into the dazzling blue, sun-lit world above, and leveling off to look down at the glistening layer of flat, white clouds below stretching to the horizon.

2. Faulkner probably flew the B-24 to Kingman Army Airfield in Arizona. It was one of around 30 depots across the country the AAF used to dispose of surplus airplanes. Over 5,000 B-17s and B-24s were scrapped there by 1948. See Roger Naylor, "Arizona's Military History: Kingman Army Air Field," February 20, 2015, *Azcentral*, accessed on September 1, 2017, http://www.azcentral.com/story/travel/local/history/2015/02/20/arizona-military-history-kingman-army-air-field/23618689/.

From the jeep, I looked at the long rows of B-24s. Each Liberator bore its own distinctive tail markings still proudly identifying its group, squadron, and airbase. Some bore the nose art and name acquired in combat. The stories they could tell! I wondered what had happened to *Lotta Laffs*. This would be the last time for decades that I would be near the plane I loved, the plane I had spent hundreds of hours inside—great times, terrifying times, joyful times, tragic times, never again to be experienced.

I thought of the old elephant in the Tarzan movie, lumbering along mountain passes in Africa in search of the enormous cave strewn with skeletal remains of his ancestors, where he would collapse to the ground, roll over, and die. Within three years, the Air Force scrapped all of these B-24s. The war was over. The B-24 Liberator bomber was already a relic of the past.

I was honorably discharged from the Air Force in November 1945 and returned to Dallas to live with my parents. I needed some time to figure out exactly what I wanted to do.[3] It was during this time that I met Ann Harrison; however, I had no idea then what was in store for us.

Ann graduated from Woodrow Wilson High School and received a full scholarship to Hockaday Junior College in Dallas.[4] Slightly pudgy at 131 lbs. and 5'7" and not among the cool crowd, she determined to slim down during that first year of college. She walked a mile and a half to Hockaday from her home and back every day, eating just an apple for lunch. After her freshman year, the caterpillar, having morphed into a beautiful butterfly, enrolled for her sophomore year at Southern Methodist University. The new and reduced Ann Harrison was stunned but delighted to find she was suddenly in demand by sororities and also by young men. Her apple diet and daily walks to Hockaday had turned her life upside down. She pledged Pi Beta Phi and many of her sorority sisters would unknowingly become her best friends for the rest of her life.

At SMU, Ann, an honor student, became a Rotunda Beauty twice, was elected a Class Favorite, and became President of Mortar Board. I always wondered why she would marry me, a guy who was

3. See Army of the United States Certificate of Service, October 21, 1945, in author's possession; and Military Record and Report of Separation Certificate of Service – Thomas P. Faulkner, October 21, 1945, in author's possession.

4. "History," The Hockaday School, accessed on September 1, 2017, https://www.hockaday.org/page/about/history.

Ann Faulkner as Shown in Rotunda Annual at Southern Methodist University, c. 1946

never elected to anything of real significance or won anything in school.

During that summer before her senior year, Ann became a model for Neiman Marcus. She performed in what would become Neiman's world-acclaimed annual Exposition. It featured a bridal event in which Ann was chosen as the bride. Stanley Marcus, who was establishing the unlikely cowtown of Dallas, Texas, as a fashion center that would compete with New York and Los Angeles, supervised the production. After the war, I remember walking on the sidewalk in downtown Dallas and thinking how much more attractive Dallas women were than those in other places. I later became convinced that it was the influence of Stanley Marcus, who had set new standards for women—and it showed.

After graduation from SMU in 1946, Ann was asked to stay and teach freshman English to accommodate the enormous influx of veterans on the GI Bill. This was the time when Ann and I met. One of my good friends was Leo Corrigan. His father,

Leo Sr., had received national accolades for his real estate achievements, acquiring major properties around Dallas, including the prestigious, downtown Adolphus Hotel and Maple Terrace, the multistory apartment building where I was now staying with my parents. At breakfast, Ann was telling her father about how she was ready to send Leo packing because of something he had said the night before just as her father opened *The Dallas Morning News* to see a front-page headline, "*Corrigan Worth Forty-five Million*." Looking over the paper at her, he said, "Now, Ann, let's not be hasty here," only half in jest.[5]

Leo brought Ann by Maple Terrace one afternoon and introduced us just after I was discharged from the Air Force in November 1945. Ann still says she fell in love with me that day. I was impressed with her, of course, but she was, after all, Leo's girl. We double-dated for the rest of SMU football games, led by future All-American Doak Walker, my former Highland Park teammate. However, it would be two years before Ann and I found each other.

I left for Washington & Lee University in Lexington, Virginia, for my sophomore and junior years, where my father, brother, and years later, my son, and nephews all graduated. I pledged Phi Delta Theta and loved Virginia and Washington & Lee, an all-boys school at the time, with a strict honor system and dress code. Coats and ties were always required in the classroom. While there was a lot of drinking on weekends, the class workload was so demanding that we had to study during the week to avoid flunking out. This was 1946 and yet, I do not recall ever talking about the war while there. There were ex-majors, ex-captains, ex-sergeants, and ex-privates, but no one knew or cared. We had frequent bull sessions that were usually confined to four subjects, religion, sports, politics, or girls. The war was no longer a subject of interest.

After being away from Dallas for almost four years, I decided that if I had any hope of having a successful career, I had better get back home and to SMU for my senior year. After returning to Dallas, I found that Leo Corrigan and Ann had actually never been more than just good friends. Leo was now vying with another good friend, Jim Cleaver, for the hand of Jo Neill a beautiful brunette,

5. For a history of the Corrigan family, see Christine Perez, "Three Generations Later, the Corrigans Are Still Shaping Dallas," *D Magazine* (January-February 2011), accessed on September 1, 2017, https://www.dmagazine.com/publications/d-ceo/2011/january-february/the-corrigan-family-is-still-shaping-dallas/.

also at SMU, who, as a sophomore, was elected president of her Kappa Kappa Gamma sorority.

It was early in 1948. I was midway through my senior year at SMU and Ann was still teaching freshman English when she and I found ourselves alone one night at a table at Louann's, the same dance hall I had visited four years earlier right after I received my wings. Ann's date and my date were out on the dance floor or preoccupied at other tables. Ann and I realized that while we had known each other for over three years, we really did not *know* each other at all. It was a delightful surprise and it was the beginning of our lifetime together.

With our dates away, Ann and I gradually discovered ourselves discussing things—personal things, experiences usually reserved only for close, intimate friends. I knew this was unusual between two people who had never had a single moment alone together. In those brief moments, I realized I had found someone whose values and views about the important things of life were just like mine and I knew then and there at Louann's that she was the girl I wanted to marry.

Still a senior at SMU, I had no thoughts of getting married before, but thirty days after the Louann's conversation, we were sitting on the piano bench in her parents' living room. The night before, I had kissed her and told her I loved her. On the piano bench, I said, "I thought we might get married." How's *that* for a proposal? She should have said, "Think again, Buster. You can do better than that." Instead, she beamed. We hugged and kissed. We still laugh about my never actually asking her to marry me and she never saying "Yes," but eight months later we made it to the church on time, and it has all worked out well, extremely well, thanks to those brief moments at Louann's when we were alone, thrown together by accident.

We married in a morning wedding ceremony on December 18, 1948. Leo Corrigan and Jim Cleaver were attendants. Steve Schneider would have joined them, but he had come down with polio not long before. My brother, Jim, was my best man. I was not very nervous at the church as he and I stepped up to the altar and waited for Ann to come down the aisle on her father's arm. However, when I looked over at my brother, standing next to me with the ring, his face reflected panic and his head was shaking.

Tom and Ann Faulkner on Their Wedding Day, 1948

This, I had not expected, and suddenly my knees began to knock. I had never experienced this. Somehow, I was able to control my knocking knees and say my vows.

The reception was at Ann's parents' home, and as we left, instead of my old car waiting at the curb, there was a brand-new 1949 Ford sedan, a wedding present from my parents. All postwar automobiles were now streamlined, a radical improvement, and to us, this shiny new model looked like a rocket ship. We headed for San Antonio and the St. Anthony Hotel. We slowly drove through downtown Dallas in our fresh smelling new car, with snow falling lightly on us as we listened to Christmas carols on the radio. Even the radio seemed to have a new, resonant sound we had never heard.

Since I had heard insurance talk at home all my life, it made sense to go in that direction for a career. I graduated from SMU with a Business Administration degree in the spring of 1948 and went to work with the marine and inland marine division of the Aetna Casualty & Surety Company. Soon after our marriage, I attended Aetna's school at its home office in Hartford, Connecticut, for six weeks. It was like an extended honeymoon. On weekends, Ann and I drove around the countryside during a beautiful snow-covered New England winter, and we visited New York City and danced to Jimmy Dorsey and his orchestra at the Plaza Hotel.

After two years in Dallas, Aetna sent us to New Orleans, where I would be in charge of an office to develop marine insurance business from independent insurance agents in three states. I travelled six days each month, leaving Ann alone with our two year

Ann Faulkner in Hartford, CT, in 1949

old daughter Linda and later, Tommy, our son who was born there. At first, we lived in an apartment near Lake Pontchartrain. It was a hot, muggy, mosquito laden summer. This was 1950, and I recall running to our car from our apartment with towels over our heads trying to outrace heavy swarms of mosquitoes trailing after us.

We had one friend in New Orleans, Kathryn Keller. Her aunt was the noted Helen Keller, whose life was the subject of the motion picture, *The Miracle Worker*. Kathryn gave us a pair of framed Chinese prints from Helen Keller's home. Kathryn had married a New Orleans native, Gordon Ewin, a member of a well-known New Orleans family, and they both wanted us to move to the section known as "Uptown," near them in the oldest residential section of the city. She found an upstairs apartment for us in an old box-like frame, four-plex. We grabbed it and paid only $60 per month because it was still under wartime rent control. It was perfect, two blocks from St. Charles Street and the streetcar line. With fireplaces in most rooms and wide mahogany floors and ceilings so tall, I could raise any of the three living room windows and walk out to the porch without ducking. We lived near the Mississippi River and could hear the soft, low moans of the passing ships throughout the day and night. We were several blocks from the New Orleans Audubon Zoo, and sometimes, we could hear the lions roaring at night.

Kathryn invited us to a party to introduce us to their friends, all longtime natives, and all very nice and friendly to us. She tried again, and again, including a private dinner for sixteen at a beautiful plantation outside the city. However, it ended there. We had gotten to know some of them. They were all personable and attractive, and I was certain they liked us, too. As much as Kathryn tried, she could not break their longstanding tradition that only New Orleans people whose ancestors were native to New Orleans would be socially accepted. It was disappointing but no great surprise. Other Texans who had lived there previously had advised us to expect this. The wife of one of our friends who had had the same experience laughingly said, "If I won a free trip around the world and the boat left from New Orleans, I'd turn it down."

Notwithstanding the social disappointment, we loved a lot about New Orleans. We would walk up and down Royal Street, noted for their fine French antique shops, swaying Ann's taste toward country French furniture, and we loved the wonderful restaurants of the French Quarter. However, having no close friends there took its toll. Ann was not happy, especially when I was away each month with our car, and I had wanted to open my own insurance agency in Dallas.

In 1955, after seven years with Aetna, I resigned from the New Orleans office. We moved back to Dallas and I opened Faulkner Insurance Agency. I had been warned that there was an insurance agent on every corner in Dallas and told that I had waited too long to start a new agency. It was a huge risk. I had little money, and I knew of six good friends from my high school days that were all well-entrenched as successful Dallas insurance agents, mostly having joined their fathers' agencies, and already taking care of everyone I had ever known.

Ann and I made the move with our six-year-old daughter, Linda, and three-year-old son, Tommy. My father had died at the age of 58, and we moved into my mother's home. Mother had moved to Virginia to become a fraternity housemother at Washington & Lee, and then she spent a year as hostess at Virginia's historic Carter's Grove, then another year back in Dallas as housemother at SMU's Phi Delta Theta fraternity. She then married an old family friend and widower from Helena, C. Jack Ritchie, living in Houston.

Opening a new office on a shoestring was a very tough challenge. I remember backing out of the driveway that first week, braking at the street, wondering which way I should turn. I had to figure out how to acquire new customers.

Having endured the ego-damaging years in New Orleans, we were now reunited with our families, with my high school friends, and Ann's sorority sisters. We were happy beyond words. Ann was taken into the Dallas Junior League and later elected its vice-president. Over time, we became members of four dinner-dance clubs, became Bible teachers at our Church of the Incarnation, and became members of the Dallas Country Club. We also joined a new Great Books Club chapter whose focus was on the Classics. Belonging to this group of nine couples was one of the most significant and enjoyable moves of our marriage. Its members became among our closest friends, and we met regularly for forty-five years, until mortality finally took its toll. Ann and I are now the sole survivors.

The insurance agency was moving along nicely. I had two fantastic employees, Eileen and Irene, who kept me out of trouble while I worked on developing new accounts. I am not a great salesman and I am not a joiner of service clubs, but I had a good knowledge of the insurance business from my Aetna training, and I worked long hours and most weekends. I also think I was very lucky.

In 1964, Ann called me at my office in the Meadows Building and insisted I meet her right away at 4304 Arcady, a house just coming on the market. I said, "Have you seen it?" She replied, "No, it doesn't matter, it's the right location at the right price and plenty big for all four of us, so be there because we're going to buy it." It was not exactly a teardown, but we spent as much on improvements as we did for the house, lived there on Arcady in Highland Park for twenty-five years, and sold it for three times what we paid. Ann had done very well.

During those years on Arcady, Linda graduated from Vanderbilt and Tommy from Washington and Lee. Linda eventually worked at Neiman Marcus and became the Public Relations Director of their prestigious downtown headquarters store. Stanley Marcus had invited Leticia Baldrige to come from Washington DC, to speak for one of their events. Linda picked her up at the airport, and they became instant friends. Later, on the way back to the airport when Linda mentioned she would like, someday, to work in a European embassy, Leticia said, "Let's wait until the election and we'll see what can happen." Letitia was well known to Ronald Reagan's transition team and before Reagan's inauguration, Linda received a call from Nancy Reagan's office to interview for the position of social secretary. After visiting with Mrs. Reagan, Linda became Assistant Social Secretary to Muffy Brandon during Reagan's first term and she became the Social Secretary for most of the second term. The Reagans entertained lavishly and often, placing Linda in personal contact with a great many American and world-renowned notables, including stars from Hollywood, governors, senators and other political leaders of most all nations. She was in charge of, and responsible for, the success of all State Dinners and all other White House entertaining, even breakfast and luncheon gatherings for President Reagan.

Linda was in charge of a large dinner and entertainment in Moscow to honor Soviet President Mikhail Gorbachev. Her most notable function was the dinner at the White House honoring Princess Diana and Prince Charles. Although not a State Dinner, a designation reserved for only heads of state, it was probably the most publicized dinner party ever given in the White House. Attended by several popular movie stars and political leaders, the party is best remembered for Diana dancing with *Saturday Night Fever* star, John Travolta. When Linda told him to cut in on President Reagan, who was dancing with Diana, Travolta said, "I can't cut in on *the President.*" Even after Linda told him that Mrs. Reagan wanted him to, she still had to push him onto the dance floor. Once they started dancing, all the other couples moved to the edge of the dance area to watch.[6]

In the spring of 1991, Linda, having finished her term as Social Secretary to the White House moved back to Dallas and established her own public relations business. I received a phone call from the Collings Foundation located in Stow, Massachusetts, to whom I had made a very small donation in support of the last combat-ready B-24 still in flying condition. Their plane, now called the *Witchcraft*, was touring the south, and they wanted me to help generate publicity in Dallas for this last, surviving Liberator. A call to Linda resulted in a great photo in *The Dallas Morning News* of their plane on its approach to the runway at Love Field with the city of Dallas skyline prominent in the background. Linda had done a great job. On that first trip, the pilot flew my son, Tommy, and me as guests to their next stop in Fort Worth, where Ann and Tommy's wife, Cindy, picked us up. I had forgotten how thunderously loud those four engines were.

It was about that time that Tommy won his first of two Clios, the national award, presented in New York City for producing the best television commercial of the year. Music is Tommy's life. Enamored of the Beatles at twelve, he led popular musical bands from his high school and college days at Washington and Lee and even after that, including the Coconuts, who became a well-known group in Dallas for years. He would later enjoy a highly successful career composing and producing music for radio and television commercials from his own studio. Best known is his *Motel* 6 radio

6. For John Travolta's memories of the dance, see Kenzie Bryant, "John Travolta Called His Dance with Princess Diana a Highlight of His Life," *Vanity Fair*, September 26, 2016, accessed on September 1, 2017, https://www.vanityfair.com/style/2016/09/john-travolta-princess-diana-dance-memory.

and television commercial, narrated by Tom Bodett ("We'll leave the light on for you"), and his "I want my Babyback, Babyback Ribs" commercial for Chili's. Tommy has also created and produced his own CDs, *Lost in the Land of Texico* and *Raise the Roof*, as well as CDs for other artists. He is now involved in entrepreneurial activities, but still enjoys performing with his guitar on occasion.

We had visited Santa Fe several times over the years and finally looked at a home in the newly constructed seven-house Stewart Compound, near the downtown area. It was small with just two bedrooms, but it was a jewel. The contractor, Betty Stewart, wanted authentic adobe homes, with solid two-foot thick walls. She wore out three concrete mixers by tumbling new red bricks to replicate the look of antique brick floors throughout the homes. The deep-set windows, arched and flanging out to the sides created a French touch. We had made an offer to the builders eight months before but were turned down. The Santa Fe real estate market is notoriously volatile and Ann had caught them on the down side. "Pack your bag," she said to me over the phone. She had called the real estate agent and discovered the house was still on the market. We hopped on the plane and in twenty-four hours owned a second home for another seventeen years. The altitude finally got me, and we sold that marvelous little house for another three times what we paid. What a girl!

I sold my insurance agency in 1990 to a larger agency and stayed on salary for another ten years. At the turn of the century, looking to the time when I would be free of business responsibilities, I enrolled in the continuing education literary classes at SMU and, during the next two years, went to New York City twice with other students, all girls, to attend sessions with authors and publishers. I decided to write a novel.

In 1998, I read two unrelated items in *The Dallas Morning News* that gave me an idea. One article concerned the United States giving an $8 billion credit to Russia to aid in its recovery. The other one revealed that thousands of Soviet scientists had been thrown out on the streets *and no one knew where they were*. I spent a lot of my time in Santa Fe writing *Starlights*. The novel seemed to write itself, a fast-paced political thriller, taking place mostly in Washington, D.C. over a short period. Failing in my three-year attempt to find an agent or publisher for *Starlights*, I finally self-published and made it available through Amazon. Because everyone who reads it gives it such high praise, I am still trying to find an agent or publisher.

In 2005, I returned to Capri with Ann. When the owner of the Quisisana Hotel learned that I had been there during the war, he invited us to dinner. He actually knew Marie quite well, and I told him about my wartime ten-minute date that was aborted because of her multiple chaperones. Marie had never married. I was not too surprised. As pretty as she was, I had wondered if all her other suitors had been forced to pass through that gauntlet of family approvers. The hotel owner also told us that Marie had become quite wealthy, owning major properties on the island.

I was looking forward to returning to San Giovanni Airfield, the place that had played such an important part in my life. I wanted Ann to see it and was curious to find out if it was still active. We had no idea if an airport would still be there. Neither of us spoke Italian, so I asked the hotel owner to write the following message in Italian for me on a card to take to the Cerignola police station:

*"I was a B-24 Liberator pilot during World War II and was stationed at San Giovanni Airfield. I would like to visit the field now and would appreciate it if you would give me directions."*

We left Capri and crossed back to the mainland. We then drove our car across Italy to Cerignola. Outside the police station, I handed the card to one of two officers standing by their police car. They nodded and motioned for us to follow them. They stopped at a rickety, wooden farm gate on a narrow road five miles from Cerignola. They left after we thanked them. We walked through the gate and discovered that the overgrown car tracks stopped after a short distance. There was no road, no airfield, no farm, only the knee-high grass covering the entire countryside. Distinctive, bright red poppies were scattered throughout. Standing alone near the gate was an old, one-story stone building. Above the doorway was a large red tile, etched with the words, "Flight Room." It could have been the briefing room for the 454th Bomb Group, the room where the entire officer corps flying that day's mission sat in the dark of early morning waiting for the curtain that would be raised to reveal the route for that day's mission.

Ann Faulkner at San Giovanni in 2005

The building was large enough, but I could not tell for sure. The windows were broken out, and inside, loose tiles littered the floor. We walked through the high grass and the red poppies, but I could find no other buildings or clues as to where our squadron was located. I could make out a shallow valley below that was probably once the double runways. It was now covered with high grass and even a few tall trees. Our tent area was on a bluff, with the runways below, and I believe Ann and I were standing near the area of our 737th Bomb Squadron tents. It had been sixty years since it had been my home for six months.

It was an emotional experience.

Ann and I are both now in our nineties. We have loved each other every minute and cherished our lives together. God has been good to us and we have been fortunate beyond words, having traveled to Europe eight times, South America twice, and taken several cruises in the Caribbean. Our son, Tommy, and his wife, Cindy, live in Highland Village, thirty miles north of us, and their children, Allie and Matthew, are in apartments near them. Our daughter, Linda, married for the first time four years ago at age 65. Her husband, Gilbert Johnston, from Alabama, was also 65, and it was also his first marriage. They have known each other since she worked in the White House

Tom Faulkner, Jr., Ann Faulkner, Tom Faulkner, Sr., Linda Faulkner

at the same time he was legal aide to an Alabama congressman. They live in Terrell, thirty miles east of us.

A few years ago, Ann and I moved to a large, new retirement community known as The Tradition. Happily, daughter Linda works here as the Vice-president of Communications and Public Relations. We see her almost every day. Ann and I have come full circle. The dance hall, Louann's, was torn down many years ago, but the balcony of our new apartment faces the corner of Greenville Avenue and Lovers Lane where Louann's once stood during those tumultuous war years. Our son, Tom, installed a wonderful sound system in our apartment. We sit on our balcony and listen to marvelous music from inside, including tangos which we learned to love during our two summer visits to Buenos Aires. We also listen to Jobim's latin lyrics, like "The Girl from Ipanima," which are Ann's favorites, and, of course, those great renditions of the big bands of the war years, which has always meant so much to us. We can recall those memories as we look out and see, not far away, that same spot where, seventy years ago, that brief, but oh so important conversation took place—the conversation that changed both our lives forever.

# Afterword

My admiration of Warner Marsh has already been expressed. He was, quite simply, the most outstanding person I have ever known in virtually every way, notwithstanding that he died at such a tragically young age.

Steve Schneider, Jimmy Cleaver and Charles (Chuck) Storey, the other three wartime pilots to which this book is dedicated, were three of the most unusual men I have ever known, each unique in his own inimitable way. Steve and Jimmy were best friends and shared the same office in the Meadows Building when I was also there on the first floor with my insurance agency. Both were World War II pilots—Steve as a Navy pilot, flying PBY twin-engine flying boats, while Jimmy became a Marine Corsair fighter pilot. It was a blast when those two, their wives, and Ann and I would get together. Martha Ann Schneider (the red head), Jo Cleaver (the brunette) and my blond wife, Ann, were all stunningly beautiful, and all three were recognized as such in their college annuals. During our early years of marriage the three of them even modeled together at the Texas State Fair in 1954 for Chevrolet, to the then well-known tune, "See the USA in Your Chevrolet."

Steve Schneider and Tom During World War II

Of all the people I have ever known, Steve was one of the most talented. His quick, sharp, dry sense of humor, occasionally cutting, was unequaled. When we were all at dinner to celebrate Jim's recovery from a life-threatening brain operation, Steve responded to one of Jimmy's wisecracks, "I liked him better when he was sick."

If Steve had not been struck down by infantile paralysis as the war ended, there is no telling what he would have achieved. As it was, Steve, forced to use steel walking sticks, and later a wheelchair, for the rest of his life, studied geology at SMU and became a prosperous independent oil producer without setting foot at the well sites.

As mentioned before, Steve enjoyed ribbing me about my spending the war skiing and ice skating at an exclusive resort hotel in Switzerland while he was valiantly protecting America's soft underbelly out of Corpus Christi, flying a naval patrol plane. He annually presided as Master of Ceremonies at the Texas Wildcatters Association dinner for oilmen, roasting the chairman each year, and he even starred in his own one-man-show at Brook Hollow Golf Club. For ninety minutes, sitting on a barstool holding

Jim and Jo Cleaver

a microphone, and with a small band behind him, he entertained over 100 guests. He sang his favorite Frank Sinatra ballads, replicated Marlon Brando's emotional *On the Waterfront* scene, *("I coulda BEEN somebody, Charley")*, and recited Gregory Peck's stirring address to his beleaguered Squadrons in *Twelve O'clock High*

Ann and I exchanged Christmas presents with Steve and Martha Ann. One Christmas, Steve handled their thank you notes. We received a printed postcard with the underlined blank spaces filled in with his handwriting:

*Dear Ann and Tom*

*Martha Ann and I have enjoyed another truly great Christmas because of friends like you who have lavished us with extraordinary gifts. We look forward to enjoying the case of vintage champagne from one friend and the Shetland pony from another. And what a beautiful sterling samovar came from Hollywood. Thank you, dear friend, for your generous gift of a sack of nuts.*

*Steve*

I sometimes would meet Steve at the early service of the Episcopal Church of the Incarnation. One Sunday, Steve, sitting in his back-row aisle-seat, watched a curvaceous blond walk down the aisle late and turned to me and said, "Wow!"

Before the service ended, the curvaceous blond left early and came back up the aisle. After she passed, I nudged Steve and said, "Did you see her give me the eye?"

With no hesitation, Steve replied, "Yeah, she leaned down and asked me, 'Is that Guy Kibbee?'"[1]

Jimmy Cleaver readily admitted that landing on a carrier was the most terrifying experience of his life. Rarely humble, Jimmy was brilliant, and he knew it. He was pictured in *Life Magazine* in 1958, along with 99 others, as one of *America's Red Hot Hundred*, the most promising men and women still in their thirties in the nation. Okay, so he personally knew the famous *Life* photographer, Alfred Eisenstadt. He still deserved the recognition. Jimmy never sold anything, but he was a *super* salesman, convincing me, a struggling insurance man with a wife and two children, to (1) buy an expensive Telefunken console for my wife for Christmas, (2) take my family to Europe for three weeks, and (3) buy an expensive Leica camera with three special lenses to record the trip.

I never regretted any of it.

Jimmy also possessed an unusual wit and was never at a loss for words or a pithy comment. "I have achieved the impossible," he once declared to me, "I have become flabby and scrawny at the same time." His definition of "business" was simple and to the

1. Guy Kibbee was a well-known character actor from the 1930s and 1940s. He was bald and overweight, and tended to play more dim-witted characters. See Guy Kibbee Biography, accessed on January 29, 2018, http://www.imdb.com/name/nm0452128/.

point: "Business is one S.O.B. trying to convince another S.O.B to do something he doesn't want to do."

Jim played the piano by ear. He would duplicate Nat King Cole's syncopated style, or any of the great jazz pianists. He played anything, *in any key.* Piano or not, having Jim to a dinner gathering was to guarantee a successful evening.

He was straight out of an F. Scott Fitzgerald novel. He was a classy dresser and the only man I knew who frequently wore a bow tie. No hypocrite, he was unabashedly candid with strong opinions. Jim savored good food and would get to know Dallas's finest chefs and they would come out of the kitchen to his table to welcome him. He had a keen mind and a keen sense of humor, always frank and honest, you knew where you stood. A man of all seasons, Jim was often drawn to the cool crowd, and I felt flattered that he liked me. He seemed to know everything about almost everything.

Jim called me "Big Knuckles" because of a letter I wrote as a boy. My dad had it copied by his secretary. Jim enjoyed reading the letter aloud to our dinner guests. It may not be all that amusing, but it was a good foil to bring forth his showmanship ability. It seemed to work. You had to be there. Jim *was* funny. Here it is:

*Johnson Smith and Co.*
*Detroit, Michigan*
*Dear Mr. Smith:*

*While looking through my third addition of "Superman", my eye caught this lovely looking piece of jewelry. At first glance, I told myself that I must be the owner of one of these astonishing rings. Of course, I am referring to the black ring with a skull with green eyes—and cross bones on either side.*

*Although it is against my principals to transact business through the mail, I am sure that such a large institution of honest dealings as yours will send only the best to me.*

*I am in hopes that you will send this wonderful, quaint and uncommon, oxidized ring with the gun metal finish to me within at least two weeks: for I just can't wait to be the owner of this popular ring.*

*I personally am not a collector of odd rings: in fact I have never even owned but one before. As a rule, I don't think rings should be worn by young men because it makes one who has no ring feel small and as if he couldn't afford one. But that feeling was overpowered when I gazed upon a picture of this ring. It's utter simplicity: it's daring, bold face, with such glaring eyes that it makes you feel as if you were under some strange, hypnotic spell if you gaze at it long enough, its sinister smile that gives you a gloomy feeling inside.*

*I believe no ring or any other object has ever stirred or inspired me so.*

*I wear a large ring; for my knuckles are unusually large. Although I could go on for hours just talking about this extremely odd, yet daring ring, I believe enough can be said about any subject. I personally believe that if you cancelled all of your other merchandise (that is, stop selling everything else) and specialized in this one object, that you, Mr. Smith, would make millions.*

*Please don't get the idea that I am trying to tell you how to run your business. I just mean to give you some special advice (that, too, is against my better principals). Although I have to leave you now, because my pen is running out of ink, I am expecting this ring by at least December 17 (if not sooner) (and one of my best policies is promptness).*

*I remain your ardent admirer for producing such a wonderful object of merchandise,*

*Tommy Faulkner*

Jim refused to believe I was just ten or eleven years old when the above letter was written. I had made the mistake of dating it. I was fourteen. Teenagers were not as sophisticated as today's brand, but even then, writing with tongue-in-cheek was a possibility. It was 1939. War had just been declared in Europe. I still have the ring. It *is* spooky looking. The ring is one of the few items of my copious collections as a boy that escaped my mother's scorched-earth policy before moving to Maple Terrace during the war.

Charles P. Storey was in the Air Transport Command in Italy at the same time as I, although we did not know it. He flew C-47 cargo planes, delivering military equipment around the Mediterranean. I look upon Chuck, along with Warner Marsh, as one of the finest men I have ever known. We first met as young boys at Camp Crockett. He later attended Woodrow Wilson High School, two years ahead of my wife, Ann, who admired him then as one of the school's outstanding leaders.

Based in Naples, there were times Chuck would fly generals and other military brass to their Mediterranean destinations, which on one occasion, included his father. His father, Robert G. Storey, a renowned Dallas attorney, was brought into the military judicial system as a colonel, and was executive trial council to Supreme Court Chief Justice Robert Jackson during the Nuremberg war crime trials of Nazi war criminals Hermann Goering, Rudolf Hess, and other high-ranking Nazi officials. After the war, Robert Storey would become the Dean of Southern Methodist University Law School.

Chuck Storey followed in his father's footsteps. In addition to being heavily involved in philanthropic activities, he was accorded top honors as one of the leading attorneys in Dallas and the state of Texas. Ann and I still look upon Chuck's great wife, Helen, as a sister. Helen's mother and mine were best friends, going all the way back to their youthful days in Helena. She and Chuck, and their three sons, were as close to our family as anyone we know.

Each one of these four men was unique and extraordinary. Although Warner was killed, his character, his personality, and his behavior have remained with me all through these many years. What an enormous impact he would have had, had he lived. Steve, Jimmy, and Chuck were, each one, a force whenever and wherever they were, leaving their individual imprint behind for others to cherish, benefit, and appreciate. Each one of them affected my life in many significant ways over the years, and for their influence and friendship, I am forever grateful.

# Appendix A

# Standard Flying Training Stages for *Pilots* (May 1944)

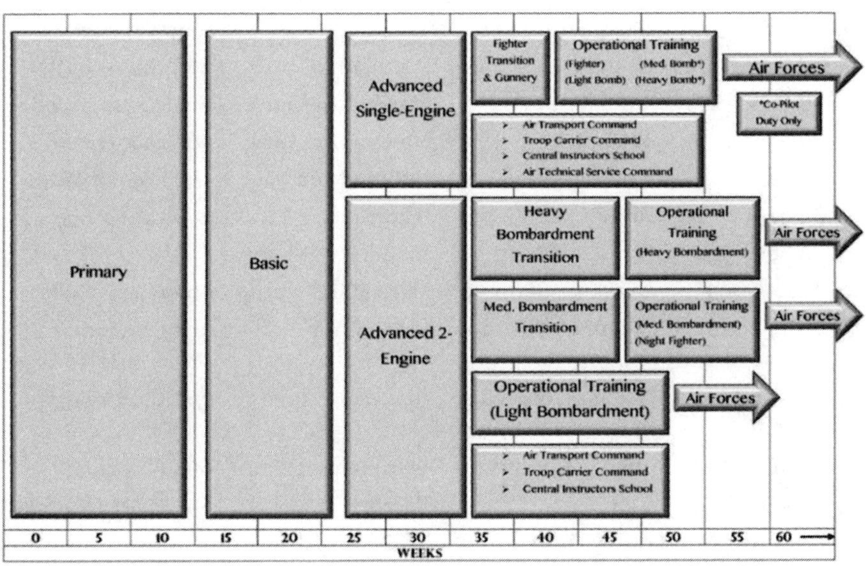

# Appendix B

# Thomas Faulkner's Combat Mission List

| Date | Destination | Target | Ship |
|---|---|---|---|
| 1) 17 Sept 1944 | Budapest | Marshalling Yard | 664 (*Lotta Laffs*) |
| 2) 18 Sept 1944 | Budapest | Marshalling Yard | 664 (*Lotta Laffs*) |
| 3) 20 Sept 1944 | *Győr*, Hungary | Marshalling Yard | 664 (*Lotta Laffs*) |
| 4) 21 Sept 1944 | *Kisköre*, Hungary | Railroad Bridge | 466 (Dinah-Mite) |
| 5) 22 Sept 1944 | Munich, Germany | Airdrome | 664 (*Lotta Laffs*) |
| 6) 23 Sept 1944 | Venzone, Italy | Viaduct | 458 |
| 7) 4 Oct 1944 | Munich, Germany | Marshalling Yard | 664 (*Lotta Laffs*) |
| 8) 7 Oct 1944 | Vienna, Austria | Oil Refinery | 264 (*Ancient & Honorable*) |
| 9) 10 Oct 1944 | Tagliamento River, Italy | Railroad Bridge | 664 (*Lotta Laffs*) |
| 10) 12 Oct 1944 | Bologna, Italy | Warehouse Depot | 664 (*Lotta Laffs*) |
| 11) 13 Oct 1944 | *Mór*, Lake Balaton, Hg | Factory | 664 (*Lotta Laffs*) |
| 12) 16 Oct 1944 | Steyr, Austria | Aero Works | 664 (*Lotta Laffs*) |
| 13) 20 Oct 1944 | Innsbruck, Austria | MarshallingYard | 264 (*Ancient & Honorable*) |
| 14) 21 Oct 1944 | *Győr*, Hungary | MarshallingYard | 387 (*Gentleman Jim*) |

| Date | Destination | Target | Ship |
|---|---|---|---|
| 15) 23 Oct 1944 | Trieste, Italy | Marshalling Yard | 886 |
| 16) 1 Nov 1944 | Graz, Austria | Supply Depot | 664 (*Lotta Laffs*) |
| 17) 4 Nov 1944 | Linz, Austria | Marshalling Yard | 417 |
| 18) 5 Nov 1944 | Vienna, Austria | Oil Refinery | 387 (*Gentleman Jim*) |
| 19) 6 Nov 1944 | Vienna, Austria | Ordinance Depot | 387 (*Gentleman Jim*) |
| 20) 7 Nov 1944 | NoviPazar, Yugo. | Enemy Troops | 387 (*Gentleman Jim*) |
| 21) 16 Nov 1944 | Munich, Germany | Marshalling Yard | 992 |
| 22) 11 Dec 1944 | Vienna, Austria | Supply Depot | 664 (*Lotta Laffs*) |
| 23) 20 Dec 1944 | Linz, Austria | Marshalling Yard | 664 (*Lotta Laffs*) |
| 24) 4 Jan 1945 | Verona, Italy | Marshalling Yard | 575 |
| 25) 15 Jan 1945 | Vienna | East Goods Depot | 009 (*San Antonio Rose*) |
| 26) 1 Feb 1945 | Graz, Austria | Marshalling Yard | 664 (*Lotta Laffs*) |
| 27) 25 Feb 1945 | Mestre, Italy | Marshalling Yard | 664 (*Lotta Laffs*) |
| 28) 27 Feb 1945 | Augsburg, Ger. | Marshalling Yard | 458 |

# Appendix C

# Diamond Shape Heavy Bomber Group Formation for 40-Planes

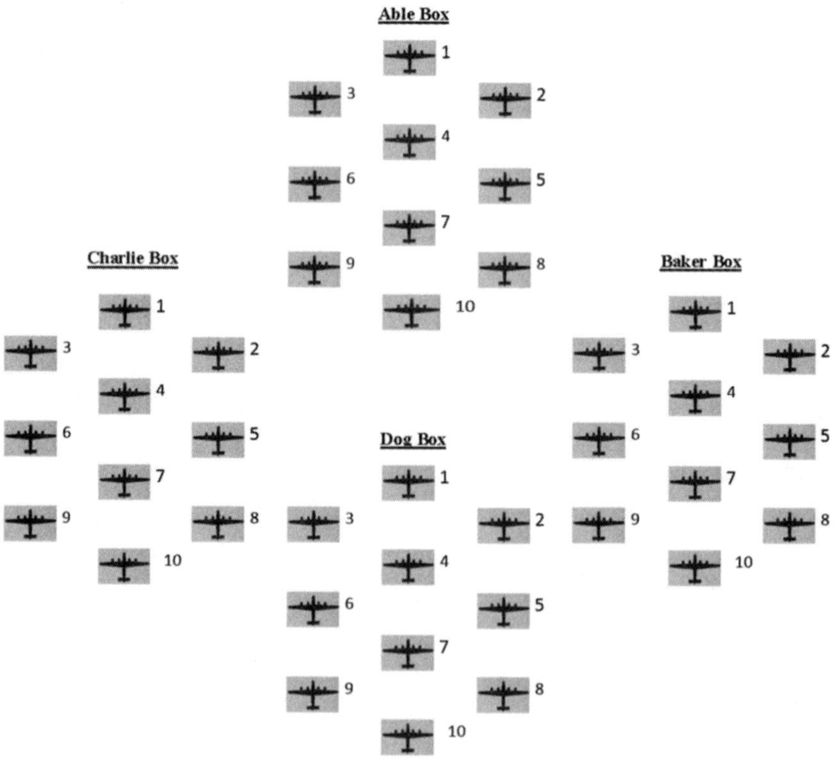


Number 10 position is the Tail-end Charlie slot.

# Bibliography


**Primary Sources**

Air Force Historical Research Agency, Maxwell Air Force Base, Alabama

Reel A6538 – 454 Records

Reel A6540 – The History of M.A.A.F. December 1943–1 September 1944

Reel A6543 – The History of M.A.A.F. 1 September 1944–9 May 1945, vol. xxxv

Reel A6544 – The History of M.A.A.F. 1 September 1944–9 May 1945, vol. xxxviii

Reel B0600 – 454 Records

Reel B0601 – 454 Records

Library of Congress, Washington, D.C.

Ira Eaker Papers

National Archives of the United States, College Park, Maryland

Record Group 18 – Records of the Army Air Forces

Record Group 331 – Records of the Allied Operational and Occupation Headquarters, World War II

Books, Diaries, and Memoirs

Ardery, Philip. *Bomber Pilot: A Memoir of World War II*. Lexington: University Press of Kentucky, 1978.

*Army Air Forces Statistical Digest: World War II*. Office of Statistical Control, 1945.

Aviation Cadet Training Video. Accessed on November 15, 2016. https://www.youtube.com/watch?v=xmFEZZkQdas.

Brochure–Aviation Cadet Training for the Army Air Forces (1943). Accessed on November 15, 2016. http://history.cap.gov/file/1432.

Callander, Bruce D. "The Aviation Cadets." *Air Force Magazine* 73, no. 11 (November 1990). Accessed on October 3, 2016. http://www.airforcemag.com/MagazineArchive/Pages/1990/November%20 1990/1190cadets.aspx.

Capps, Robert S. *Flying Colts: Liberator Pilot in Italy, Diary and History, World War II, 456th Bombardment Group (Heavy), 15th Air Force*. Alexandria, VA: Manor House Publications, 1997.

Carigan, William. *Ad Lib: Flying the B-24 Liberator in World War II*. Manhattan, KS: Sunflower University Press, 1988.

Chalker, Joseph. *The Flight of the Liberators*. Rochester, NY: The Du Bois Press, 1946.

*Chandu the Magician*. Directed by William C. Menzies and Marcel Varnel. Fox Film Corporation, 1932.

Convention (V) respecting the Rights and Duties of Neutral Powers and Persons in Case of War on Land, The Hague, 18 October 1907, International Committee of the Red Cross. Accessed on May 18, 2017. https://ihl-databases.icrc.org/applic/ihl/ihl.nsf/Article.xsp?action=openDocument&documentId=3C5ACCA7CF58497CC12563CD00516A15.

Cubbins, William R. *The War of the Cottontails: Memoirs of a WWII Bomber Pilot.* Chapel Hill, NC: Algonquin Books of Chapel Hill, 1989.

Currier, Donald R. *50 Mission Crush.* No place: Burd Street Press, 1992.

Davis, James M. *In Hostile Skies: An American B-24 Pilot in World War II*. Edited by David L. Snead. Denton: University of North Texas Press, 2006.

Dubuque, Jean H., and Robert F. Gleckner. "The Development of the Heavy Bomber, 1918 to 1944." 1951. Air Force Research Historical Agency. Accessed on October 13, 2016. http://www.afhra.af.mil/Portals/16/documents/Studies/1-50/AFD-090602-028.pdf.

Eisenhower, Dwight David. *Crusade in Europe*, repr. ed. Baltimore: The Johns Hopkins University Press, 1997.

"Flash Gordon." King Features Syndicate. Accessed on June 9, 2017. http://flashgordon.com/history/.

Fletcher, Eugene. *Mister: The Training of an Aviation Cadet in World War II.* Seattle: University of Washington Press, 1992.

Fortier, Norman "Bud." *An Ace of the Eighth: An American Fighter Pilot's Air War in Europe*. Novato, CA: Presidio Press, 2007.

*454th Memories*. Dallas, TX: Taylor Publishing Company, 1991.

Greer, Thomas H. "Preflight Training in the AAF, 1939–1944." November 1946. Air Force Research Historical Agency. Accessed on October 13, 2016. http://www.afhra.af.mil/Portals/16/documents/Studies/1-50/AFD-090602-105.pdf.

Harwell, Ursel P. *Jaws Over Europe: B-24 Bombers in World War II*. Private Publisher, no date.

Hibbits, John Joseph. *Take 'er Up Alone, Mister!*. New York: Whittlesey House, 1943.

Hollon, W. Eugene. "The Preflight Schools in World War II." June 1953. Air Force Research Historical Agency. Accessed on October 13, 2016. http://www.afhra.af.mil/Portals/16/documents/Studies/51-100/AFD-090601-131.pdf.

Interview with Lt. "Pep" Petrocine, 398th Bomb Group Pilot, 600th Squadron, Eighth Air Force. 398th Bomb Group Memorial Association. Accessed on November 14, 2016. http://www.398th.org/History/Veterans/Voices/Transcriptions/Interview_Petrocine_Pep.html#PP_Feathering.

Layman, Martha E. "Organization of AAF Training Activities, 1939–1945." June 1946. Air Force Research Historical Agency. Accessed on October 13, 2016. http://www.afhra.af.mil/Portals/16/documents/Studies/51-100/AFD-090529-105.pdf.

LeMay, Curtis E. with MacKinlay Kantor. *Mission with LeMay: My Story*. Garden City, NY: Doubleday & Company, Inc., 1965.

Leslie, Conrad. "Welcome to the Diary of Conrad Leslie's 35 Bombing Missions over Germany as a 21 Year Old B-24 First Pilot." Unpublished memoir in author's possession.

Mason, Keith W. *My War in Italy: On the Ground and in Flight with the 15th Air Force.* Columbia: University of Missouri Press, 2016.

McNarney, Betty J. "Pilot Transition to Combat Aircraft." September, 1944. Air Force Research Historical Agency. Accessed on October 13, 2016. http://www.afhra.af.mil/Portals/16/documents/Studies/1-50/AFD-090602-044.pdf.

Myers, Jack R. *Shot at and Missed: Reflections of a World War II Bombardier*. Norman: University of Oklahoma Press, 2004.

Okerstrom, Dennis R. *The Final Mission of Bottoms Up: A World War II Pilot's Story*. Columbia: University of Missouri Press, 2011.

Rogers, Will, and M. Jane Johansson. *The Papers of Will Rogers: The Final Years, August 1928-August 1935*. Norman: University of Oklahoma Press, 2006.

Sanders, Chauncey E. "Legislation Relating to the AAF Training Program, 1939 to 1945 (Revised)." May 1946. Air Force Research Historical

Agency. Accessed on October 13, 2016. http://www.afhra.af.mil/Portals/16/documents/Studies/1-50/AFD-090602-030.pdf.

"Selective Service and Training Act of 1940." *World Affairs* 103, no. 3 (September 1940): 179–86.

Stewart, John L. *The Forbidden Diary: A B-24 Navigator Remembers*. New York: McGraw Hill, 1998.

Stiles, Bert. *Serenade to the Big Bird*. No place: Howland Associates, 1947.

Tailspin Tommy – Comic Strip, Pioneers in Aviation. Accessed on May 22, 2017. https://av8rblog.wordpress.com/2013/05/22/tailspin-tommy-comic-strip/.

10 U.S. Code § 8749 - Distinguished Flying Cross: Award; Limitations, Cornell University Law School, Legal Information Institute. Accessed on May 16, 2017. https://www.law.cornell.edu/uscode/text/10/8749.

*The Return of Dr. Fu Manchu*. Directed by Rowland V. Lee. Paramount Pictures, 1930.

*The Statistical History of the United States: From Colonial Times to the Present*. New York: Basic Books, 1976.

Thompson, Robert "Bob". *Flying in Coffin Corner*. Sahuarita, AZ: McAlister Press, 1995.

Thompson, Robert L. "Initial Selection of Candidates for Pilot, Bombardier, and Navigator Training, November 1943." Air Force Research Historical Agency. Accessed on October 13, 2016. http://www.afhra.af.mil/Portals/16/documents/Studies/1-50/AFD-090602-023.pdf.

Thurston, Grace, et al. *My Magic Husband: Howard Thurston Unmasked*. No place: Phil Temple Publication, 1985.

War Department Pamphlet, No. 21–1 – When You Are Overseas These Facts Are Vital, July 29, 1943. Accessed on August 7, 2017. http://penelope.uchicago.edu/Thayer/E/Gazetteer/Places/America/United_States/_Topics/history/_Texts/US_Government/War_Department/Pamphlets/21_dash_1/pamphlet*.html.

Watry, Charles A. *Washout! The Aviation Cadet Story*. Carlsbad, CA: California Aero Press, 1983.

White, Jerry. "Combat Crew and Unit Training in the AAF, 1939–1945." August 1949. Air Force Research Historical Agency. Accessed on October 13, 2016. http://www.afhra.af.mil/Portals/16/documents/Studies/51-100/AFD-090601-030.pdf.

White, Wayne. *It Wasn't My Time*. Lulu.com, 2011.

Wiener, Willard. *Two Hundred Thousand Flyers: The Story of the Civilian-AAF Pilot Training Program*. Washington D.C.: Infantry Journal Inc., 1945.

Williams, Howard D. "Basic Military Training in the AAF, 1939–1944." November 1946. Air Force Research Historical Agency. Accessed on October 13, 2016. http://www.afhra.af.mil/Portals/16/documents/Studies/1-50/AFD-090602-106.pdf.

WWII Army and Navy Venereal Disease/VD Scare Film. Periscope Film. Accessed on October 4, 2016. https://www.youtube.com/watch?v=aro1HE1KB0w.

Secondary Sources

Adams, Noah. "At 75, A World War II Legend Gets A Full Makeover." West Virginia Public Radio. Accessed on July 14, 2017. http://www.npr.org/2017/04/22/525106154/at-75-a-world-war-ii-legend-gets-a-full-makeover.

"Adriatic Island Base Succors Allied Airmen." *Torretta Flyer* 11 (Winter 1984): 27.

Airplanes of the Past. Accessed on September 4, 2017. http://www.airplanesofthepast.com/wwii-bomber-production-numbers.htm.

Ambrose, Stephen E. *The Wild Blue: The Men and Boys Who Flew the B-24s Over Germany*. New York: Simon & Schuster, 2001.

______. *Citizen Soldiers: The U.S. Army from the Normandy Beaches to the Bulge to the Surrender of Germany, June 7, 1944-May 7, 1945*. New York: Simon & Schuster, 1997.

______. *D-Day, June 6, 1944: The Climactic Battle of World War II*. New York: Simon & Schuster, 1994.

American Air Museum in Britian. Imperial War Museums. Accessed on August 4, 2017. http://www.americanairmuseum.com/place/152480.

Asch, Alfred, Hugh R. Graff, and Thomas A. Ramey. *The Story of the Four Hundred and Fifty-Fifth Bombardment Group (H) WW II: Flight of the Vulgar Vultures*. Appleton, WI: Graphic Communications Center, Inc., 1991.

Ashcroft, Bruce. *We Wanted Wings: A History of the Aviation Cadet Program*. Lackland AFB, TX: HQ AETC Office of History and Research, 2005.

Astor, Gerald. *The Mighty Eighth: The Air War in Europe as Told by the Men Who Fought It*. New York: A Dell Book, 1997.

Aviation Archaeological Investigation and Research. Accessed on August 4, 2017. http://www.aviationarchaeology.com.

Aviation Museum at Garner Field. Accessed on November 5, 2016. http://txhillcountrytrail.com/plan-your-adventure/historic-sites-and-cities/sites/aviation-museum-garner-field.

Barker, John S. *Flight of the Liberators: The Story of the Four Hundred and Fifty-Fourth Bombardment Group*. Nashville, TN: Battery Press, 1946, 1986.

Beck, Earl R. *Under the Bombs: The German Home Front, 1942–1945*. Lexington: University of Kentucky Press, 1986.

Berg, A. Scott. *Lindbergh*. New York: Putnam, 1998.

"Bert Early, Former ABA Executive Director, Dies at 91." August 8, 2013." *ABA Journal*. Accessed on November 7, 2016. http://www.abajournal.com/news/article/bert_early_former_aba_executive_director_dies_at_91/.

Birdsall, Steve. *Log of the Liberators: An Illustrated History of the B-24*. Garden City, NY: Doubleday & Company, Inc., 1973.

Blow, Steve. "War Wound Finally Heals for WWII Pilot from Dallas," September 18, 2013. *Dallas News*. Accessed on May 16, 2017. https://www.dallasnews.com/news/news/2013/09/18/blow-war-wound-finally-heals-for-wwii-pilot-from-dallas.

Bowman, Martin W. *The B-24 Liberator, 1939–45*. Wellingborough, England: Patrick Stephens Limited, 1989.

______. *The USAAF Handbook, 1939–1945*. Stackpole Books, 1997.

Brokaw, Tom. *The Greatest Generation*. New York: Random House, 1998.

______. *The Greatest Generation Speaks: Letters and Reflections.* New York: Random House Trade Paperbacks, 2005.

Bryant, Kenzie. "John Travolta Called His Dance with Princess Diana a Highlight of His Life." *Vanity Fair*, September 26, 2016. Accessed on September 1, 2017. https://www.vanityfair.com/style/2016/09/john-travolta-princess-diana-dance-memory.

Caddick-Adams, Peter. *Snow and Steel: The Battle of the Bulge, 1944–45*. New York: Oxford University Press, 2014.

Cameron, Rebecca Hancock. *Training to Fly: Military Flight Training 1907–1945.* Washington D.C.: Air Force History and Museums Program, 1999.

Capps, Robert S. *Flying Colt: Liberator Pilot in Italy.* Manor House, 1997.

Carigan, William. "The B-24 Liberator—A Man's Airplane." *Aerospace Historian* (March 1988): 11–24.

Chandler, Graham. "Travels with Churchill: A World War II Flight Engineer Dishes on the Most 'I' of the VIPs He flew With." *Air & Space Smithsonian*. July 2009. Accessed on August 4, 2017. http://www.airspacemag.com/history-of-flight/travels-with-churchill-136166507/.

Childers, Thomas. *The Wings of Morning: The Story of the Last American Bomber Shot Down over Germany in World War II*. New York: Addison-Wesley Publishing Company, 1995.

Clifford, J. Garry, and Samuel R. Spencer, Jr. *The First Peacetime Draft*. Lawrence: University Press of Kansas, 1986.

Controversial Refugee Policy. Swiss Federal Archive. Accessed on May 18, 2017, https://www.bar.admin.ch/bar/en/home/research/searching/topics/die-schweiz-im-zweiten-weltkrieg/umstrittene-fluechtlings politik-im-zweiten-weltkrieg.html.

Cornelius, Deborah S. *Hungary in World War II: Caught in the Cauldron*, 3rd Ed. New York: Fordham University Press, 2011.

Crane, Conrad C. *Bombs, Cities, Civilians: American Airpower Strategy in World War II*. Lawrence: University Press of Kansas, 1993.

Craven, Wesley Frank, and James Lea Cate, eds. *The Army Air Forces in World War II*, Volume 1 – *Plans and Early Operations, January 1939 to August 1942*. Chicago: University of Chicago Press, 1948.

______. *The Army Air Forces in World War II*, Volume 2 – *Europe: TORCH to POINTBLANK, August 1942 to December 1943*. Chicago: University of Chicago Press, 1949.

______. *The Army Air Forces in World War II*, Volume 3 – *Europe, Argument to V-E Day, January 1944 to May 1945*. Chicago: University of Chicago Press, 1951.

______. *The Army Air Forces in World War II*, Volume 6 – *Men and Planes*. Chicago: University of Chicago Press, 1955.

Crown Zellerbach Corp. Lehman Brothers Collection – Contemporary Business Archives, Harvard Business School, Baker Library, Historical Collections. Accessed on November 14, 2016. http://www.library.hbs.edu/hc/lehman/company.html?company=crown_zellerbach_corp.

Daso, Dik Alan. *Hap Arnold and the Evolution of American Airpower*. Washington, D.C.: Smithsonian Institution Press, 2000.

Davis Monthan Aviation Field Register, Delta Mike Airfield, Inc. Accessed on June 9, 2017. https://dmairfield.com/people/turner_ro/.

Davis, Larry. *B-24 Liberator in Action*. Carrollton, TX: Squadron/Signal Publications, Inc., 1987.

Dorr, Robert F. *B-24 Liberator Units of the Fifteenth Air Force*. Botley, Oxford, UK: Osprey Publishing, 2000.

Douglas, Graeme. *Consolidated B-24 Liberator Owners' Workshop Manual: 1939 Onwards (all marks): An Insight into Owning, Servicing and Flying the American Second World War Heavy Bomber*. Somerset, U.K.: Haynes Publishing, 2016.

Eby, Cecil D. *Hungary at War: Civilians and Soldiers in World War II*. University Park: The Pennsylvania State University Press, 1998.

Ehlers, Jr., Robert S. *The Mediterranean Air War: Airpower and Allied Victory in World War II*. Lawrence: University Press of Kansas, 2015.

Flynn, George Q. *The Draft, 1940–1973*. Lawrence: University Press of Kansas, 1993.

454th Bombardment Group. Accessed on June 27, 2017. http://www.454bg.org/737th-squadron.cfm?LN=S.

455th Bombardment Group Association. Accessed on August 4, 2017. http://www.455th.org/index.htm.

459th Association. Accessed on July 14, 2017. http://www.459bg.org/index.cfm.

461st Bombardment Group (H). Accessed on June 27, 2017, http://www.461st.org/Cerignola/Cerignola.htm.

Freeman, Roger A. *B-24 Liberator at War*. London: Ian Allan, LTD, 1983.

______. *The Mighty Eighth: Units, Men and Machines (A History of the US 8th Army Air Force)*. Garden City, NY: Doubleday and Company, Inc., 1970.

______. *Mighty Eighth War Manual*. London: Jane's Publishing Company, 1984.

______. *Mighty Eighth War Diary*. London: Jane's Publishing Company, 1981.

Gander, Terry, and Peter Chamberlain. *Weapons of the Third Reich: An Encyclopedic Survey of All Small Arms, Artillery and Special Weapons of the German Land Forces 1939–1945*. Garden City: New York: Doubleday and Company, Inc., 1979.

Gilbert, Elizabeth, and Phil Fountain. "WWII Pilot Presented Distinguished Flying Cross, after 68 Years," October 17, 2013, Air National Guard, 136th Airlift Wing. Accessed on May 16, 2017. http://www.136aw.ang.af.mil/News/Features/Display/Article/866721/wwii-pilot-presented-distinguished-flying-cross-after-68-years/.

Glantz, David M., and Jonathan M. House. *When Titans Clashed: How the Red Army Stopped Hitler*, rev. and exp. ed. Lawrence: University Press of Kansas, 2015.

Goldstein, Erik. "Ray's Story: The Lost Air Gunner of the 454th Bomb Group." Accessed on May 16, 2017. http://www.454thbombgroup.it/Ray's%20Story%20EMAIL%20614.pdf.

Granfield, Alun. *Bombers over Sand and Snow: 205 Group RAF in World War II*. South Yorkshire, UK: Pen and Sword Aviation, 2011.

Graser, Marc. "First Superman Comicbook Sells for $3.2 Million." August 25, 2014. *Variety*. Accessed on June 9, 2017. http://variety.com/2014/biz/news/first-superman-comicbook-sells-for-3-2-million-1201289733/.

Guests of the Third Reich: American POWs in Europe, National World War II Museum, New Orleans. Accessed on August 7, 2017. http://guestsofthethirdreich.org/capture/.

Harley, R. Bruce. *A Brief History of the Fifteenth Air Force, "Aggressive in War, Alert in Peace". Silver Anniversary, 1 November 1943–31 October 1968.* March Air Force Base, California, Headquarters Fifteenth Air Force, 1968.

Henderson-Elder, Tracy, and Keith Myhrer. *The History of the World War II Tonopah Army Air Field, Nevada*. Nellis Air Force Base, NV: United States Air Force Air Combat Command, 2009.

"Helena-West Helena (Phillips County)." *The Encyclopedia of Arkansas History and Culture*. Central Arkansas Library System. Accessed on June 8, 2017. http://www.encyclopediaofarkansas.net/.

Herndon, Dallas Tabor. *Centennial History of Arkansas*, Volume 3. Chicago: S. J. Clarke Publishing Company, 1922.

Historic California Posts, Camps, Stations and Airfields: Hamilton Air Force Base (Air Corps Station, San Rafael; Hamilton Field, Hamilton Army Airfield). Accessed on November 13, 2016. http://www.militarymuseum.org/HamiltonAFB.html.

Holland, James. *Italy's Sorrow: A Year of War, 1944–1945*. New York: St. Martin's Press, 2008.

Hoseason, James. *The 1,000 Day Battle*. Suffolk, Great Britain: Gillingham Publications, 1979.

Huber, Peter. "Passive Countermeasures," *Frontline Defense* 8, no. 4 (2011). Accessed on August 4, 2017. http://defence.frontline.online/article/2011/4/1907-Passive-Countermeasures.

Johnsen, Frederick A. *B-24 Liberator: Rugged but Right*. New York: McGraw Hill, 1999.

Kennedy, David M. *The American People and the Great Depression: Freedom from Fear*. New York: Oxford University Press, 2003.

Lake Balaton. Hungarian Tourism Agency. Accessed on July 24, 2017. http://balaton.gotohungary.com/.

"Lamar Bathhouse." National Park Service, U.S. Department of the Interior. Accessed on June 9, 2017. https://www.nps.gov/hosp/learn/historyculture/lamar-bathhouse.htm.

Lambert, John W. *The 14th Fighter Group in World War II*. Atglen, PA: Schiffer Military History, 2008.

Leslie, Conrad. *Conrad Leslie's Guide for Successful Speculating: Stocks, Commodities, Gold*. Chicago: Dartnell, 1970.

Lewis, Adrian R. *Omaha Beach: A Flawed Victory*. Chapel Hill: University of North Carolina Press, 2001.

Levine, Alan J. *The Strategic Bombing of Germany, 1940–1945*. New York: Praeger, 1992.

Mahoney, Kevin A. *Fifteenth Air Force Against the Axis: Combat Missions over Europe During World War II.* Lanham, MD: Scarecrow Press, 2013.

Makos, Adam. *A Higher Call: An Incredible True Story of Combat and Chivalry in the War-torn Skies of World War II*. New York: Berkley Caliber, 2012.

Manning, Thomas. *A History of Military Aviation in San Antonio.* Washington D.C.: Department of Defense, 2000.

Maurer, Maurer. *Combat Squadrons of the Air Force, World War II*. Washington, D.C.: Government Printing Office, 1982.

McCarthy, Bob. *Hell at 30,000 Feet: The World War II Experiences of Pittsburgh Lieutenant Fran Goldcamp as a B-24 Bomber Copilot over Europe.* Baltimore: Publish America, 2006.

McElvaine, Robert. *The Great Depression: America, 1929–1941*, rep. ed. New York: Times Books, 1993.

McFarland, Stephen, and Wesley Phillips Newton. *To Command the Sky: The Battle for Air Superiority Over Germany, 1942–1944*. Washington, D.C.: Smithsonian Institution Press, 1991.

McGuire, Melvin W. and Robert Hadley. *Bloody Skies: A 15th AAF B-17 Combat Crew, How They Lived and Died.* No place: Yucca Tree Press, 1993.

McManus, John C. *Deadly Sky: The American Combat Airman in World War II*. Novato, CA: Presidio Press, Inc., 2000.

Mears, Dwight S. "Better Off as Prisoners of War: The Differential Standard of Protection for Military Internees in Switzerland during World War II," *The Journal of the History of International Law* 15 (2013): 173–99.

______. "Interned or Imprisoned?: The Successes and Failures of International Law in the Treatment of American Internees in Switzerland, 1943–45." Ph.D. dissertation, University of North Carolina at Chapel Hill, 2012.

______. "To Intern or Not to Intern? Neutral States and the Application of International Law to United States Airmen in World War II," *The Journal of the History of International Law* 15 (2013): 77–101.

Mets, David R. *Master of Airpower: General Carl A. Spaatz*. Novato, CA: Presidio Press, 1997.

Mighty Eighth Air Force Museum. Accessed on September 5, 2017. http://www.mightyeighth.org/.

Miller, Donald L. *Masters of the Air: America's Bomber Boys Who Fought the Air War Against Nazi Germany.* New York: Simon & Schuster, 2006.

Millet, Jeffrey R. *The Fifteenth Air Force Story: A History 1943–1985.* March Air Force Base, CA: Fifteenth Air Force Association, 1986.

Morris, Rob. *Untold Valor; Forgotten Stories of American Bomber Crews over Europe in World War II.* Sterling, VA: Potomac Books, 2006.

Mrazek, Robert J. *To Kingdom Come: An Epic Saga of Survival in the Air War Over Germany*. New York: NAL Caliber, 2011.

Murray, Williamson, and Allan R. Millett. *A War to Be Won: Fighting the Second World War*. Cambridge, MA: The Belknap Press of Harvard University Press, 2000.

Murrmann, Mark, and Elizabeth Gettelman. "The Enemy in Your Pants: The Military's Decades-long War against STDs." *Mother Jones* (May/June 2010). Accessed on October 4, 2016. http://www.motherjones.com/media/2010/05/us-military-std-posters.

National Geographic Society. *The Alps*. National Geographic Society, 1973.

Naylor, Roger. "Arizona's Military History: Kingman Army Air Field," February 20, 2015, *Azcentral*. Accessed on September 1, 2017. http://www.azcentral.com/story/travel/local/history/2015/02/20/arizona-military-history-kingman-army-air-field/23618689/.

Neillands, Robin. *The Bomber War: The Allied Air Offensive Against Germany*. New York: The Overlook Press, 2001.

1940's Morocco: World War Two. Accessed on November 14, 2016. http://marocmama.com/1940s-morocco-world-war-two/.

"Obituary for Billy Joe Jacobs, 1920–2014." *Reno Gazette Journal*. Accessed on May 16, 2017. http://www.legacy.com/obituaries/rgj/obituary.aspx?pid=171244606.

O'Leary, Michael. *Consolidated B-24 Liberator*. Oxford, U.K.: Osprey Press, 2002.

______. *North American Aviation P-51 Mustang*. Oxford, U.K.: Osprey Press, 1998.

______. *Lockheed P-38 Lightning*. Oxford, U.K.: Osprey Press, 1999.

O'Neill, William L. *A Democracy at War: America's Fight at Home & Abroad in World War II*. Cambridge, MA: Harvard University Press, 1993.

Overy, Richard J. *The Air War, 1939–1945*. New York: Stein and Day Publishers, 1980.

______. *The Bombers and the Bombed: Allied Air War over Europe, 1940–1945*. New York: Penguin Books, 2013.

Parks, Tom. "A Box of Old Letters: WWII, Family Letters, & Strange Tangents," Stories – WWII. Accessed on July 14, 2017. https://aboxofoldletters.com/tag/wwii/.

Parton, James. *"Air Force Spoken Here:" General Ira Eaker and the Command of the Air*. Maxwell Air Force Base, AL: Air University Press, 2000.

Peeler, Tom. "Remembering Louann's." *D Magazine* (February 1977). Accessed on September 1, 2017. https://www.dmagazine.com/publications/d-magazine/1977/february/remembering-louanns/.

Perez, Christine. "Three Generations Later, the Corrigans Are Still Shaping Dallas." *D Magazine* (January-February 2011). Accessed on September 1, 2017. https://www.dmagazine.com/publications/d-ceo/2011/january-february/the-corrigan-family-is-still-shaping-dallas/.

"Personal Decorations – Distinguished Flying Cross." The Institute of Heraldry, Office of the Administrative Assistant to the Secretary of the Army. Acessed on, May 16, 2017. http://www.tioh.hqda.pentagon.mil/Catalog/Heraldry.aspx?HeraldryId=15249&CategoryId=3&grp=4&menu=Decorations%20and%20Medals&ps=24&p=0.

Polk, David. *World War II Army Airborne Troop Carriers.* Nashville, TN: Turner Publishing Company, 1992.

Prince, Cathryn J. *Shot from the Sky: American POWs in Switzerland.* Annapolis, MD: Naval Institute Press, 2003.

Pro Football Hall of Fame. Accessed on September 10, 2016. http://www.profootballhof.com/.

Reed, Cary. "Remembering Will Rogers: 80 Years On, How The 'Cowboy Philosopher' Popularized Political Humor." August 15, 2015. NewsHour Production LLC. Accessed on June 8, 2017. http://www.pbs.org/newshour/rundown/remembering-will-rogers-80-years-cowboy-philosopher-popularized-political-humor/.

Rives, Timothy Rives. "The Ike Jacket," November 11, 2014, The National Archives Pieces of History. Accessed on November 8, 2016. https://prologue.blogs.archives.gov/2014/11/11/the-ike-jacket/.

Rust, Kenn C. *Fifteenth Air Force Story … in World War II.* Temple City, CA: Historical Aviation Album, 1976.

Ryan, Cornelius. *The Longest Day: The Classic Epic of D-Day, June 6, 1944*. New York: Simon & Schuster, 1959.

Schaffer, Ronald. *Wings of Judgment: American Bombing in World War II*. New York: Oxford University Press, 1985.

Second Bomb Group. Accessed on September 5, 2017. http://www.2ndbombgroup.org/15thairforce.htm.

"2nd Lt. Warner H. Marsh and His P-47 Soon to be Uncovered?" *Argunners Magazine*, April 15, 2015. Accessed on August 14, 2017. https://argunners.com/2nd-lt-warner-h-marsh-and-his-p-47-soon-to-be-uncovered/.

Shlaes, Amity. *The Forgotten Man: A New History of the Great Depression*, repr. ed. New York: Harper Perennial, 2008.

Sherry, Michael S. *The Rise of American Air Power: The Creation of Armageddon*. New Haven, CT: Yale University Press, 1987.

"67 Years Ago: The 362nd FG Moves Airfields." Flat Spins and Milk Runs. Accessed on August 14, 2017. https://obscureco.wordpress.com/2011/11/06/67-years-ago-the-362nd-fg-moves-airfields/.

Skelton, William Paul, III. "American Ex-Prisoners of War," Veterans Health Initiative, Department of Veterans Affairs. Washington, D.C.: U.S. Government Printing Office, 2002.

Spick, Mike. *Fighter Pilot Tactics: The Techniques of Daylight Air Combat*. New York: Stein and Day Publishers, 1983.

Spink, Barry L. "Distinguished Flying Cross and Air Medal Criteria in the Army Air Forces in World War II." June 25, 2015. Air Force Historical Research Agency. Accessed on May 16, 2017. http://www.afhra.af.mil/Portals/16/documents/Timelines/World%20War%20II/WWIIDFCandAirMedalCriteriaCommand.pdf?ver=2016-08-30-150741-427.

Stapfer, Hans-Heiri, and Gino Kunzle. *Strangers in a Strange Land; Vol. II: Escape to Neutrality.* Carrollton, TX: Squadron/Signal Publications, 1992.

Swansborough, Gordon, and Peter M. Bowers. *United States Military Aircraft Since 1909.* Washington D.C.: Smithsonian Institution Press, 1963.

Swiss Internees Association, Inc. Accessed on May 16, 2017. http://swissinternees.tripod.com.

Tanner, Stephen. *Refuge From the Third Reich: American Airmen and Switzerland During World War II.* Rockville Centre, NY: Sarpedon, 2000.

*The Outlaw Journals*. Accessed on June 9, 2017. http://www.babyfacenelson journal.com/melvin-purvis.html.

Thole, Lou. *Forgotten Fields of America: World War II Bases and Training Then and Now*. Missoula, MT: Pictorial Histories Publishing Co., Inc. 1996.

Thomas, Roy. *Haven, Heaven, and Hell - Part 1: The United States Army Air Force Aircraft and Airmen Interned in Switzerland During WWII.* Monroe, WI: Puka Press, 1991.

398th Bomb Group Memorial Association. Accessed on November 14, 2016. http://www.398th.org/History/Veterans/Voices/Transcriptions/Interview_Petrocine_Pep.html#PP_Feathering.

Tillman, Barrett. *Forgotten Fifteenth: The Daring Airmen Who Crippled Hitler's War Machine.* Washington D.C.: Regnery History, 2014.

Tull, Matthew. "Trauma, PTSD, and OCD," January 31, 2017, Very Well. Accessed on May 16, 2017. https://www.verywell.com/ptsd-and-other-anxiety-disorders-relationship-2797549.

United States Strategic Bombing Survey. *The Effects of Strategic Bombing on the German War Economy*. Washington, D.C.: U.S. Government Printing Office, 1945.

_____. *Over-all Report (European War)*. Washington, D.C.: U.S. Government Printing Office, 1945.

Uvalde: Aviation Museum at Garner Field. Accessed on November 5, 2016. http://txhillcountrytrail.com/plan-your-adventure/historic-sites-and-cities/sites/aviation-museum-garner-field.

Van Buren, Abigail. "Vet Urges Release of Wartime Films on 'Social Disease'." *Desert News*, January 27, 1992.

"Venereal Disease Propaganda." Welcome to the Home of Psywarrior. Accessed on October 4, 2016, http://www.psywarrior.com/PSYOPVD.html.

Waldron, Daniel Waldron et al. *Blackstone, A Magician's Life: The World and Magic Show of Harry Blackstone, 1885–1965*. David Meyer Magic Books, 1999.

Weinberg, Gerhard L. *A World at Arms: A Global History of World War II*. New York: Cambridge University Press, 1994.

Westermann, Edward B. *Flak: German Anti-Aircraft Defenses, 1914–1945*. Lawrence: University Press of Kansas, 2001.

Widner, Robert. *Aircraft Accidents in Florida: From Pearl Harbor to Hiroshima*. Lulu.com, 2009.

Wiener, Willard. *Two Hundred Thousand Flyers: The Story of the Civilian-AAF Pilot Training Program.* Washington D.C.: Infantry Journal Inc., 1945.

Winkler, Alan M. *Home Front U.S.A.: American During World War II*, 2nd ed. Wheeling, IL: Harlan Davidson, Inc., 2000.

Wright, Stuart J. *An Emotional Gauntlet: Life in Peacetime America to the War in European Skies*. Madison: University of Wisconsin Press, 2004.

Yagoda, Ben. "'Bacon, Beans and Limousines' --Will Rogers (October 18, 1931)," Library of Congress. Accessed on June 8, 2017. https://www.loc.gov/programs/static/national-recording-preservation-board/documents/WillRogersSpeech.pdf.

YMCA of Metropolitan Dallas. Accessed on June 9, 2017. http://campgradyspruce.org/our-story/camp-history/.

Zaloga, Steven J. *Operation Nordwind 1945: Hitler's Last Offensive in the West*. Osprey Publishing, 2010.

Zimmerman, Dwight Jon. "A War Won with Spam (and a Few Other Things)," May 19, 2011. Accessed on July 13, 2017. http://www.defensemedianetwork.com/stories/war-won-spam-things/.

# Index